Yahuwah's Game

It's Just A Ride In The Matrix

by

Sandy Bergen

RoseDog Books
PITTSBURGH, PENNSYLVANIA 15238

The contents of this work, including, but not limited to, the accuracy of events, people, and places depicted; opinions expressed; permission to use previously published materials included; and any advice given or actions advocated are solely the responsibility of the author, who assumes all liability for said work and indemnifies the publisher against any claims stemming from publication of the work.

RoseDog Books
585 Alpha Drive
Pittsburgh, PA 15238
Visit our website at www.rosedogbookstore.com

ISBN: 978-1-4809-3917-2
eISBN: 978-1-4809-3940-0

Contents

Chapter 1

Waking up in Orwell's 1984 in December 2012

Wow. We made it through another New Year...2016. Another powerful year for the shift. As the shift is getting stronger and stronger I pray, with a crystal in each hand, for my mind to be clear, my heart pure, and my path straight. What a glorious time to be alive and awake. I'm standing strong in my faith, with my heart wide open, writing what I need to say. I've been putting the pieces of the puzzle together and have realized there is a pattern to maneuvering the matrix. First, we have to realize that this is a virtual reality game, and we came in to play the game with certain tools we acquired from learning in other lives and between lives here in the third dimension. My tools were the ability to write and type. I brought the scripture, Yahuwah and Yahushua, the Word. I practice yoga, meditation and love and pray for Mother Earth (Gaia). Yahuwah ("GOD") and Yahushua's (Jesus Christ) breath is in my nostrils, Word is written in my heart and love is in my temples (on each side of my brain). We are in the end of a 26,000-year cycle, and those who do not wake up will have to endure another cycle of incarnations here on earth. I'm not Alan Watts, a great philosopher with many YouTube videos, but I remember one of his quotes as basically saying, "Just write."

I believe that reading and writing are the most nour-
ishing forms of meditation anyone has so far found.
By reading the writings of the most interesting
minds in history, we meditate with our own minds
and theirs as well. This to me is a miracle.[1]

-Kurt Vonnegut

First, I want to thank you for reading this book. I've re-read this in-
spiring quote many times. It has helped me to realize how important
we all are to the cosmic universe and how important it is that I share
my experiences and love for the scriptures with others. Marianne
Williamson wrote in her book *A Return To Love: Reflections on the Principles of a Course in Miracles*:

Our deepest fear is not that we are inadequate. Our
deepest fear is that we are powerful beyond measure.
It is our light, not our darkness that most frightens
us. We ask ourselves, who am I to be brilliant, gor-
geous, talented, fabulous? Actually, who are you not
to be? You are a child of God. Your playing small
does not serve the world. There is nothing enlightened about shrinking so that other people won't feel
insecure around you. We are all meant to shine, as
children do. We were born to make manifest the
glory of God that is within us. It's not just some of
us; it's in everyone. And as we let our own light shine,
we unconsciously give other people permission to do
the same. As we are liberated from our own fear, our
presence automatically liberates others.[2]

---

[1] Kurt Vonnegut, *Palm Sunday: An Autobiographical Collage.* (Place of publication [include
the state if it is an unfamiliar town]: publisher, date of publication), page numbers.

[2] Marianne Williamson, *A Return To Love: Reflections on the Principles of a Course in Miracles.* (Place of publication [include the state if it is an unfamiliar town]: publisher, date of
publication), 190-191.

We have to liberate ourselves from the perception that we are small with little power.

Since sharing my experiences and memories of the MK Ultra (mind experimentation), I have become what is modernly known as a "targeted individual." Learning that I am an MK Ultra (mind experimentation) survivor has been a traumatic experience. MK Ultra, M=Mind, K=Kontrolle (German for control), Ultra – extremely secret. I just learned the term "targeted individual" in May 2015 when I did my interview with Miles Johnston on his thebasesproject.org website. I am Bases 44, Sandy Bergen. The interview is on YouTube. Just type in "Sandy Bergen" and it will come up. He did a not-so-great job on that interview but, thus far, I have over 12,000 views on the first hour. I just want the information to get to as many people as possible. I didn't come this far to lay down and say, "Oh, it is just the way it is." We want to change the things we cannot accept, not accept the things we cannot change. Funny, back in 2013 when I was in the first stages of my awakening and my sister JoAnn was still talking to me, she said, "My God, Sandy! They're naming hurricanes after you." I thought to myself, *Yeah, Sandy on Jersey Shore*, but when I typed in Sandy Bergen on YouTube, "Sandy Bergen County Hurricane" comes up. So, it is literally my name on that hurricane in 2012. The second hour of that interview has a blackout in the beginning and at 45:55 there is a cut or a glitch, and it is where an obvious cut was taken. I had said that during an astral dream my mother said, "Sandy, the government has been after you all your life," but it now says, "Sandy, the government has been after you." The "all your life" part is cut out. I guess that "they" don't want people to realize how they select children and torture them from birth and definitely from as young as three years old. With all the technology today and crisis actors and look-a-likes, so much can be altered and so much information can be deleted or scrambled.

I am a survivor of extensive mind control. I saw a video of another mind control victim, and he said that a Cathy O'Brien technique for deprogramming is writing incidents down. Cathy O'Brien (also from

Michigan), a high presidential mind control sex slave, has proven the fact that she was mind controlled. She stressed that traditional cursive was more beneficial than typing them, but I have been typing this for three years and could not have accomplished all of this if I had been handwriting it. I am sure that is why my higher powers keep saying to write it down. It's important. It's been revealed to me that we must remember who we are. We have all reincarnated through many lives. Edgar Cayce, a well-documented psychic of the 20th century, said, "All souls were created in the beginning and are finding their way back to whence they came."[3]

If we create our own reality then I certainly would not have created this. If it is true, the mind creates the reality then by fragmenting my mind, brainwashing me, constant abuse would explain why I created this. The Edgar Cayce readings emphasize the spiritual nature of humankind. Because of the demands of life, however, we frequently overlook the truest part of ourselves which is our connection to spirit. Although we possess physical bodies and mental attitudes, ultimately our deepest connection is to our spiritual source. *"The spirit is life. The mind is the builder. The physical is the result."*[4]

Just last night, reliving AGAIN ALL the sex I had as a child, realizing I was taught to be a child sex star, remembering how much I enjoyed all the sex games. Being given a huge, thick graphic cartoon pornography book to play with and read countless times throughout my childhood. Playing all sorts of sex games with my cousin and brother. The neighborhood boys. To be deliberately taught that sex is what a child does. Knowing now that we were filmed. It happened so often, night after night, year after year with never one parent ever once interrupting us or teaching us morals and respect for our bodies. I am ever eternally grateful to have had my awakening. Reliving the horrific childhood is part of the healing. I will detail below many of my experiences.

---

[3] Edgar Cayce, psychic reading 3744-5 February 1924.

[4] Edgar Cayce, *A.R.E., Readings Advice On Personal Spirituality,* Meditation, and Prayer.

I can't change the past, but I can hope to make something positive out such a negative violation of my free will. I will not accept the things I cannot change, but I will change the things I cannot accept. My writing this book is for the generations that are growing up here in this crazy world (whirled) and for all the generations to come. I have to accept that I cannot change the past and not be a prisoner of the past but a pioneer for the future. I truly don't like the old adage "forgive and forget." Forgive but never forget. "The memory of the just is blessed: but the name of the wicked shall rot." (Proverbs 10:7)

I remain grateful and full of thankfulness that I never forgot my childhood…that hospital stay when I was about three years old…the first time I ever had sexual relations with my cousin. It all fits together perfectly into building a mind control, sex slave. By revealing the details, I hope to make a change in the world.

How long have we been waiting for the world (whirled) to change? It changes when we change. When realizing selflessness not selfishness must be our first instinct. A choice of being a service to self or a service to others. "Injustice anywhere is a threat to justice everywhere. We are caught in an inescapable network of mutuality, tied in a single garment of destiny. Whatever affects one directly, affects all indirectly."[5] Martin Luther King The system is rigged against us. My peaceful protest against the United States government is to never vote in this system of corruption. If all Americans just said, "No I'm not having it. I know the election is rigged. You give us an illusion of choice when it doesn't matter who is voted in. Either party is run by the same puppet master behind the curtain. It's all an illusion." Getting the masses to believe in the illusion is the key to control. Letting people think they are free when they are not. As I'll say many, many times, the perfect mind control victims do not know they are mind controlled; the perfect host doesn't know it has a parasite, and the perfect slave doesn't know he is one. Zbigniew Brzezinski, a presidential advisor and author, said, "We

---

[5] Martin Luther King, Jr., Letter from the Birmingham Jail, April 16, 1963.

have a large public that is very ignorant about public affairs and very susceptible to simplistic slogans by candidates who appear out of nowhere, have no track record, but mouth appealing slogans."[6]

I'm going to start with scripture that revealed to me what an evil time we live in and how important it is to wake up and open up to the fact that we are not alone in this universe. If we are all specks of the universe than the UNIverse is in us. We are all ONE and must stop thinking of selfishness and thinking with selflessness. Spell live backwards and it's evil. Spell evol[ve] backwards and its love. David Icke, a pioneer of the awakening, says, "Infinite love is the only truth, everything else is an illusion."[7] David's infinite love etc. conclusion is so powerful that he actually named one of his many books the same. Thank you, David Icke.

> Blessed are they that do his commandments, that they may have right to the tree of life, and may enter in through the gates into the city. For without are dogs, and sorcerers, and whoremongers, and murderers, and idolaters, and whosoever loveth and maketh a lie. (Revelation 22:14-15, underline added)

Wow. Written 2,000 years ago and did I learn that in Catechism? The Lutherans had me worshiping on the wrong day. Falsifying his name. Spell god backwards and it's dog. There are mighty men of renown who snuck in unawares. A whole hour church service could be used explaining each and every warning written there and how we are living in these exact times. At this time question everything, seek the truth in all things, and it will be revealed to you. It's our hearts we have to listen to. "Redeeming the time, because the days are evil, wherefore be ye not unwise, but understanding what the will of the Lord is." (Ephesians 5:16-17)

[6] Zbigniew Brzezinski, *The Grand Chessboard.* (1997) 190-191.

[7] David Icke, *Infinite Love Is The Only Truth, Everything Else Is Illusion: Exposing the Dreamworld We Believe To Be Real.*

These times are indeed very difficult. We must keep in mind that Jesus Christ (Yahushua) did not come to bring peace. He came to separate the wheat from the tares.

> Suppose ye that I am come to give peace on earth? I tell you, Nay; but rather division: For from henceforth there shall be five in one house divided, three against two, and two against three. The father shall be divided against the son, and the son against the father; the mother against the daughter, and the daughter against the mother; the mother in law against her daughter in law, and the daughter in law against her mother in law. (Luke 12:51-53)

> Think not that I am come to send peace on earth: I came not to send peace, but a sword. For I am come to set a man at variance against his father, and the daughter against her mother, and the daughter in law against her mother in law. And a man's foes shall be they of his own household. (Matthew 10:34-36)

Adding yet another scripture to stress the times we are in. If our own parents and government and children betray us, where do we stand a chance? By not acquiescing to the system anymore.

> And ye shall be betrayed both by parents, and brethren, and kinsfolks, and friends; and some of you shall they cause to be put to death. And ye shall be hated of all men for my name's sake. (Luke 21:16-17)

Micah, from the Old Testament reveals much in these three verses:

Trust ye not in a friend, put ye not confidence in a
guide: keep the doors of thy mouth from her that
lieth in thy bosom. For the son dishonoureth the father, the daughter riseth up against her mother, the
daughter in law against her mother in law; a man's
enemies are the men of his own house. Therefore I
will look unto the LORD [Yahuwah]; I will wait for
the God of my salvation; my God will hear me.
(Micah 7:5-7)

Yea, mine own familiar friend, in whom I trusted,
which did eat of my bread, hath lifted up his heel
against me. (Psalm 42:9)

These verses touched me so profoundly I am sure because of my betrayal by family members. If it relates to me then it could relate to
you. Trust in reading the Word for yourself. Pray to GOD [Yahuwah]
and Jesus Christ (Yahushua) for the truth, the light, and the way. Pray
for Yah to reveal the truth to you in ALL things.

But the Comforter, which is the Holy Ghost, whom
the Father will send in my name, he shall teach you
all things, and bring all things to your remembrance,
whatsoever I have said unto you. (John 14:26)

Those reading, I hope, understand then why this may have repeats
and fragments, but I so want to get this out there and then maybe
work on another. I originally had a lot of scripture in my first pages,
and I took them out of this version and was going to make a separate
book with just scriptures. Then I realized that scriptures are part of
my programming and have actually helped and comforted me, just as
they were intended to do. Thus, this book is a compilation of what I
have learned in the last three years from reading the Bible and other

books. When my last alter kicked in, triggered by the code word *antichrist*, I could not stop reading the Bible for eight to ten hours a day, every day for about a year. I was reading the Psalms and I kept reading, "I know your commandments, precepts, testimonies, judgments." So I decided to go back to the beginning. I went right to the beginning of the Bible and read it cover to cover. I still spend hours per day reading the Bible. I've read most of the book many times over. I had to go back to a Hebrews Roots Bible to find out the name of God. There are learning tools there. It has also been altered, changed, watered down, and falsely interpreted by man. Yahuwah uses the word *conspiracy* regarding his own priests and prophets. Ah, yes that great conspiracy word. So many times in the past three years have I heard from persons I'm sharing information with and trying to awaken, "Ah, you're one of those conspiracy theorists." The term *conspiracy theorist* was put in the psyche of the American public after the JFK assassination to deter any persons questioning the official story. Nope, the government doesn't want any of the "sheeple" to question any of their perfidy.

I am under 24/7 surveillance. My whole life has been a series of predators, setups, and many, many sex films. There is a cult, you see, a very secretive and powerful cult, centuries old that have chosen victims for their sick game. It's governmental in nature with strong freemason ties. Throw in Satanism and alien mind control and there is the perfect targeted individual. Basically, we are just pawns in a universal experiment. Humans are just rats in a cage being attacked by mind maggots. I've had people say, "At least you're doing what you want to do now," and I say, "I wonder if I've ever had an original thought of my own." The mind control has been so extensive on my brain. Is there anything unique about me? It is hard for many to understand the frustration in knowing that you have been targeted for extensive mind control and that you have no choice but to keep pushing forward through every day, every week, one Sabbath at a time, Saturday to Saturday.

We have to remember that we are in 2017, and the technology is so very advanced that a common person has literally no idea how extensive and pervasive the tracking tools are that are available to the NSA, CIA, TSA, do as I say, alphabet soup agencies. Fritz Springmeier, an expert on MK Ultra/Monarch Project programming: *[I'll spell it out for the reader, but we must remain calm. A fear-based response only makes things worse.] Yes, it is true that the NSA can remotely track people if they know the specific EMF waves (evoked potentials from EEGS in the 30-50 Hz 5 milliwatt range) of a person's bio-electric field. Each person's emissions are unique, just like their fingerprints, palm prints, and voiceprints. This means that the NSA can remotely track anyone in public. And yes, it is true that the NSA's RNM system can remotely send EMF brain stimulation signals which create visual images, subliminal audios which appear to be audible sounds, and thoughts into people's minds. Yes, it is true that bodysuits of implants are used to control people's minds and bodies, as well as to track them. Yes, it is true they have voiceprints of hundreds of thousands of Americans and can identify & track via their computers all electronic communications in this nation. Most phone calls go through about thirty computers before they reach their destination. The phone companies' computers, according to someone who worked for AT&T and witnessed it, record ALL phone calls using computers.*[8]

I will have incidents shared in this book regarding my childhood, my handlers, lots of scripture and things that happen to targeted individuals, information acquired since my awakening in 2012. Some may be of little interest to you, other information may resonate with you and lead you to more information regarding that topic. Nonetheless, this is what I have to share thus far.

The below is an email I sent to my attorney in Georgia for a DUI I received in August 2015. It sums up what a targeted individual goes through.

---

[8] Fritz Springmeier, *Project Monarch.*

Darrell & Jennifer:

Hope you both are well. I have mailed today the $500.00 balance due on my account for Daryl's representation for me for my DUI hearing. I hope to have a decent outcome...fingers are crossed. I will call a couple weeks before the January 22, 2016 hearing date to discuss the probable outcome and if my presence is necessary at the hearing. I'm not sure what the videos will reveal, but for what it's worth, I don't recall Officer Nettles reading me any rights at the police station. He just said, "Come here, Ms. Goodridge, sit down. You're going to blow into this machine." I didn't think I had an option but to abide since I was already arrested. I know my alcohol level proves I was drinking and driving, but I was deserted on Tybee Island, and I think that was a setup, too. I was only a few miles from my motel room in Savannah, and I was not speeding or driving recklessly. I may have looked down at my GPS and went out of my lane, but I don't think I deserved to go to jail my second day in Georgia. But I also know I should not have gotten behind the wheel. I appreciate any and all help you can provide for me.

Below you will find a few links to an interview I did in England back in May 2015. Although I am not crazy about the outcome, as Miles edited it and posted it without my review first, I have had over 9,000 [now over 10,700] views on the first hour. I plan on creating my own presentation with a link for my book which I plan to self-publish in the near future. Please let me know if you wish to postpone the hearing. I need to know ASAP if my presence makes a difference to the outcome of my case. If it does, I will definitely be there. If not, I trust you to do the best you can. I do need my bond money back. It is $4,600 just to get out of jail, and I lose 15% to the bondsman even though my own money was used. If I do not appear, will that money be mailed back to me? I am so glad I met both of you and I know you are both very busy, but my story is true and the Monarch project/MK Ultra/Mason Ritual Abuse program/Alien mind control must be exposed.

I also got my van window shot out on Tybee Island a couple weeks after the arrest and my telephone stolen. I am indeed a targeted individual but am so glad to be alive and awake. The perfect mind control slave doesn't know they are mind controlled. I will never be out of the program, but am doing my best to make a difference for mankind. As Martin Luther King said, "Anyone's injustice is our injustice," but the almighty dollar sure does buy souls. Thanks for taking the time to read this. Here's to the ride.

My attorney's assistant told me a person called impersonating me asked if we were going forward with the hearing or passing. It was not me who called. I waited for my attorney to call me and when no call ever came I finally called them a day before the hearing. The assistant explained she didn't call me because I had called her on Monday morning and spoke with her. The assistant said the person said she was Sandra Goodridge and that her voice was similar, but in hindsight it wasn't me. I never called her and spoke with her that Monday morning. The hearing was supposed to be on Friday, January 22, 2016. Someone sure has an interest in my whereabouts. Probably another shipment was going to be planned around my having to go back to Savannah, Georgia for my hearing.

My goodness, the energy that was sucked out of me. The tears I cried in that jail cell. I bonded out within three hours and still had to sit there for another eleven or so, about fourteen hours. I begged the officer to let me go. I was not swerving or speeding. I didn't hit or hurt anyone. I was all alone in Savannah, Georgia, the second night I got there. It was $4,600 to get out of jail and another $4,000 on attorney fees. I was tracked and followed in Georgia, and I realized I had to get out of there so I went back to Michigan. Go to Georgia on vacation and leave on probation.

Why would I even go to Georgia...the state with the Georgia Guidestones? The Georgia Guidestones is a monument that was erected in 1980 in Elbert County, Georgia, in the United States. A set of ten guidelines (commandments) are inscribed on the structure in eight modern languages, and a shorter message is inscribed at the top of the structure in four ancient language scripts; Babylonian, Classical Greek, Hindi and Egyptian hieroglyphs. The principles are engraved on the Georgia Guidestones in eight different languages, one language on each face of the four large upright stones. Moving clockwise around the structure from due north, they are as follows: English, Spanish, Swahili, Hindi, Hebrew, Arabic, Chinese and Russian. In June 1979, an unknown person or persons under the pseudonym R.C. Christian hired Elberton Granite Finishing Company to build the structure. The monument was unveiled on March 22, 1980.

Georgia Guidestones—8 languages for NWO—opening date 3/22/1980

I also have an incident that I will be sharing below regarding having been tricked into a mental hospital for a week, all for sharing the truth by a forensic nurse, an advocate, and three police officers.

The latter pages will share the experiences I went through as a child and throughout some of my life. There is so much to it, so much to share, that I am not sure how well a reader may follow this, but I'm giving it a try. One must remember this is a spiritual, energetic world and thus, spiritual warfare prayer is essential to keeping the dark forces off your back. I pray every day. I pray for the millions of children in global sex slave rings. Over 700,000 children were reported missing in 2015 in the United States alone, and only about 200,000 are attributed to family abductions, i.e., the father stealing the child from the mother or the mother stealing the child from the father. The number in 2016 was over 800,000 children. When I was still watching television in 2013, surprisingly a news show shared this story. The Super Bowl was being held at the Meadowlands in New Jersey. A stewardess noticed a couple children on a flight with a man in route to New York City, and the children were acting very peculiar. Thus, the stewardess reported the man, and those children along with eighty-five other children were freed from ONE sex slave ring. There is so much money in child pornography and prostitution that governments across the globe do nothing to stop it.

I pray for Gaia, this beautiful earth spirit, mother Gaia, that is being destroyed right under our noses by the radiation in the ocean, oil spills perpetrated on purpose, fracking, constant bombing in the Middle East, destroying the rain forest. The Palestinians are in an open-air prison. The Gaza strip is only twenty-five miles long and four miles wide according to Max Igan. Max Igan has been sounding the alarm since about 2008 or so. Listening to him will really inform you on the situation with the Palestinians. Over a million people live there and many are young adults and children. There is a constant struggle for fresh drinking water and their electricity is cut off on a regular basis. The Israeli soldiers snipe Palestinian children on their playgrounds. The Palestinians are often harassed and woken up in the middle of the night by Israeli soldiers. That Israel is not the true Israel of Yahuwah. Israel and the United States should be tried and held accountable for their war crimes against humanity. All these topics could have pages written, but I am hopeful that most will have done their research already on these topics. Our water is fluoridated, our foods modified (GMO through Monsanto), our bodies bombarded with radiation. Give me a reason it has to be this way.

Remembering that it's just a ride and flowing through life like water, that flows and moves with the tide of the ocean or the river that ripples and glides through the closest crevice, we must flow and sit back and meditate and enjoy the NOW. Now spelled backwards is Won. We win when we realize there is no death, only transition, there is no time, no past, present or future. They are simultaneously *now*. It's a hard concept to grasp but once you have felt the timelessness of an out-of-body experience or astral dream, it becomes more real than this virtual reality game. There are many names for this place: loosh farm, slaughterhouse, matrix, prison planet….all pertain to this experience. Loosh is energy that is food for the inter-dimensionals. They are like crackheads for it and suck on low vibrational energy and sexual innocence energy. They are pedophiles and suck on the children's energy, the younger, purer, and more innocent, the better. They have been harvesting our energy for thousands and thousands of years.

Robert Monroe, in his book *Far Journeys*, writes of contact he had with a light being in an out-of-body experience (OBE). (Monroe is arguably the world's foremost researcher on OBE's; he started an institute with trainee/researchers to scientifically investigate the phenomenon.) Reportedly, the light being told Monroe that when humans die, their energy is released and harvested by trans-dimensional beings who use it to extend their own life spans. The claim is that the earth is a garden created by these beings as their food source.

According to Monroe's story, animals are intentionally positioned on this planet to feed on plants and on each other, thereby releasing the life force of their victims so it can be harvested. In a predator-prey struggle, exceptional energy is produced in the combatants. The spilling of blood in a fight-to-the-death conflict releases this intense energy which the light beings call *loosh*. Loosh is also harvested from the loneliness of animals and humans, as well as from the emotions engendered when a parent is forced to defend the life of its young. Another source of loosh is humans' worship.

According to Monroe's informant, our creators, the cosmic "energy farmers," intentionally equipped animals with devices like fangs, claws and super-speed in order to prolong predator-prey combat and thereby produce more loosh. In other words, the greater the suffering, the more life force is spewed from our bodies, and the tastier the energy meal for our creators.

This story told to Monroe (which threw him into a two-week depression) corresponds to reports in some of the world's oldest scriptures — the Vedas, Upanishads, and Puranas of India. There we read that "the universe is upheld by sacrifice (Atharva Veda) and that "all who are living (in this world) are the sacrificers. There is none living who does not perform Yagya (sacrifice). This body is (created) for sacrifice, and arises out of sacrifice and changes according to sacrifice."[9] Robert Monroe quotes, *"You are not your physical body,"* and *"Remember your ultimate goal is not physical survival."* Another thing Robert Monroe shared in his books is the necessity to get out of a belief system. He said that when people pass over they are confused and are asked what their beliefs were while they were incarnated in the Earth reality. Then they get sent to the dimensions (heaven) according to their belief. A Christian goes to the Christian heaven. The Muslims go to Muslim heaven and so on.

I have been jailed six times and put in three mental hospitals (twice against my will, and in the first case I was too young to see what was going on). I was a drug addict, beaten up many, many times (at

---

[9] Garbha Upanishad.

least 50 beatings) by boyfriends and husbands, molested my entire childhood, a child whore and adult whore. Having sex with many, many men in many, many motels, hotels, on top of the Pan Am Building in New York City, on top of a movie theater in Savannah, Georgia, and in one of the head offices at a law firm in New York City called Stroock, Stroock & Lavan. I didn't put it together that there were cameras up in that record center that conveniently had a couch. I had sex with a handler, Dan Farley, up there many times and went to many hotels with him in New York City. He now works for the New York City prosecuting attorney's office. Oh Sandy, what were you looking for? I was used and abused my entire life, all the way through this year. I lasted two years with Dan.

Working as a legal secretary for almost thirty years, I never knew the bar association fees I paid for my attorneys every year went to the Crown, which is the Templars, which is the Masons. After doing years of corporate law, liquor law (New York State Liquor Authority…government), and landlord/tenant law, my specialty became intellectual property (patents, trademarks, copyrights…all U.S. Patent Office). For at least sixteen years I worked for law firms specializing in intellectual property. I've asked myself, *How could I have been surrounded by such "intelligent" persons and never have heard a word about the Masons or the corrupt government?* Then there was that ah-ha moment and when I realized my entire life was setup from the cradle. I remember a co-worker asking me what I was doing on my next vacation (we got four weeks' vacation each year), and I said, "Driving to Michigan." She replied, "We might as well call you road warrior." I didn't realize then how accurate she was. I went back and forth to Michigan countless times, probably at least forty.

I have been passed around at least fourteen to sixteen handlers (boyfriends, husbands) which I will share as well.

Still feeling more stuck here than wanting to be here playing this 3D virtual reality game…a game that the programmers have a cheat sheet for. It's hard to explain, but it is just that my life is so bizarre with so many predators, and so much advance technology that I have no access to, that I would much less choose to be more with technology than with nature. Being a targeted individual, we are constantly attacked with ELFs, EMFs, constant sound frequency interruptions, and human/hybrid predators. The following is an example of a recent incident that happened to me.

I met with Detective Neumann, Warren Police Department, and special victims unit today. He is a portly man with blonde hair and blue eyes, an average-looking sort of guy with a heavy breathing problem. Detective Neumann called me several times to meet with him, and I spent an hour with him regarding a possible date rape. This isn't the first time it has happened to me, but this time I am making sure to go forward. I reported it on December 16, 2015 and ended up being held against my will in a mental hospital for a week, just for telling the truth about my childhood and the stalking that goes on in my life. I got out of the mental hospital on December 24, 2015. Don't say MK Ultra, Masons or Illuminati as then you are labelled "conspiracy theorist." I was confined in a mental hospital for telling the truth. I made my police report and was told to meet a nurse to do a rape kit. Through conversation, she asked about my childhood and I shared my story about the program I was put through. The nurse and advocate called police (three officers) and held me for two and a half hours until I'd agree to go to a hospital to do the kit rather than at the clinic. They said the hospital kit is more advanced and that I would only be there a few hours.

I told them, "No way. I know you're going to do to something to me."

They reassured me and even said (and I quote), "We are the good guys."

The nurse went ahead and did a petition for the hospital to hold me, and then I was court ordered to a mental hospital for a week. The forensic nurse marked a box on the petition that said I may be harmful to myself or others, yet all of her "quotes" in her notes of what I had said only shared what I said about MK Ultra, Masons, and being a targeted individual. There were no quotes where I said anything indicating I wanted to hurt myself or others. I never once indicated that I was at all extremely depressed or suicidal. I just wanted to get the kit done and get out of there. Funny how things happen. Anyway, I got through it. There are so, so many people being held in mental hospitals, left there to rot away. The same as in nursing homes. The rape kit takes months but I did do the kit, and I would not have if I wasn't convinced something happened to me. Not the first time but hopefully the last. The program is from cradle to grave, generation after generation of predators and generation after generation of victims, a.k.a. targeted individuals. Here's to the ride!

"Our society is run by insane people for insane objectives. I think we're being run by maniacs for maniacal ends and I think I'm liable to be put away as insane for expressing that. That's what's insane about it."[10] Yes, and unfortunately, the psychopaths rule in the top governmental/political/military positions as well as the local police stations (now militarized) and the medical industry.

The mental hospital was under lock and security so there is really no escaping once there. What a feeling of betrayal when I was secured in the emergency room overnight and then transferred to a mental hospital. It is a terrible feeling wondering how long "they" may hold you. I was lucky to get out within a week. I played the game, took the meds, went to group meetings, ate all my food and got out after a week. It felt so good to experience fresh air and sunlight again. There were some very sad people there, all doped up and barely alive.

This is an ongoing true story of a mind-controlled survivor who is not out of the program but using every bit of power and courage I have to keep my sanity, clarity and spiritual essence. I had my awakening in December 2012, exactly with the Mayan calendar. What an awakening. My parents sold me out at birth. Interestingly, on my parents' gravestone they even have two monarch butterflies. That makes me inclined to feel that my programming was definitely Monarch programming

---

[10] John Lennon, Beatles Interviews Database: John Lennon Interview: Release 6/6/1968

under the MK Ultra mind control. From December 2012 through today, I have been learning, growing, watching videos, ordering books to read, dot connecting, and writing this book. My understanding is that my mother was sexually abused by boyfriends of her mother and that her mother was repeatedly abused and beaten by my mother's father before he died. All the boyfriends came in to abuse my mother. So apparently, it is multi-generational. Maybe that is why my mother thought it was alright to turn me over to the government and allow me to be sexually exploited and experimented on.

My parents' headstone with Monarch Butterflies

The name MONARCH is not necessarily defined within the context of royal nobility, but rather refers to the monarch butterfly. When a person is undergoing trauma induced by electroshock, a feeling of light-headedness is evidenced; as if one is floating or fluttering like a butterfly. There is also a symbolic representation pertaining to the transformation or metamorphosis of this beautiful insect: from a caterpillar to a cocoon (dormancy, inactivity) to a butterfly (new creation) which will return to its point of origin. Such is the migratory pattern that makes this species unique.[11]

When I was still speaking to my living brother and told him about my suspicions of the Freemasons in our family, he said he remembers our mother telling him that she and Daddy had been invited to a secret meeting. I'm sure if they were invited, they went. She probably couldn't say any more than that. When my father and my mother forsake me, then the LORD [Yahuwah] will take me up. (Psalm 27:10)

It was in May 2015 when I turned the key to the realtor and walked away from my home and twenty acres in Lake, Michigan. I sold all my possession except a few totes and packed my van, parked it in long-term parking and flew to England. That was on May 14, 2015. I flew to England for an AlternativeView6 conference and then a week of "sightseeing". I did some sightseeing but ended up filming a three-hour interview to speak out about the nefarious programs of the government, the Freemasons and alien mind control. The England trip proved to be very insightful.

There were many speakers at the conference. One speaker was Samantha Bachman. Samantha has websites and workshops to assist people to their true empowerment. Samantha Bachman held a workshop on the Monday morning after the conference, and I attended. She actually turned sideways toward me, as I was leaning on the side wall of a crowded room, pulled her pants down, revealed her buttocks with two all-seeing eyes tattooed and pointed her ass right at me. I mean she had to really turn to aim her ass at me. During her workshop, she kept using Miles as a key word, saying it was her grandson's name.

She kept saying, "Myles, Myles, Myles," as a way for her to stay focused and keep her vibration up since it is her grandson. She would lean forward and with her right hand point straight out and go up and down and repeat, "Myles, Myles, Myles," but I think they were key words to get me to go with Miles Johnston. I've emailed about her

---

[11] Ron Patton, *The Evolution of Project MKUltra Project Monarch, Nazi Mind Control*

eyes on the butt and she said in an email back that it was a young mistake. She also said, "Oh those? They're just cartoons."

She showed up at a conference in Philadelphia, Pennsylvania in April 2016, and said she knew I shared with others about my strong suspicion that she works for "them" and was programming me. As many years as she has been doing these events, she has to know that many attending are seeking healing, and then she does that symbology. I just don't get it.

Right after her workshop I was introduced to Miles Johnston. Miles Johnston is a UFO and mind control researcher. I ended up doing a half hour interview with him on that Monday morning. He introduced me to the term "targeted individuals." In hindsight, I knew nothing about Miles Johnston and totally put any intuition and discretion to the wind and let him film me. Then Samantha "took me under her wing" and we drove to Bristol where she and Ian Crane were speaking that night. Then the next day we went to Stonehenge. She would not let me talk about my story, and I realize now in hindsight that I'm being monitored, followed, with my probable behavior, predictive programming, and that I will never be out of the program. She even said she hates Santos Bonacci, who most know is just trying to wake people up to the secrets of the universe and our existence. Condemned him saying he is leading people astray and commented how Santos is sleeping in his car now. There are many speaking out who have their lives manipulated and are harassed and forced into difficult situations. Santos Bonacci is a researcher and is fluent in astrotheology. I could be totally wrong, but I don't really think so.

After Samantha and I separated, I spent a few days with Miles Johnston to film a three-hour interview. The YouTube interview is separated into three parts. The first hour has over 12,000 views, but in the second hour there is a blackout and I am really not happy with the interview. The second hour has had over 6,000 views, and the third over 5,000 views. Hopefully, by the time you are reading this I will have my own presentation available to be viewed.

Miles had me painting his house and preparing a guest room. He kept me busy, took me to mind control spots and basically works for them as well. Just the way he wouldn't directly answer anything in my emails to him when I specified I did not want him posting my interview until I saw it first, as I saw what he did to my first interview. At the conference, I had been so excited that someone wanted to record my testimony, I totally didn't check him out. He worked for the BBC ,and I distinctly believe he is a hybrid. Miles, sue me if you want to, but let's call a spade a spade. All of our DNA is twicked and most of us are implanted in some way.

Also, my luggage was delayed for two days upon arriving in England. Just very bizarre. At this point coming as far as I have, there are no coincidences in who I meet and decisions I make. The mind control is so prevalent in people like us who were hijacked as children and mind controlled our entire lives.

During my flight back to the United States I sat at the boarding gate at the Birmingham, England airport waiting for the boarding call when a man sat in a seat directly across from me. He looked me up and down and stared at me for a minute or so. I should have known then that he was a programmer sent to destabilize me. He was in his mid-thirties, nice looking, trim haircut, well dressed. As the boarding call came, I arose and thought nothing of the man until he sat next to me on the plane. My seat was a window seat and this man, who introduced himself as Carl, was in the middle seat. In the aisle seat next to him was a black man appearing to be in his twenties who introduced himself as Matthew.

The flight was long, my guard was down, and I began to have conversations with both of these men. It wasn't until I was back in my van in the United States that I realized that they were both sent to try and reprogram me. Carl had nothing but propaganda to share and discuss. He told me he was an electrical engineer and flies back and forth to Malaysia all the time. He told me practically his entire life story, sharing long detailed stories about fights he was in, his family, his job. I wrote it in script form below and yes everyone is entitled to their own opinion and this may be interpreted as me judging but please read and draw your own conclusion.

Carl: I love the queen. She is so good, and it is parliament that is bad.

Sandy: The queen owns enough land to feed the hungry and educate the poor across the world six times over. Her servants have to walk backwards when they leave the room because they cannot show their backs to her.

Carl: Oh, she owns everything. She owns my house for ninety-nine years. That's fine with me since I won't live to be ninety-nine years old. It is rude to turn your back on anyone. I was taught never to turn my back on anyone.

Carl: Americans think Obama is good. He's done a lot to bring about change.

Sandy: (laughing) You have to be kidding me. He should have been impeached when he enforced ObamaCare. If U.S. citizens don't get ObamaCare, a tax penalty is imposed when filing their income tax. He has done nothing but continue wars and write executive order after executive order. The last election (as all) had to be fixed to get him re-elected. That was the last year I voted. I voted for Mitt Romney, but now I know it doesn't matter who a person votes for, whether republican or democrat (demo[n]crat…just saying, had to put that in. I didn't say it to Carl), it doesn't matter. Once elected, either candidate will be run by the same behind-the-curtain puppet master.

Sandy: I think there is something more to the moon. Have you ever heard of the lunar wave? I bet there are space stations all over the moon. I just learned the other side of the moon has a lunar operations center.

Carl: Oh, did you know there is no dark side of the moon? The truth is the moon rotates and the government and NASA have been lying all this time about there being a dark side. There is no dark side of the moon.

Sandy: Nikola Tesla was so brilliant and insightful and I never learned about him in school. His inventions were far more advanced than was exposed to the public.

Carl: Oh, did you know that his air conditioning coil is still being used today?

Sandy: His inventions were way more advanced than what the public was ever told. He had lasers and many other inventions. There is a video called "The Secrets of Tesla" and I read his autobiography. He was in tune with nature, the breath and the Vedic hymns. Tesla said, "If you want to know the secret of the universe, think of energy, vibration and frequency."

Carl: Blah, blah, blah about the air conditioning apparatus still being used today.

Carl was chatting away about his personal life when he shared, about his cousin Jane's wife.

Sandy: What? Your cousin Jane is gay?

Carl: Well, she has a girlfriend but doesn't call herself gay.

(NOTE: Doublespeak is a big programming tool. He said "my cousin Jane and her wife numerous times.)

Carl: Bill Gates is so good, donating so much money to all those charities.

Sandy: Bill Gates gets huge tax write-offs for those donations. Bill Gates funded a vaccination program for polio in India and over 40,000 children are now paralyzed. India is suing Gates.

Carl: (dumbfounded) Oh.

Carl: (Pulls out a book and shows it to me) Have you ever read *Salem's Lot*? I hear it is a very good book. *Salem's Lot* is supposed to be Stephen King's best book.

Sandy: I read it years ago. I don't read that garbage anymore. I read books that educate and inform now.

Carl: Well, *Salem's Lot* is supposed to be very good.

Sandy: What do you think about Freemasons?

Carl: I'm not a Mason but my dad is a mason. An honorary mason two years ago.

Sandy: The Freemasons are not good. Anything that is secret is not good.

Carl: Oh, they do charity work and it's a wonderful brotherhood.

Sandy: Your Dad is a Mason but you're not?

Carl: (No comment.)

Sandy: War should be ended. If the military soldiers would just put their arms down and say, "Nope, I'm not shooting another human being," war would not be the money-making machine it is.

Carl: Oh, I was in the military. It is honorable to serve your country.

Sandy: I don't think most of the military soldiers even know what they are fighting for. This endless war has to stop.

Sandy: I was a legal secretary for almost thirty years and only got paid twenty-five to thirty dollars an hour.

Carl: I'm an electrical engineer in London and only get eighteen pounds an hour.

Sandy: (Disbelieving) That sounds remarkably low for an electrical engineer.

The man, Matthew, in the aisle seat, said he was a dancer for Azealia Banks. Azealia Banks is an American singer/rapper. Through conversation, he said that the hotel threw Azealia and him out of the hotel because they were talking loudly. He was sure it was because they were black. Matthew asked me what I was in England for so I told him the AlternativeView6 conference and proceeded to tell him about some of these topics. He right away said he knows what I am talking about and asked me if I knew about the Illuminati.

Sandy: So Azealia Banks is Illuminati.

Matthew: Oh yes, but she knows what is going on. They are really watching her. We were in a hotel once and noticed an automatic air freshener in the wall that wasn't working. We got up and looked inside and there was a camera.

Matthew: Here watch her video. The video is listed under Illuminati on YouTube. (He handed me his phone and there she is dancing with a huge eye behind her, weird stuff with her eyes). We have to do whatever we're told to do.

Sandy: So you answer to the Illuminati.

Matthew: Yes, we basically sit around a table and they tell us what to do for our fame and fortune.

Sandy: Well, I will be travelling around the United States.

Matthew: You know where you have to go? To Salem. Salem is really a great place. I love Salem.

NOTE: Interesting both men had the code word *Salem*.

Matthew: I perform witchcraft. I drink baby boys' blood. (Seeing my reaction, he said) Oh, actually chicken and goat's blood. The blood keeps us young.

Sandy: So you are about thirty years old?

Matthew: (offended) Why would you guess me at thirty? I am twenty-four years old.

(NOTE: My gut told me he was older than twenty-four years old. The Illuminati drink blood to stay youthful.)

Then Azealia Banks came back to see Matthew. I didn't put it together at the time that he should have been sitting with her and the other dancers in first class.

He introduced me to Azealia and said to her, "This is Sandy. Isn't she beautiful. She is really smart and anointed.

Azealia said, "So you know about David Ickey?" very childish sounding, pronouncing David Icke's last name as Ickey.

Waiting for our luggage at JFK Airport, I noticed one of the persons in the Azealia Banks' group was a man dressed as a woman. It was obvious it was a man. They kept calling her/his name, Jacqueline. The whole group kept staring at me while at the luggage carousel. I got my luggage, checked how long of a layover (ugh, two hours) and headed to my gate to take a nap.

I was heading to my gate on the far left of aisle when I heard, "Hey Sandy! Hey Sandy!"

Sitting on the right side of the aisle at a gate on the way to my gate was my friend Carl. Looking back, he had to be watching for me.

I turned and said, "Oh, hi Carl."

He said, "How long do you have to wait for your connection?"

I said, "A couple hours."

"Oh, then sit here with me for a little while."

Still not reading him for what he was, I sat with him. He immediately pulled out the book *Salem's Lot*. Oh this book is so good." Then there was more doublespeak about his cousin Jane's wife and his visit with her.

Looking back, it was so surreal. At the baggage center all the dancers and Azealia were hanging around and kept looking at me. There was a dancer from the group who was clearly a man but dressed and acted like a woman. They kept calling her Jackie. I know there are many, many homosexuals but with the extent of mind control performed on me, I'm sure that had some sort of trigger type image for me. A lot of my handlers would call themselves lesbians but then they would kiss a man right on the lips in front of me as well.

Just a warning to all late awakened! The game is on and the alternative world is infiltrated by the CIA/Mossad/NSA/Tri-Lateral, who knows who. I've had to learn the hard way, but now I will be careful with interviews. Trust me. It's humbling to have to admit and share all these outrageous, horrific stories, but they are true and others need to put the pieces together. We awakened have to wake up every day and just keep pushing on, letting the breath flow, recapture our minds, using heart knowledge and intuition. Let love be our primary guide. Abolish all fears. Seek wisdom. Ask for the truth in all things, all the time, every day. And if it suits you, praise his name. Ohhhh, there is so much power in that name, Yahuwah…the Great Spirit in the sky, the one I knew before the book. The inter-dimensional being we call "God."

I did an interview back in 2014 on Freemanflytv.com. That interview had to be hacked. They stood me up the first interview date of Friday, October 10, 2014. I sat there waiting for the call in front of a super nice computer I had rented from Rent-A-Center so I could have a good Skype video conversation. Then 7:00 p.m. came and went. I called Freeman around 7:15 p.m. and was sent straight to voicemail.

The next day I got a call from Freeman saying that there was a mix-up between him and Jamie Hanshaw. They each thought the other had notified me of the cancellation. He was eager to reschedule, but due to two more postponements, one by him and one by me as I couldn't get to my computer at the designated time, still thinking the interview was going to be by Skype. I even have an email from Jamie asking me how long I would have the computer available for my interview.

This is the actual email text from Jamie Hanshaw to me on October 11, 2014:

> Hi, Sandra. Sorry about the mix up. I thought Free-man had emailed you and he thought I had. Sorry for the inconvenience. We still want to record with you, but our other guest for this week fell through which we were going to add your show to. How long do you have your computer rented for? I just saw that we missed your call last night. The phone has been acting weird. Let me know when you have to get the computer back. Sorry for the mix up. :(

So the interview finally got recorded…not by Skype but by telephone.

Live and learn. Ah yes, Paul's good words, that we are not going against flesh and blood but principalities and spirits in high places. "For we wrestle not against flesh and blood, but against principalities, against powers, against the rulers of the darkness of this world, against spiritual wickedness in high places." (Ephesians 6:12) I didn't put it together why Freeman had been to every Mason lodge all over the world. I have multiple texts between him and me regarding the botched interview. In one he said, "Don't accuse me of any wrongdoing." The few people I shared the interview with said they could tell it was hacked. Words were cut off, a bunch of "ya knows" added, I mean a ridiculous amount. Then when Freeman called me on the telephone and I asked him if he was ready to Skype me. He said, "Oh, we're doing the interview right now. We don't video." Then why ask how long I would have the computer for? I have the interview saved. I have the original and the one he cut. He admitted to cutting but he said nothing but chit chat. That is a boldface lie. We slaves have excellent memories.

The interview was chopped up and hacked. The interview was recorded two to three weeks before it was aired, and I know a lot of what I shared was deleted and cut. I am so disappointed that my speaking out ended up like that. My beginning is cut off when I say I am being watched 24/7 and being attacked with ELFs and EMFs. I know I said I was speaking out for the glory of Yahuwah and my three daughters and two granddaughters. I started with and it was not in there, "The perfect host doesn't know it has a parasite, just like the perfect mind control victim doesn't know they are mind controlled." I know I said my birth name, Sandy Bergen, and the year I was born and not just the month and date. The interview just has, "My name is Sandy. I was born November 15th." The year 1959 is a key year for all this mind programming and I wouldn't have omitted it or my last name. I also talked about scripture that was taken out of the interview, i.e. the aliens and cockatrices. "Behold I will send serpents and cockatrices and they will not be charmed." (Jeremiah 8:17) So I google a cockatrice and it is a reptile egg. The cockatrice is also mentioned three times in the book of Isaiah and described as fiery-winged serpents. I know I plugged Sherry Shriner who is an expert between the Bible and the aliens (although a bit fanatical to me — she wants to kill them all). I said, "Sherry Shriner speaks candidly about the aliens." I was stuttering a lot and I know I mentioned my handler's name, Thomas Byrnes, and that seems to be cut out. I asked Freeman to look into it. I don't know the good guys from the bad guys anymore. I know I plugged Sherry Shriner and James Bartley. I spoke with James through emails and he didn't want me sharing his name but it came out anyway, and I do remember saying his name and regretting it. I did say Sherry Shriner's name, and I did not hear one word about her or the alien aspect. I said a few things about the aliens, I know I did. I regretted not mentioning David Icke. I have listened to it twice and I couldn't find my alien part of the scripture that I wanted to point out so imperatively. I don't know, I talked to Freeman for about an hour about the possibility of "them" altering the interview and he promised to get back to me. I know I might sound paranoid, but they have been watching me my entire life and I am just seeking and sounding the alarm for my brothers and sisters to wake up. I went over the interview in my mind afterward and regretted not mentioning the synchronicity of some key informational websites that have led me to airing that interview. I know I didn't mention John Lash (*Not In His Image*) or Jay Weidner. I know what I said and what I listened to was not all what I said. I mentioned Mt. Clemens General Hospital, the hospital I was in when I was three years old, around 1962. It has now been renamed McClaren General Hospital in Mt. Clemens, Michigan, and when I called to get the records, the hospital told me that all records twenty-five years and older are destroyed. I know I shared that and it was not aired in the interview.

I know I said I was married to a freemason, my third husband, and that he even put a black and white floor in our kitchen and had owl lamps, but it just cuts off. When I mentioned my husband in New York, there was a weird cut again. I know when Freeman asked if I had any last words I said, "Infinite love is the only truth. Everything else is an illusion, you know, a belief." I remember him saying "Uhm." That was omitted. There were a bunch of "you knows" added. I mean so many and I know I don't say "you know" like that all the time.

Freeman didn't even put my last name on the webpage. I am not speaking out, revealing all the disgusting things done to me throughout my life to be anonymous. This is characteristic of the big brother problem on people who are awakened and want to speak out. David Icke talks about the awakened being targeted and I would love to reveal this as well. I just want to make a difference. Freeman's interview was the first time I was ever recorded, and I didn't even think of the possibility of it being aired altered.

Freeman basically said, "Don't accuse me of any wrongdoing." It was so obviously a set up, standing me up the original time/date of the interview to put me off-balance. Oh, what a test for patience. I confronted Freeman at the Freeyourmind4 Conference in April 2016 in Philadelphia and he repeated numerous times, "I did nothing, I did nothing…" If he did nothing why didn't he offer to listen to the interview and address the issues? The last evening of the conference, he finally came over to speak to me. Once I said I knew the interview was hacked, he made a big scene and kept yelling, "You're calling me a liar! You're calling me a liar!" He turned his back on me and yelled, "Your calling me a liar!" over and over again to embarrass me. I told him I was leaving the incident in my book and walked away frustrated. The scene was so ugly.

Chapter 2

Operation Paperclip/MK Ultra

I said to myself in June 2015, *How did my life end up like this?* Sitting at a campground in Halls Crossing, Utah, overlooking Powell Lake, the landscape is breathtaking. Purple, blue, pinks across the early evening sky. A beautiful view of the lake nestled in a cove with mountains and rocks surrounding it. A warm breeze caresses my face. *Stay grateful Sandy. You are still alive and you are awake and determined to recapture your mind* I can relate to how Winston had to feel in Orwell's *1984*, wanting to break out but getting beaten down. In the end, though, he said, "God bless The Brotherhood." That I will not ever do. I have absolutely no fear of death and I actually would prefer to be out of this reality now.

I am a survivor of MK Ultra/Monarch Project, Freemason Ritual Abuse, and alien mind control. Hard to believe one person could be preyed upon and experimented on by all these groups. Few people will understand or even care about the life living under Big Brother (CIA NSA, do as I say), mason ritual abuse, and alien mind control. Acknowledging the fact that this is from cradle to grave and that I will be used until I depart this human existence is half the battle to keeping any sanity. I have been diagnosed with a "mental disorder." Yep, just a mental disorder, not bipolar, manic depressive, schizophrenic under United States Social Security, which is fine for me to be considered not sane in this psychopathic insane world. What a blessing to be able to say I paid in since 1976, almost thirty-five years and am getting some of it back.

I have been living with constant surveillance and harassment my entire life. It was like a bag was taken off my head and my critical thinking returned and empathy and compassion tripled. I'd rather be dead in this experience than do nothing and let this horrendous mind control continue to be performed on the masses. Writing this is for the future. Wisdom dwells with prudence and finds out knowledge of witty inventions.

According to Fritz Springmeier, who has written a number of books regarding mind control and the New World Order, over two million Americans have been programmed by trauma-based mind control since 1947. The CIA admitted its Mind Control publicly in 1970, and yet the existence of the mind control is still secret to the general public. A few years ago according to someone who had access to the computers which contain all the names of actively monitored human Monarch slaves, there are 40,000.

I am living in the program, knowing I am programmed, knowing all my decisions are prearranged and everywhere I go is surveillance. The technology that is being used today was already being secretly used by the CIA/NSA/military/government for at the very least forty years. This is a frequency game, and those brave enough to decode the matrix and break out of the herd mentality and free themselves from a belief system are the ones who will evolve and enlarge their hearts.

I was born Sandra Marie Bergen on November 15, 1959, the youngest of five children. There was a full moon the day I was born. I was always a quick learner and had a sharp memory. My childhood days were spent in Utica, Michigan. Unfortunately, since birth I have been mind controlled and used for child sex porn, used as a mule, used as an adult sex slave, and hooked on drugs. It is clear that the perfect mind control victim is not aware of the mind control. Just like the perfect host doesn't know it has a parasite. That is why energy has been continuously sucked out of humans by the many multi-dimensionals. People are not aware that it is happening. It is important to remember that victims are chosen from a diverse array of families.

> A former military officer connected to the CIA, told this writer, "In the 'big picture' these people [MONARCH victims] are in all walks of life, from the bum on the street to the white-collar guy". In corroboration, a retired CIA agent vaguely discussed the use of such personnel to be used as "plants" or "chameleons" for the purpose of infiltrating a designated group, gathering information and/or injecting an ulterior agenda.[12]

I realized that my life was deliberately manipulated by the government/aliens/masons and I am under constant 24/7 surveillance. "They", let's call them The Brotherhood, knew I was going to wake up in December 2012 and begin to deprogram. I don't think they expected me to remember the hospital stay when I was about three years old. The hospital stay I never forgot, just tucked it away until my awakening when I started putting the pieces of the puzzle together. The hospital stay where I was kept in a cage and sexually abused and electro-shocked to fragment my mind, among other mysterious tests. I am a survivor of mind control/brainwashed programs known to have been implemented during the time of my mysterious hospitalization.

> One of the biggest secrets kept from most of the slave's alters is that their System was demonized while a fetus. First, this would give religious front alters the information they need to get them on the right track towards healing, and it could also adversely affect the programming lies of some of the

---

[12] Ron Patton. Project Monarch: Nazi Mind Control.

front alters who don't realize how premeditated all the trauma and torture is. The front alters of victims remember the cover story that the moon children were produced via torture in the cages as little children.[13]

A lot of information can now be found regarding the MK Ultra/ Monarch Project program. I will testify under oath that the incidents that I share are completely true. I will take a lie detector test. I have no reason to make this up. Many are very embarrassing and I've had to muster the courage to write them down. All my intuition says the inclusion of every incident makes a difference. I am not trying to get negative attention or to make an excuse for my compulsive behavior. This has been a soul searching journey that I am sure was planned. I was directly triggered when I learned about the antichrist.

That's when all this enlightenment came to me. Since all of this has been done before, I am sure my birth was well anticipated. I know I am being watched right now. My life has been an obstacle course of stumbling blocks to keep me engulfed in guilt and disgust. I don't know where all this is going, but I know I have to make the best of this lifetime. I would like to make something positive out of all this. The nefarious crimes of the hidden puppeteers who run this country via the visual political puppets must be exposed and stopped.

I was blessed with time on my hands on a beautiful twenty-acre piece of land in Clare County, Michigan, purchased in July 2012. The vibrations up there were incredible. I have a constant vibrational buzz in my head that is overpowering at times. I'm just learning to live with it and realize that it is the heightened vibrational energy I am experiencing. I am in the middle of all that is happening today, firsthand, on purpose. I keep meditating and focusing on not staying stuck in a belief. Realizing my religion that I followed from childhood, Lutheran, is a religion that led me away from honoring the Father's

---

[13] Fritz Springmeier & Cisco Wheeler. The Illuminate Formula Used To Create An Undetectable Mind Control Slave, Chapter 1: The Selection and Preparation of the Victim.

commandments has brought me through some life changing experiences. My life has been no bed of roses. All my higher consciousness keeps telling me to do is write it all down. I remember a remarkable lot from a very early age. I know that I have been tracked by the government all my life. That was one of the first revelations that came to me. but I do believe there is a reason for me to put my life in words and I am going to discuss some horrifying things. There are other victims beginning to deprogram and recapture their minds. My programming was done with help from my family. Cathy O'Brien, born in Muskegon, Michigan in 1957 was a high level governmental sex slave. She was given to the government by her father who was caught selling pornography. He was given an ultimatum…go to jail or give up your daughter. Gerald Ford came right to her house when she was a little girl. With the help of Mark Phillips, a former programmer for the CIA, she was able to deprogram and write her book Trance Formation of America. She has since written more books.

After my awakening in December 2012, I was led to videos and books to learn about Operation Paperclip. MK Ultra was started through Operation Paperclip in 1953 as a mind control experimental program. It was signed off by the then leader of the new CIA, Allen Dulles. There were Nazi doctors, scientists and psychiatrists who performed and perfected their mind control programs on the Jewish prisoners, but not just on Jews but also on Germans, gypsies, gays, and the disabled. These scientists, psychiatrists, and doctors were secretly brought into the United States and Canada through Project Paperclip by the CIA. They came with their records of the experiments done involving surgeries, electrodes, hypnosis, and drugs. They were scooped right into the CIA. This was a completely logical, detached, electronic program. There were 149 subprograms under MK Ultra. It wasn't until the Church Committee Congressional hearings in 1975 that many of the CIA's activities from MKUltra would come to light. Unfortunately, we'll never know the full extent of the program after former CIA director Richard Helms ordered the destruction of documents and had them burned in 1973, sensing the heat from the Watergate scandal in 1972. A New York Times article in December 1974 would allege the CIA had conducted illegal domestic activities on unsuspecting American citizens. The article prompted an investigation by Congress into the allegations, and a committee was appointed to head the investigation. Senator Frank Church was appointed the chair of the committee named for him; however, the Church Committee kept everything hush hush regarding the activities. In 1977 the U.S. Senate released a report on the findings of Project MKUltra. Senator Ted Kennedy revealed to the U.S. the CIA had indeed been testing on unwitting citizens, that the tests involved LSD, and that there had been known deaths from the activities. A follow-up report from the U.S. General Accounting Office in 1984 would reveal that between 1940 and 1974, the CIA exposed thousands of human test subjects to hazardous substances. Of course, with no remaining program documents and few witnesses willing to talk, most expect the true numbers to be higher.

In 1953, Allen Dulles, then director of the USA Central Intelligence Agency (CIA), named Dr. Sidney Gottlieb to direct the CIA's MKULTRA programme, which included experiments conducted by psychiatrists to create amnesia, new dissociated identities, new memories, and responses to hypnotic access codes. In 1972, then CIA director Richard Helms and Gottlieb ordered the destruction of all MKULTRA records. A clerical error spared seven boxes, containing 1738 documents, over 17,000 pages. This archive was declassified through a Freedom of Information Act Request in 1977, though the names of most people, universities, and hospitals are redacted. The CIA assigned each document da number preceded by "MORI", for "Management of

Officially Released Information", the CIA's auto-
mated electronic system at the time of document release. These documents, to be referenced
throughout this chapter, are accessible on the Internet. (see: abuse-of-power.org/modules/content/
index.php!id=31) The United States Senate held a
hearing exposing the abuses of MKULTRA entitled
"Project MKULTRA, the CIA's program of research
into behavioral modification.".[14]

In 1995, President Clinton called for the Human Radiation Experiments Committee. They went through the children that had been deliberately injected with radiation, just to see what happens. Then along
came many victims from MK Ultra programs that were still going on.
Many victims don't have the courage to go back to those terrifying
memories of men and women with PhDs and medical degrees performing these atrocious experiments on them. I will share below, my
clear recollection of the hospital stay when I was three years old.

*By the time Cheryl Hersha came to the facility, knowledge
of multiple personality was so complete that doctors understood how the mind separated into distinct ego states,
each unaware of the other. First, the person traumatized
had to be both extremely intelligent and under the age of
seven, two conditions not yet understood though remaining consistent as factors. The trauma was almost always
of a sexual nature...*[15]

*Fracturing of the psyche is said to be conclusive to creating
the phenomenon that has been termed sleeper assassins.*

[14] Orit Badouk Epstein. *Ritual Abuse and Mind Control: The Manipulation of Attachment Needs.* 1977

[15] Cheryl Hersha. *Secret Weapons: How Two Sisters Were Brainwashed To Kill For Their Country*, p52

According to such theories, the first psychiatrists employed to master mind control studied mental patients who had been diagnosed with Multiple Personality Disorder, which medical science has since renamed Dissociative Identity Disorder. Many of those psychiatrists are said to have been Paperclip Nazi doctors who were brought to the US after conducting radical psychiatric experiments on patients during the Holocaust – the same doctors whose victims not only included Jews, Gypsies, political agitators and homosexuals, but also the mentally ill.[16]

Working simultaneously, though seemingly without a conscience, was Dr Ewen Cameron, whose base was a laboratory in Canada's McGill University, in Montreal. Since his death in 1967, the history of his work for both himself and the CIA has become known. He was interested in "terminal" experiments and regularly received relatively small stipends (never more than $20,000) from the American CIA order to conduct his work. He explored electroshock in ways that, offered such high risk of permanent brain damage that other researchers would not try them. He immersed subjects in sensory deprivation tasks for weeks at a time, though often claiming that they were immersed for only a matter of hours. He seemed to fancy himself a pure scientist, a man who would do anything to learn the outcome. The fact that some people died as a result of his research, while others went insane and still others, including the wife of a member of Canada's Parliament, had psychological problems for many years afterwards, was not a concern to the doctor or those who employed him. What mattered was that by the time

---

[16] Lance Morcan. *The Orphan Conspiracies 29 Conspiracy Theories From The Orphan Trilogy.*

Cheryl and Lynn Hersha were placed in the programme, the intelligence community had learned how to use electroshock techniques to control the mind. And so, like her sister, Lynn was strapped to a chair and wired for electric shock. The experience was different for Lynn, though the sexual component remained present to lesser degree... [17]

Multi-generational sexual child abuse is such a common cause of the proliferation of pedophilia that Hitler/Himmler research focused on this genetic trait for mind control purposes. While I personally could not relate to the idea of sex with a child, I had parents and brothers and sisters who did. I still believe that George Bush revealed today's causation of the rapid rise in pedophilia through justifications I heard him state. The rape of a child renders them compliant and receptive to being led without question. This, Bush claims, would cause them to intellectually evolve at a rate rapid enough to "bring them up to speed" to grasp the artificial intelligence emanating from DARPA. He believed that this generation conditioned with photographic memory through abuse was necessary for a future he foresaw controlled by technology. Since sexual abuse enhanced photographic memory while decreasing critical analysis and free thought, there would ultimately be no free will soul expression controlling behavior. In which case, social engineering was underway to create apathy while stifling spiritual evolution. Nevertheless, to short sighted flat thinking individuals such as Bush, spiritual evolution was not a consideration anyway. Instead, controlling behavior in a population diminished by global genocide of 'undesirables' would result in

---

[17] Cheryl Hersha. *Secret Weapons: How Two Sisters Were Brainwashed To Kill For Their Country*

Hitler's 'superior race' surviving to claim the earth. Perceptual justifications such as these that were discussed at the Bohemian Grove certainly did not provide me with the complete big picture. It did, however, provide a view beyond the stereotyped child molester in a trench coat that helped in understanding the vast crimes and cover-ups being discussed at this seminar in Houston.[18]

I had a couple astral dreams with my mother since 2012. In the first I met her and she said the government had been after me my whole life. In another dream I asked her how much my parents were paid for selling me into the program and she said $20,000. Back in 1962, that was quite a bit of money. People may think that these were just dreams but they were very real spiritual contacts. Interestingly, the second hour of my interview with Miles Johnston has a weird glitch/cut at 45:55 where I share about the dream. I know I said my mother told me in an astral dream "Sandy, the government has been after you all your life." There is a stop of my lips and the "all your life" is cut out. Apparently "they" don't want people to know that children are traumatized and stalked from the time of their birth. If there was no relevance in an astral dream, why take it out? I know what I said and I know the "all your life" was deliberately cut out and the cut is apparent. By cutting out the "all your life" the context of the statement is completely changed. It sounds like my mother just said "the government has been after you." So Sandy is paranoid now that she learned about Snowden in 2013 revealing all the surveillance and read George Orwell's 1984. Very clever way to change the power of a statement.

The victims of Monarch Project/MK Ultra programming are generational. My parents did it to me, my first daughter Amy may be doing it to her daughters. At Heidi's preschool graduation she flashed her little titty. The classroom was jam-packed full with parents, grand-

[18] Cathy O'Brien, *ACCESS DENIED For Reasons Of National Security: Documented Journey From CIA Mind Control Slave To U.S. Government Whistleblower*

parents, siblings. All the graduating preschoolers were lined up in front of the room singing songs. During a song I notice my granddaughter fiddling with her strap on her little sundress. Then boom, she pulls down the strap and flashes a full view of her little breast. I gasped, "No!" and turned but neither my daughter, Amy, her boyfriend Bruce (Heidi's parents) nor the teacher seemed to notice or care or have any kind of response. That same summer (2014), the last summer with my granddaughters, Amy, Heidi, Baylie and I were going to the community swimming pool. I was in the bathroom putting on my suit when Heidi came in and said, "Grandma, let me see your boobies."

I said, "These are Grandma's boobies" as I covered mine up and added, "and don't you show yours to anyone."

God bless her heart, she got puffed up and boldly said, "I'm showing them to everybody."

That same afternoon while I left the pool and went to buy lunch for us, Amy said, "While you were gone, Heidi pulled her bathing suit down and proudly stood at the edge of the pool with a big smile on her face and basking in the sun."

I said "Don't you find that unusual?"

Amy said, "Well, I don't want her to be ashamed of her body."

By that fall (October 2014), I was cut off from any contact with my granddaughters or Amy and, of course, Bruce seemed to have a particular grudge against me. In around December 2014, I showed up at Amy's house and parked outside her house; however, in November 2015, I showed up at their house with balloons and presents for Heidi's sixth birthday on November 12th. Amy had no choice but to let me in when the girls saw me outside with presents and balloons. So I was able to visit for a couple hours, and actually was hoping for some type of visitation, even once a month, something. Nope. Amy said if I ever do that again that they will issue a personal protective order. I don't want the drama for the girls. During that visit, Heidi and Baylie were showing me pictures that were taken of themselves with a tablet. Many were of Heidi taking selfies with no shirt on, etc.

Baylie would seductively pose and Heidi would snap a shot of her. I mean six-years old and taking naked selfies. What happened to childhood innocence? Also, since Heidi was as young as about two years old, after a bath she would run through the house naked. I would be on the couch in the living room and Heidi would run in and say, "Look, Grandma!" and bend over and spread her butt cheeks open so I could see her little butt hole. She would laugh and she taught Baylie how to do it, too.

I would shake my head and say to myself, *Well, she must know way more than me 'cause I was having extensive sexual relations at that age with my cousin and brother yet I never once ran through the house naked and bent over.* I'm sharing this because the generational aspect to the chosen victims for the mind control.

Amy has the signature butterfly tattoo on her back shoulder. When Amy was only about two years old, I left her with my parents for several years. It is really hard to have to face the fact that your own daughters are a part of the cult/program or whatever you want to call it and that they actually have no conscience or empathy toward me. How can I smoke crack on and off for seven years in the same household with daughters (ages fourteen, sixteen, and twenty-six at the time) and not one of them ever say, "Hey, Mom, we hear you drive out of the house at 3:00 a.m. and return at 3:15 a.m. and go right into your room. We know you are doing something. We love you. You're better than that." Nope, even after they knew I was in jail for twenty-three days for violating my probation for possession of crack cocaine did any one of them say, "Let's get you help. We're here for you." I can't blame them. I was the one who was so screwed up and am so glad that I would never, ever do crack, coke, meth, or heroin again. I know they were not the parent but I can't help feeling some betrayal.

My daughters Amy and Kristi have completely shut me out of their lives. I have absolutely no contact with my two beautiful granddaughters because their father and mother do not want anything to do with me. My granddaughters' father, Bruce Drinkwater, told me he is a Mason. I have many texts saved from him such as, "You're not going to the One. There's a much worse fate for you. You should have paid attention to your gifts," and "Mind your own business, stop judging, and most of all keep your mouth shut. I am prepared to escalate this matter. You have your memories. Enjoy them." I will never keep my mouth shut. It breaks my heart the way I have been exiled from Amy and my granddaughters. All I can do is pray.

I want to also point out that the blood Rh factor is also key in choosing victims for mind control. Blood has an Rh factor and most are positive, in fact about 85% are Rh positive. but there is a small percentage that has Rh negative blood. There is no Rhesus factor in their blood. Growing up my mother told me my blood is Rh negative. It is odd that through the years I never had one doctor tell me what my blood type is and I never asked. Other survivors have told me their Rh factor is negative. The Illuminati bloodline is Rh negative factor and they intermarriage with first cousins and second cousins.

The NSA could track and monitor those that have a distinct genetic marker, which is the Rh negative blood factor. It is said the tribe of Dan which would be mixed with the Nephilim (the hybrids between human women and "fallen angels" a/k/a other species, interdimensionals, aliens have this blood type. Interestingly, the tribe of Dan is not mentioned in Revelation as one of the 12 scattered tribes of Israel that have their names written on the new foundations. People in western nations have mandatory blood tests whenever a new child is being brought into existence. The blood type of the child is recorded within a permanent medical record. These medical records are kept in a government owned electronic database. Anytime you visit an emergency room within a government run hospital or your very own family doctor, your medical history is logged into an electronic database under your health card number. So it would be very easy for the NSA to find and track all Rh negative individuals by accessing this electronic database.

Rh negative human tissue and organs are more than likely in high demand when it comes to black market organ sales If only 15% have this Rhesus factor missing, how valuable is it? So it shouldn't surprise anyone that Rh negative people are worth more dead than alive.

Chapter 3

The Hospital Stay – Three Years Old

My earliest memory I always carry with me is from when I was about two years old. I was riding a tricycle on the sidewalk. I also have one memory of my mother's mother when I was also about two years old. She was lying in my parents' bed dying; however, the memories of a hospital stay that I had when I was about three years old have haunted me all my life. I recall throughout my childhood wondering what that hospital stay was about, never forgetting parts of it, and then for quite some time I never thought about it again. Then the massive flashbacks started in December 2012 and continue to this day. Memories I never forgot, just tucked away until my awakening in December 2012.

I remember very vividly the morning I was taken to the hospital. It was a hectic morning with my two older sisters and two older brothers getting ready for school. It was not a large house for five children and two adults. It had three bedrooms, one bathroom. I walked from my bedroom through the kitchen to the bathroom. I was rubbing my eyes, feeling happy, no type of ill feeling at all, no pain, fever or sickness and urinated. As I turned to flush the toilet, my urine appeared to be red. I called my mother to come and look and she panicked. She didn't take my temperature, ask me if I was in pain, didn't call a doctor. She just called my cousin Roslyn and asked her to immediately drive me to the hospital. Why to the hospital, not a doctor appointment? My mother wrapped me in a blanket and held me in her arms and rocked me all the way to the hospital. Roslyn pulled up to the emergency room door and my mother got out of the car with me in her arms and was put into a wheelchair. We were wheeled into the emergency room, and my mother handed me over to the nurses. Then she was gone. I ended up spending days at that hospital. I always remembered the hospital stay as three days at Mt. Clemens General Hospital, Mt. Clemens, Michigan, the same hospital I was born in. Through therapy and meditation I know I was there longer than three days. Unfortunately, my parents are dead and when I called the hospital to ask for my records, the hospital informed me that any records dating back over twenty-five years are destroyed. I don't understand the purpose of records if they are not all retained. The hospital is now McClaren Macomb Hospital. There is an air force base less than five miles away, Selfridge Air Force Base, built around World War I. It is still an active base. From reading about the program, most hospitals where the mind control program is implemented have military bases nearby.

I wasn't sick and had no stomach or urinary pain, no fever or illness whatsoever. During deep meditation I saw an image come into my mind with my mother handing me something in a drink to change my urine color. My mother smiling, handing me a drink and telling me to drink it all. That is not one I carried forever, but that is irrelevant; they got me to the hospital. I was put in a caged bed, yes an entire cage. I was taken to a big room full of cages. The beds were flat and the cages had black steel bars all the way to the top of the ceiling. I remember sitting in that cage and being examined. My parents came one time to visit me during that hospital. I will never forget seeing them walk into the room toward my cage. My parents were holding hands and my mother walked in like a star. She had a dress on and waltzed across the room like she was royalty. My father had a bag in his hand. My mother reached into the bag and handed me puzzles. I never forgot they brought me a stack of puzzles. I sat there and solved those puzzles - one, two, three - just I like always could. Puzzles are a part of preparing the child's mind for the electroshock programming. That is the only visit I had from my parents. I had to be sedated after they left because I cried so hard and became so upset.

I have no memories of any vitals taken such as temperature, blood pressure, or heartbeat during that hospital stay. There were other children in cages in the room, and we were let out of our cages to go into the game corner. There were puzzles, blocks with numbers and symbols on them and we played in the game corner many times. There was a room behind my cage with a closed door and I asked the nurse what was in that room. She said a little girl with a hole in her heart. What a thing to tell a three year old frightened child. I still remember how that devastated me, not wanting to eat and being so sad.

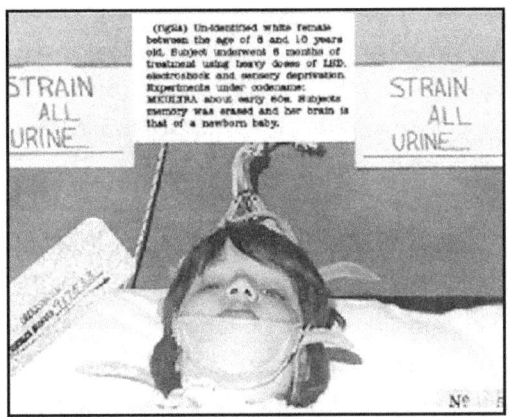

I remember something on my head and attached to my temples

I was electroshocked during that hospital visit. The electroshock is so traumatic that most don't remember. I have been praying for the strength to remember all that I encountered. Bits and pieces have come back to me, but some of it will always be blocked off. I had a flashback seeing something on my head with attachments on my temples. A nurse was wiping drool off the corner of my mouth. I have indents on my temples that I noticed since a very young age. By electroshocking the brain is fragmented and honeycombed and compartments and alters created. I also have many moles which I understand is a byproduct of electroshock treatments. I have a large mole above my mouth on the left of my lip.

> 8. Victims almost always possess multiple electric prod (stun gun) scars and/or the resultant moles in the muscled areas of the back, arms, neck and thighs. Some victims are also (in addition to) vaginally mutilated through "body piercing" (rings placed in nipples, vaginal lips, or clitoris) or through actually elaborated carving the vaginal area. Also, scars from branding irons or knives throughout the body will depict pentagrams, animals, crosses, even certain cartoon characters. There is also a group that "forces" moles through electric shock and/or chemical application to the neck and face to further identify to abusers the victim's training/programming.[19]

One incident during that hospital stay I always remembered. An orderly came and took me out of the cage and wheelchaired me down a long hall and into an area where I sat in the hallway for a few minutes next to an empty wheelchair. A female child about four years old was carried out of the room and put into the wheelchair. Then a male and female that I thought of as being doctors (but I distinctly always remember them being humanoid type beings, very robotic, very cold with weird eyes) carried me into a room and put me on a table. Then they stepped away and looked through a rectangular hole in the wall, tilted their heads toward each other and said, "Smile," and zapped me in the area of the lower three chakras (there are seven chakras in our bodies). The solar plexus (the third), the chakra for self-esteem and self-worth, and/or the sacral chakra (the second) sex/emotions chakra, could have been altered at that time or my root chakra (the first) could

---

[19] Mark Phillips. Operation Monarch.

also have been targeted. I will explain more on chakras below. I know it sounds like an x-ray but if it was an x-ray there would have been some covering put onto me. From what I've learned, victims that the controllers have such free access to have the technology to attach an entity to the root chakra. With the technology available being so advanced and hidden, anything is possible.

On what I always "thought" of as the third day, I was moved to another room.

"Here you go, Sandy. You're not in the cage anymore. This was your sister JoAnn's bed." JoAnn was hospitalized for her appendix removal." She was only about twelve years old and she, too, was in the hospital. The nurses and doctors knew how much I loved my big sister JoAnn.

In the new room another girl was in a bed beside me. She had thick black hair and a dark complexion. It may have been the same girl who was carried out of the room where the zapping was done. Her father, dark haired and dark skinned, was there and noticed I wasn't eating. He came over to my bed, buttered my toast and told me I had to eat. I would not eat. I was so depressed. I only remember my parents coming one time to visit me. That was when they brought me puzzles to solve. I truly do not think they came any other time except to pick me up.

After my hospital stay, neither my parents nor sisters and brothers ever spoke about the hospital stay or why I was there in the first place. They never said what was wrong and never talked about it ever. Nothing was ever said about anything found to be wrong. What caused me to urinate red? Was it really blood? Could my mother have given me something the night before to turn my urine red? I know I already said this, but it baffles me so much that I contacted McClaren Macomb Hospital to find out exactly what tests were performed on me during that stay, and the hospital destroys any records more than twenty-five years old. How convenient. What is the point of having health "records" if the records are not retained for an entire lifetime?

More flashbacks started coming throughout 2013 of why it felt so good and familiar the first night "my cousin" woke me up in my bed and we began our sexual child marriage. I was in bed with Danny, sleeping, and a rough arm started rubbing my tiny breasts and vagina and my eyes popped wide open, as if on command, and it felt good and it felt familiar. I remember my eyes popped open and I said to myself "it's time." The fondling hand felt familiar because that is the same way we children were woken up in the hospital to play "sex". The memories flooded back of being in bed with the boys in the hospital and taught how to grind, kiss, fondle. Our bodies were naked and we were extremely sexual.

Another flashback that revealed to me why my thumbnails always had deep ridges growing from the thumb bed. As long as I can remember my thumbs have had ugly deep ridges horizontal across my nails that would grow from the thumb bed up. I would read about it and would read that damage had to have been done to the thumbnail bed to make it always grow with the ridges from the base. Well through meditation and spiritual guidance I remember being tortured and held by my thumbs. It is not a memory I always carried with me but it something that I have been being led to for about a year now and it feels so true that I just wanted to share it. The image I saw was me on an examining table with my arms outstretched with clamps attached to the thumbs. I saw two nurses on one side of me and a doctor looking at a monitor on the other side of me.

Chapter 4

Early Years of Childhood and Teen Years

The house I lived in until sixth grade (when I was eleven or twelve years old) was on a corner lot at the end of Pinecrest and Durham in Utica, Michigan. It was a small, three bedroom home that my dad had built. My dad was a welder in a shop and my mom stayed at home. My dad drank beer every night and bowled a few times a week on bowling leagues. He always worked ten to twelve hours a day so he was not around much. I have two older sisters, born in 1950 and 1952 and two older brothers born in 1954 and 1956. All five of us were born in Mt. Clemens General Hospital.

When I got home from the hospital, I had ear pain. My mom gave me drops for my ears. One bottle would burn and another bottle would tickle. What were in those drops? Why did I need drops put into my ears? Where did the pain come from? Could the pain be from implants?

I started kindergarten when I was a little over four and a half years old. By age four or five I was having regular sexual activity with my cousin Danny all the time. He is a year or so younger than me. I always remembered the first time that the sex started with Danny and me. It had to be sometime when I was three, not long after the hospital stay. I was so excited, Danny was staying overnight, and we were given a bath together. My mom put him and me in the same double bed in my bedroom. We had a couch but she didn't make him a bed there. No, she put him in bed with me. As I shared above, I remember the first time like it was yesterday. I was awoken with a rough arm rubbing on my chest and vagina area. My eyes popped open and it felt good *and it felt familiar*. I said to myself, *It's time*. The next thing I knew my cousin and I were kissing, fondling, grinding. Wow, it felt good and it felt familiar. Because that was how the children would be wakened in the hospital. I remember him rubbing all over me. Why would my mother deliberately put children of different sexes in bed together. This child sexual passion went on for years with my cousin. It was like we were husband and wife. It disgusts me to the bone when I think about it now.

I was a beautiful child, with long dirty blonde/brownish hair and big brown eyes with long eyelashes. I had a beautifully shaped face with high cheekbones, a cute pug nose and sweet lips. My cousin Danny was a beautiful little boy, with amazing blue eyes and white blonde hair. A longer nose than mine but perfect lips. A typical sex time between Danny and I was at bedtime. We would be told to go to bed together and we would lie down and start kissing. Not just little pecks, passionate kissing, fondling, making out. Heads moving back and forth, tongue sucking and nuzzling. We would undress each other very sexually and grind on each other. He would rub his penis between my legs and on my body and buttocks. It was passionate lovemaking by two children. There were times he would get on top or I would get on top. He would rub his penis on my behind to wake me up sometimes. I loved my cousin and was eager for the hugging and kissing and the feelings it created in my groin. I mean this sexual perversion was night after night, year after year.

We played sex games our entire childhood, at least until our early teens. I knew his penis like a toy. I would suck on his penis and he would get hard. This went on with my cousin until our teens. The thought of my granddaughter, now seven years old, doing the things I was doing since I was three breaks my heart. Since this mind control is generational, I am concerned that my granddaughters will be exploited.

This sexual activity would happen at both my house and his house. I would spend summer vacations at Rich and Sharon's house, my cousin Danny's parents. Sharon would put us to bed by ourselves. We would kiss and grind and do disgusting stuff two children should never have been doing. Sharon never walked in on us and no stop came to it. I was attracted to my cousin. How can a little girl be attracted to a blue eyed, blond haired boy? I started carrying guilt around about that for years before my awakening. Comments about uneducated "hillbilly" types having sex with their cousins would trigger the memory. But I DIDN'T tell. I was bred to be a whore. The shame I felt realizing the improper behavior that occurred between my cousin, Danny and I. There was another cousin, Diane, who played with Danny and I a couple times, too. During one of our threesomes, I remember Diane saying, "We call it playing ghost." All the summers I spent at Sharon and Rich's house, all the sexual games played with my cousin and not once were we ever caught. We had to have been filmed for child pornography. So many nights I fell asleep with my cousin nursing on my little titty, with his penis in my hand. The cameras were hidden and we had no clue.

Too much time spent with me sleeping with my cousin Danny and nothing being done about it. Sharon would put me in the bathtub with her boys. That was child exploitation. It went on for too many years not to have been a setup.

I called my cousin Danny and asked him if he remembers all the sex we had as children and how young we were when it started. He said, "Oh Sandy, we were so young and it happened so often, at your house, at my house, I don't remember the first time it happened."

I said, "Well I do. Don't you see we were set up?" I told him about my hospital stay when I was three years old.

He was like, "Well, I was never taken to a hospital like you, but I do know we started to have sex at such a young age, it seems like for as far back as I can remember."

Sharon hung a picture up in her living room when I was there one summer during my early childhood. It was a picture of a little girl and a little boy kissing. She said, "kissing cousins, ha ha." I didn't put it together at the time obviously. My mother also had the same picture in her living room. This may sound innocent enough but when both these women were allowing their son/daughter to be sexually active night after night, year after year, there is something to both having that same picture.

As will be further explained below, Sharon had a litter of puppies and gave me a Poodle/Pomeranian mix when I was in around seventh grade. That puppy was supposedly killed about five months after I had it, a known torture to a child in a mind control program.

Sharon knowingly encouraged all the sexual activity between her son, Danny and I. I have a niece, Kari, now thirty-eight years old, and she told me how another one of Sharon's sons, Ricky, molested her as a young child many times. She also felt Sharon knew about it and it was a setup. Fortunately for her, she figured it out much sooner than me. Her counselor suggested she write a letter to both Sharon and her third son, Ricky, and tell them how she feels. She said it gave her great relief to write that letter. I have tried to contact Sharon through messages to her sons but she won't contact me.

The movies *The Wizard Of Oz* and *Alice In Wonderland* were movies my parents made sure I watched. I remember being taken to my dad's sister's house to watch *Alice In Wonderland*. All the adults stayed in one room and made sure I sat and watched that movie. These movies are known to be trigger/command movies involved in the programming. *Alice In Wonderland* has been mentioned by many MK Ultra authorities as a prime movie to hold Monarch programming triggers, i.e., the transformation of the caterpillar, as well as other butterfly symbolism. It's said that *The Wizard Of Oz* movie is actually used during Monarch programming to plant triggers into the minds of subjects. Certain symbols within the movie are later used to activate them (such as rainbows). I used to sing "Somewhere Over The Rainbow" throughout my childhood.

My parents had a clothesline in the backyard. Our yard was not very large and the clothesline went across with a perfect view out of the kitchen window over the sink. The large steel poles were exceptionally thick for a clothesline. I mean probably double the size of a standard pole used for clothes that I've since seen in my adult years. We lived in that house until I was in sixth grade so I had to have played on this pole from as soon as I could climb up the pole (which probably was pretty young) until we moved when I was probably eleven or so years old. I would wrap my legs around that pole and shimmy up and grind on the top of the pole holding the top pole that went across and held the lines. Because it felt good, I would grind for a long time. My mother never once came into the yard and told me to stop. Almost comical if you can imagine seeing a kid grinding, practically drooling, on a pole in the yard. I'm sure that I was supposed to be stimulating my sexual desires at such a young age.

As a child I would be watching TV and then suddenly get an urge to go look through my parents drawers. I had no idea what I was looking for. I came across a cartoon pornography book in my dad's drawer. It was right on top of his T-shirts, in plain sight, not under anything. That became my go-to toy. It was a big, thick detailed book with many, many explicit sexual stories and graphic sex drawings with grandpa doing granddaughter and sex with dogs and other animals. I'm sure I was triggered to go into my dad's drawer just to find that magazine. I read that magazine for years. I learned to masturbate at a young age. My mother noticed when I couldn't have been more than five years old and snuck in my dad's drawer and took some hankies of his and wrapped them for a Christmas present for him. Christmas morning I remember having my arm around my dad and watching him open his present from me. But, oh, he opened it, and there were brand new hankies for him. I felt so embarrassed, I ran into my bedroom. If my mom caught the hankies, I am sure she knew I was going into my dad's drawer and getting his big, thick, cartoon pornography book almost every day, taking it into my room and then returning it when I had read enough for the day. I mean I started reading that thick, graphic cartoon pornography book at a very young age, probably six or seven years old. To this day, I have graphic images of pedophilia.

An incident I never forgot, being in second grade (six or seven years old) and at a neighbor boy's house, Terry Savage. Terry lived a couple blocks away from my house in what we called the "new subdivision". The homes are typical brick middle-class homes. We were in his bedroom, in the bed, naked and he was trying to put his penis in my butt. I was nuzzling up and rubbing my little butt on his penis.

His mother slammed open the door and yelled, "What are you two doing?"

I remember being embarrassed and *disappointed* that his mother walked in and caught us. That was the one and only time there was ever an interruption in all the sex I had as a child with other children.

During early 2013 and since, I started having flashbacks of my brother molesting me. I apparently blocked most of the incidents out. I called him in 2014 and said, "Billy, do you remember undressing me in Mom and Dad's bed?" He said, "Oh, that was in the tent." Then, boom, it was like a veil was taken off my mind, and I had about twenty more flashbacks of my brother fondling, molesting me, even as far back as him climbing in my crib. He is three and a half years older than me. I said to Billy "Do you realize how many times you molested me?" He replied: "I was just a kid too. I never penetrated you." Like that makes it alright all those years of doing everything except penetrating me.

I do extensive meditation and deep breathing and have even gone back as to seeing my mother changing my diaper. She took my diaper off and started stimulating my clitoris.

An incident that to this day I cannot fully understand happened to me when I was probably five years old. I was walking down Betty street in Utica, Michigan by myself. The Mollett brothers, Donnie and Tommy, called me into their garage. I have the memory of them lying me on a table in the garage and then the next memory I have is walking in the driveway back to Betty St. There was no memory of what happened in the garage and I walked home in a daze. When I told my brother Bill about it when I was still speaking to him, he immediately said, "Oh, they raped you." To this day I recall going into the garage, the boys lying me down and then nothing and then walking back to the street.

In my entire childhood, my brother Bill constantly called me names and told me I was fat and ugly. My parents did nothing to stop it. Day after day, year after year, he would sing songs, a particular polka song, "I don't want her you can have her she's too fat for me, she's too fat for me. Oh, I don't want her…" My brother Bill was taken from our regular elementary school and bused to a special education class in a school at least ten miles away. A "special bus" would pick him up and take him to a special classroom in a school miles away from our home. Probably two years he was bused to that special classroom. I remember asking my mother why Billy had to go to that school. My mother replied, "Because he daydreams."

My parents would go to the grocery store every Thursday, Daddy's payday, and fill two grocery baskets. I grew up on junk food and TV dinners. I doubt my mother ever thought about what was healthy for us to eat. I had a Hostess cake in my lunch every day.

My sister JoAnn would put makeup on me, do my hair, and put a fake fur on me as young as five years old. I was a pretty girl but was always brought down by my brother about my looks. The name calling and teasing were relentless and constant. This was not normal brother/sister rivalry. I don't know how many times I'd say, "I'm made of rubber, your made of glue, everything you call me bounces off me and sticks on you." He had names like Baby Buffalo, Fatty Sandy, and others that he would shout at me all the time. He would tell me I had thunder thighs.

Throughout my childhood there were numerous incidents with boys, mostly a few years older molesting me. Larry Perrin took his penis out and made me suck it when I was about 8 years old. We were left in the care of my best friend Linda Perrin's brother, Larry's care. He proceeded to show both Linda and I his penis. He put it in my face. I played with it and kissed it and sucked on it for a while. I never told. I had to run from Danny Barnes who started kissing me and then trying to undress me at his house, probably around 9 years old . I never told. Billy Bracket chased me down the street pulling my pants down. I never told.

I clearly remember groups of fifth and sixth grade boys and girls (9-11 years old) gathering behind Auburnshire Elementary School in Utica, Michigan on recesses (2-3 per day) and kissing and fondling. We all wanted the same boy, Teddy, but I ended up with Jimmy. Where were the teachers and staff aides? Why was this allowed the entire school year? The school system wasn't for our protection. There were endless hours of groping and kissing. A generation encouraged to be sexual. I confirmed with a gal I grew up with who went to the same school about the group of girls and boys that would go on the side of the school and kiss and fondle. When I mentioned it to her, she said, "Oh, I wasn't a part of that group," So other kids even knew what was going on.

Throughout my early elementary grades there were hearing tests given. Any kind of subliminal message could have been given to set off a trigger. They went through all the work when I was three years old, they know my social security number so they know what school I went to. I had no control over the teachers requiring I participate in the many hearing tests. That school was torn down. I wonder how many tests were actually performed. Now I did screw up back in 2009 and participate in a radio-sponsored three hours of songs being played into individual headphones to a survey of about one hundred people. Immediately after that survey, I got introduced by the same person who went with me to do the survey to Ray Goodridge, a handler I fell in love with and married within three months. Time with Ray will be shared in a later chapter.

During the 1980s, a remote viewing project called Stargate was done at Fort Meade. It used binaural beat tones, transmitted through earphones, that altered brain waves. A hemi-sync that device played two different frequencies into each ear was found to produce altered states of consciousness. Perhaps this technology was derived from these experiments done in the 1960s on MKULTRA subjects.[20]

Throughout my childhood, I spent a lot of time in front of the television. What a mind control object. Throughout the 60s and 70s and even today, there are subliminal messages everywhere. It's heartbreaking really. I started getting overweight by about fifth grade. So when I was starting around seventh grade, my mother said a doctor could see me and give me a shot to help me lose weight. This shot was twice a week and was supposed to help me lose weight. We called it my "fat shot". What was really in those shots? Where did she get the idea to take me for a shot to lose weight? Why would a young teenager be given shots every week? In my early twenties, I started using drugs. I ended up being controlled by drugs and the need for acceptance by my abusive husbands and boyfriends.

My brother Bill had an extensive pornography magazine collection that I became very familiar with by the time I was about eleven years old and throughout my teen years, Billy had a huge box of pornography books, i.e. Penthouse, Playboy that he kept under his bed. I would go into his bedroom and take a few into my bedroom and read them. I would lay on my stomach, place a pillow between my legs and read the graphic sexual stories while grinding on the pillow. I had orgasms all the time. Why would my mother let my brother have so many magazines? Once my mom and sister JoAnn found a few magazines I had forgotten under my pillow when they changed my sheets for me. They just laughed and did nothing about me looking at pornography at thirteen years old. There was no scolding or

---

[20] Alison Miller. *Healing the Unimaginable: Treating Ritual Abuse and Mind Control.*

punishment or advice not be looking at the magazines.

My brother Bill tortured me daily. He would lock in me the shed in the yard for hours at a time. Billy would tie me up and make me pull him around in a wagon. Hostile arguments often turning physical. Daily he would call me names and verbally and mentally abuse me. For some reason though I always loved my brother and kept contact with him until my awakening. My brother, like my parents was a handler of mine.

I was a Brownie during the first few years of school and then a Girl Scout. There was a picture taken of the Brownie troop and I remember my girlfriend and I laughing at me. I was sitting in the front row in a chair with my legs wide open. A clear shot of my little legs all the way to my panties. I don't know what it is about these organizations but I remember Cathy O'Brien saying she was molested while on a Brownie troop outing. There were trips that our troop took that I had lost time. A really weird camping trip in the winter to Camp Whispering Woods. It was so cold, I remember shivering so bad my teeth were chattering.

My parents bought a party store when I was in sixth grade (ten or eleven years old). My father with a seventh grade education and my mother with a tenth grade education became business owners. The store had living quarters attached and my family moved into the attached living quarters. Shortly after moving into the living quarters behind the store, my dog Duffy was taken away from.

I had a dog, Duffy, in seventh grade given to me by my cousin Sharon. She had a box of puppies and told me I could choose any puppy I wanted. The cute little puppies were all so fluffy, adorable and affectionate. A box of Poodle/Pomeranian mix puppies. I chose my dog and fell in love with that dog. Duffy and I spent the entire summer together. My best friend growing up with me would call the dog "my son" because he was always with me. Then school started and I always missed my puppy so much and he would greet me at the door and leap into my arms after school. I remember in every detail the day I was told he died. I had to walk a block from the school bus stop to my house. My neighbor, only a few houses away from the bus stop, was walking with me. When he approached his house, his dog came running out to greet him. I remember saying, "Oh, David, my dog greets me the same way when I get home. That little guy jumps right up into my arms." I'll never forget the feeling that overcame me when I walked into the house and he wasn't there. I immediately confronted my dad and asked, "Where's Duffy?" He said, "Your mother took him to vet."

I immediately started crying, rationalizing in my little head that the dog didn't have a vet appointment. I instinctively knew something was wrong. My dad said he had an extension cord leading out the side door and the dog got out and went into the street and Duffy got hit by a car. My mother said he was still alive and the lady who hit him drove her to the vet. She said the whole ride to the vet she kept rocking the puppy in her arms, saying, "Oh my God, Sandy is going to be so brokenhearted." I was. She said the vet couldn't do anything to save his life. I didn't go to school for three days.

Dogs are used all the time in the mind control program. Looking back, I realize I never questioned my mother. How I wish I would have asked to see my dead dog and give him a proper burial. He probably was simply taken away from me on purpose. I remember my dad coming home from bowling and hearing him say to my mother, "Is she still crying over that dog?" My parents never once comforted me, hugged me, or consoled me over that dog. They deliberately took that dog away from me. It never occurred to me at the time that my mother and father would betray me but now I spiritually know they did.

Upon learning about the program, the puppy trauma is often used. Sometimes a child is even forced to kill the puppy.

All energy that is harvested from a child is valuable. I truly believe that humans' energy is harvested by other beings and that entities are tied into individuals from birth. They know who is coming through. Our energy patterns have been watched through centuries and through many incarnations. They can especially attach entities when a child is inflicted through the mind control program. This was a definite tactic to traumatize me and collect my grievous energy. The inter-dimensionals also are addicted to the sexual energy from young children. I cried for days over that puppy.

From as early as I can remember, every night I said my prayers and committed my soul to God. I always wondered who taught me to pray. How odd it must have been for a little girl to say her prayers to bless her family and even her enemies and then turn and have sex with her cousin. Because of some inherent need to seek goodness, when I was about thirteen years old I started going to Catechism for three hours every Wednesday for three years. I was confirmed at Gethsemane Lutheran Church in Auburn Hills, Michigan. They would have a record of it. Pastor Ott taught the class every Wednesday evening. Then I found out at fifty-three years old that thirteen books of the doctrine of the New Testament primarily relied on by Christians are written by Paul, a fake apostle. He wasn't even an apostle named by the Lamb yet he starts most of his books written with, "I, an apostle of Jesus Christ." Then there is the fact that Christians go to church on Sunday. Yahuwah clearly states to worship on the Sabbath which is the seventh day, which is Saturday. Right in your face and this has been going on for thousands of years. I don't think it is a coincidence that people are just now figuring this out. I'm sure through the last thousand years many persons have been killed because of this knowledge. The whole idea is it doesn't matter what you believe in, as long as you believe in something more powerful than yourself.

The following incident is one of the most embarrassing of all for me. I have to reveal it though for the reader to understand the magnitude of this mind control. I have a defense mechanism in me trying to dissuade me from sharing this story but I have to push on regardless of the consequences. This is a true story from a person who has never condoned molestation of children and had a husband who molested my niece in my own living room. I didn't think much about this incident at the time. I just blocked it out of my head. But now, with my daily meditations, it was revealed to me that I have to share this. To relieve my mind and my nephew's mind. I'm sure he's asked himself through the years if that really happened or not. Or maybe he has always known and never told. Anyways, here we go.

Like I mentioned earlier, I have two older sisters and two older brothers. The oldest two are my sisters, ten and nine years older than me. They each had four kids. I was their number one babysitter. All the years I babysat for my sisters and earned money babysitting for neighbors, I never had sexual thoughts toward any of the children, but there was an incident that occurred while babysitting my nephew, Scott Parker. Kathy had Scott when she was sixteen and I was nine years younger than her so I had to have been about eleven or twelve years old. Scott was two or three years old. I really don't think it traumatized Scott too much. He has a beautiful wife and lovely children, a good job, but it has been in the back of my mind for a long time now. Scott was a very sexual little boy. He would often play with his penis and Kathy would literally go up and smack his hands to get him to stop. He was also always grabbing at my boobs. Well, one night Scott and I were watching TV on the couch and he started groping at my chest. I remember thinking at the time that I might as well let him see them. Don't ask me why I would do that but I put my top down, threw up my bra and let him fondle my breasts. For maybe a minute or two and then as it sickened me to what I was doing I immediately stopped him. It was perfectly casual and he obviously never told his mother. We never had another sexual encounter and I don't know why I felt like I was doing him a favor. I don't know if he even remembers it. But I do and I feel awful about that. There has never been an incident that any child can say that I sexually approached them in all my life, so I had very distorted views on sex from a very young age.

There was never very much affection from my parents for me or for my siblings. My brother and I were arguing one day when I was probably ten or eleven, and I remember my mom jumping me and throwing me on the bed and straddling me and punching me with her fists in my face. My sister Kathy and brother Billy were there, and I remember Billy saying, "Kathy, we have to get Mom off her." The beating went on for at least five minutes. I was terrorized and face bruised. Beatings are what help for the mind control victim to disassociate.

When I was probably five years old I remember standing outside my bedroom window, crying as I listened to my dad whip my sister JoAnn with his belt while she lay across the bed because she was smoking cigarettes. What a hypocrite. He smoked all his life.

Another incident when I was about ten or eleven I remember my sister Kathy, the second oldest sibling in my family, tying my ankles together and my wrists together and tying a rag around my mouth. She locked me in the bedroom and put a record on the record player that kept playing over and over again. I was in that bedroom for hours. The song was "Gimme Dat Ding." I laid on the floor on the side of the bed and tried pulling myself up the skirt of the bed with my teeth. That song still repeats in my head over and over again. I had several black eyes caused from fights with my brother Bill. I was literally abused by my siblings as well as my parents.

My parents decided to move out to a little town, Memphis, Michigan, when I was starting the eleventh grade. My mom got the house she dreamed about. I'm reminded of an eleventh and twelfth grade school teacher, Victoria Patterson, who taught us about horoscopes and got me started buying the books on it. I totally got interested in the horoscope and bought many books on the subject. Upon checking the zodiac signs, they all give an indication about what explains one's behavior. Not surprisingly, my zodiac sign explained my personality to be an addictive personality and controlled by sex organs and highly sexual, but now I realize the importance of the power of the stars (spaceships), planets, sun, and moon (there is a possibility that the moon is fake). The planets are energy as well that affects us here on earth. Yahuwah even mentions the zodiac in Job. Job 38: Canst thou bring forth Mazzaroth in his season? Or canst thou guide Arcturus with his sons? Mazzaroth is the Hebrew word for zodiac. There is an importance to the time and date for each of us incarnated here on starship Earth.

That same teacher, Mrs. Patterson, suggested I become a legal secretary, and that's what I became. I became Mrs. Patterson's aid in twelfth grade and worked in the high school office until I graduated in 1977. I later ended up working for attorneys for almost thirty years, specializing in Patent and Trademark Office filings (Intellectual Property Law – the U.S. government.) All those Jews I worked for and not one said, "Psst, Sandy…hey, your worshiping on the wrong day and going against the Ten Commandments wearing that cross." They watched me go to bible study three days a week on my lunch hour. A group of God's people would gather seeking the true Word of our Lord known as God, but it was deliberately hidden. They were going to church on Sundays as well. I know that I have a maker, and I know that he is watching me as well as the watchers here. It's all been done before. That is why this is so sophisticated. God is the top archon. He's the ringleader and he allowed all this to happen on purpose. There is nothing we can do about it. It all had to happen like this, but I know the female souls are definitely being harvested and sold. It's all about money as well.

When I was in eleventh grade (15 years old) I starting dating my first serious boyfriend. Ronald Nash was a year older than me and drove a van. We would have sex all the time in his van, my car, my parents' house, his parents' house, go to motels on the weekend. Ron's mother told me that Ron was born with six fingers, and the sixth finger was removed in the hospital when he was first born before he was brought home from the hospital. The giants were born with six fingers and six toes but that genetic defect has mostly been eliminated. Ron had thick curly red hair and I've since read of the red-haired giants. Remains have been found of giants and their hair pigment was red. Giants remains have been found at Serpent Mound in Ohio estimated to be about 2,000 years old.

And there was yet a battle in Gath, where was a man of great stature, that had on every hand six fingers, and on every foot six toes, four and twenty in number; and he also was born to the giant. (II Samuel 21:20)

And yet again there was war at Gath, where was a man of *great* stature, whose fingers and toes were four and twenty, six on each hand, and six on each foot: and he also was the son of the giant. (I Chronicles 20:6)

Ron recently contacted me on Facebook and I reminded him about the six fingers. He replied that he couldn't believe that I remember that.

Ron's parents went out of town for a weekend. Another couple and Ron and I watched porn films all weekend at his house. Not soft porn films by any means. The films were old fashioned type on a reel-to-reel camera. There was a lady having sex with a horse and another a lady masturbating with a big bottle. I was only in eleventh grade of high school.

Chapter 5

The Handlers

Clifford Donald Morgan (1st husband)

After I graduated high school, I went to college for a semester and was going to major in legal secretary. I dropped out after my car crashed in the beginning of the second semester. I decided to go to Professional Bartenders School and after graduating got a job at an Elks club in Troy, Michigan. Through a waitress there, I was invited to a party and met Clifford Donald Morgan. Cliff was tall and handsome. He had dark hair and brown eyes which was unusual for me to be attracted to. Within a couple months we ended up getting pregnant. I did the right thing and married him and kept the baby. We went to church together. He was the father of my child. He didn't have good work habits though, and I did find pornography magazines hidden in the closet. He said he got them from my brother. That didn't surprise me. Because he couldn't hold a job too well, he joined the Navy. I remember how sad I was with him gone. All the energy sadness brings forth. The way a woman misses the man in her life is definitely stimulated out of proportion. He knew how disappointed I was to hear that he might not be with me during the delivery of our first child. The Navy had promised him time off when he joined. Then at boot camp Cliff was told he couldn't be promised to have the time off when my due date was near, so Cliff got out by acting crazy. He even said he wet the bed in order to get out. So he was with me at the birth of my daughter, Amy, now thirty-seven years old.

From the first day I met Cliff he would say, "I'm not going to live past the age of thirty." During the two years I was with him there were countless times I heard him say that. He was a victim of mind control as well. That is a typical belief for mind control victims and most don't live past thirty. He died when he was twenty-five years old. My understanding that the code word "freedom train" is the trigger for slaves to do acts to lose their lives. The programmers/masters program them with the expectation that they will be "thrown from the freedom train" when they get to age thirty. *Freedom Train* is the code word for the Monarch trauma-based mind-control. He would say many times that he wanted the Elton John song "Funeral For A Friend" played at his funeral. I made sure that it was played. I'm sure many would think he deserved to die for molesting my niece. He deserved help not death.

> The Illuminati and other organizations have also programmed individuals who are simply expendable. These are sex slaves who are used up and killed very early in life, one-time use as saboteurs, breeders, soldiers, drug couriers and so forth. The bodies of these people will often show visible torture scars. The expendable are the children of parents who were blackmailed into turning their children over to the CIA. This is all hidden by the power of the National Security Act. These are children, who have been sold by pedophile fathers, or pornographic parents. The programmers/masters program them with the expectation that they will be "thrown from the freedom train" when they get to age 30. (Freedom Train is the code word for the Monarch trauma-based

mind-control. To be thrown from the Freedom Train means to be killed.) The CIA and Illuminati are skilled at blackmailing parents to give up their children. They would watch the mail for porn. Pedophile and murderers who abuse their children are warned that they will go to prison for long lengths of time if they do not cooperate by selling their children into mind-controlled slavery.[21]

A terrible thing happened one Friday night when my daughter was about one-year-old. One of my nieces, Sherry, asked if she could spend the night. She was about ten years old at the time. I told her yes and made a bed for her on the couch. It got to be about 10:00 p.m. and Benny Hill was coming on television. I didn't like that show and told my husband, Cliff, I was going to bed but to remember he had work in the morning so not to stay up too late. I've felt guilt most of my life for leaving him alone with my niece. It never ever occurred to me that he would molest her. What messages could that Benny Hill show have been sending?

I woke up around 1:00 a.m. and could hear whispering. I came down the dark hall and saw my niece sitting on his lap. I said, "What do you think you're doing?" and they both jumped a mile. I still didn't put two and two together. I said, "You know you have work in the morning."

He must have wiped his forehead off and thought, *Wow that was close. She didn't even realize what was happening.* My niece ended up staying the entire weekend, not telling me anything was wrong. On the following Monday evening I was at the gym with my sister JoAnn, my niece's mother, and asked her if Sherry came home and said Aunt Sandy scared her. I told my sister what happened and a lightbulb went off in her. She went home and asked her daughter what she was doing on Uncle Cliff's lap. My niece turned ten shades of red and said it was

---

[21] Fritz Springmeier and Cisco Wheeler, *The Illuminate Formula to Create an Undetectable Total Mind Control Slave.*

their secret. It all came out that my husband molested my niece. My Aunt Mary Ann even called and said, "You know he was finger fucking her, don't you? And he'll do it to your daughter, too." I fell to my knees. Of course, he denied it, and I had no choice but to take my daughter and move in with my parents. He even told me that when he got up to go to work that Saturday morning, he saw my niece playing with herself.

I moved in with my parents and got a job bartending in Port Huron, Michigan. Within a month of that job, I met with an attorney to file divorce papers.

Bobby Craven, a tall 6'4" blond haired, blue-eyed steamfitter with a New York accent came into my life via the bartending job at the hotel he was staying at the same time. He had a good job and seemed to really like me. He had all the characteristics of and what I now know he was, a Nordic hybrid (perhaps Nephilim). I was overwhelmingly attracted to him. Little did I know that through my social security number anybody could find out where a person works. Not long after the dating began, I remember us having an argument and him spitting in my face before I pulled away. That same night I got a telephone call from my husband's brother Ronnie that Cliff was dead.

I'll never forget that telephone call. It was about 11:30 p.m. on Friday, October 10, 1980. I answered the telephone and Cliff's brother Ronnie said, "Sandy, this is Ronnie. Cliff's dead." I was shocked and called for my mom to get out of bed. So there I was trying to deal with my husband molesting my niece and divorcing him, and then he was killed in a car accident. They said he was passing another car and lost control and crashed into a tree. His car was the only car involved. Wrapped right around a tree. Only several months after he molested my niece, he happened to die in a car accident all by himself.

My niece's father, Wade Vires, I think has connections with the Freemasons. The city that Wade is retired in, Stanford, Kentucky, has a Freemason lodge. Some cities he lived in, Pontiac and Pickney, both have Freemason lodges. His father's name was even "Mason". As later detailed, I married his nephew and he clearly used Freemason symbols in our home. I never asked to see the police report for Cliff's death. He was supposedly in a hurry and was passing another car and lost control. I don't believe he was passing another car. I think he was deliberately run off the road. The direction he was supposedly going would mean if he lost control passing another car he would have hit the opposite side of the road. He was killed in front of my parents' party store, the same street and area that my puppy was killed. Mason Vires lived on the nearest side road to the accident, Pinecrest, from the main road, Auburn Road. Of course, because the Freemasons are such a secret society, members' names are never revealed, and I can only go with the truth vibrations that only recently have been with me. Another victim was killed on that same road in the same spot in about 1970. That victim was a lady and she was killed on a motorcycle in that same spot that Cliff was killed at.

Because of this sad news, I called Bobby, who immediately consoled me and came right over. I remember him consoling me while I was sitting on his lap. I bet he was sucking up all my energy. I went through all the motions, making funeral arrangements, the viewing and then having to bury Cliff. As will be detailed later, Bobby was a disgusting man and was brought into my life as a "handler". I was so obsessed with him.

The night I got the telephone call from Ronnie, Cliff's brother, that Cliff was dead, Bobby and I had an argument. I remember him spitting in my face before I left him. Then after I got a telephone call that my husband had been killed in a car accident, I called that same person who had spit at me. I had absolutely no self-esteem.

Robert ("Bobby") Emmett Craven

As soon as Cliff was dead, I let Bobby move right in on me. I never put it together until my awakening. Bobby was working in Monroe, Michigan at a nuke plant, at least two hours away, but stayed at the Hotel Harrington in Port Huron, Michigan, where I bartended. Why stay at a hotel over two hours away from the jobsite? Bobby and a few other members of the crew drove 2 hours each way from the job site and hotel. Bobby had the perfect answer to my despair. Get high and forget the problem. It was subtle at first. Just a biweekly suggestion at first. "Hey, it's Friday night. Want to get high?" Then it became more and more often until Bobby got me hooked on drugs. I followed him blindly. Like a slave. He would beat me and then say how sorry he was. He bought me an engagement/wedding ring and pretended to love me. One night, feeling so trapped in a violent, drug-infested relationship, I got so depressed that I took some Valium and went into the bathroom, locked the bathroom door and cut my wrist with a razor blade. Bobby had to break down the bathroom door. He called an ambulance, and that time I went willingly. I got my wrist stitched up in the emergency room at a hospital in Port Huron, Michigan, and then I was checked in the mental ward. I was there for what I remember as being three to four days. I remember my parents coming up to see me. I remember Cliff's pastor coming to see me. Cliff had prayed with the pastor the week before he died in the car accident. I was so depressed and sad. Bobby came to visit me and when he would leave I would cry and miss him. I had no thoughts about my daughter and actually thought she was better off with my parents.

Bobby and I moved to California with my daughter Amy. Throughout the three to four years I was with him, he repeatedly and brutally beat me numerous times. We drove my Cordoba across the country with my two-year old daughter to California. There was clearly something wrong with me. Why would I be so obsessed with someone so destructive to me? Bobby beat me up and destroyed all my furniture in California. He was beating on me so I ran to a neighbor's apartment, and we watched from the window Bobby carrying each piece of furniture out to the dumpster. My coffee table, kitchen table, and chairs. It never ever occurred to me to call the police as there was cocaine at the apartment I was hiding out at. I remember I flew back to Michigan with Amy. Bobby started calling me within a few days at my parent's home. He talked me into flying to California to get him and my vehicle. My parents were all happy with that idea. "Sure, Sandy, you go and find yourself. We'll take care of Amy." I left my daughter with my parents and traveled the United States with Bobby. I signed Cliff's monthly social security check over to my parents. Thinking I was only hurting myself and feeling I didn't deserve anything better, I spent at least three or four years without my first daughter Amy.

All those years I missed my daughter. I would mail her gifts weekly. I remember going to see her at least nine times in one year. I blocked out the trauma of leaving her and only since 2012 have I faced the sadness of leaving her behind all those times I would see her and then leave. I was a terrible mother. I didn't know that my parents did what they did to me until 2012. I was oblivious to most everything until my awakening. I can only pray for my daughter Amy. Amy won't even let me see my granddaughters. As I've said many times, the perfect mind control victim doesn't know they are mind controlled, and the perfect mule doesn't get paid, pays for the trip, and doesn't even know they transporting anything. Nine times in one year, mostly from different states did I go back and forth to see my daughter Amy. The perfect mule is one that doesn't know they have anything, cartels the product, and pays for the trip. I presume it was drugs that I was transporting. As I will have mentioned elsewhere, I counted how many times I went back and forth between New York and Michigan alone, and it had to be well over forty times. I lived in New York City sixteen years and still went back and forth after I moved back to Michigan. I was a mule my entire life as will be detailed below time and time again.

Through therapy experts, I have learned that the beatings caused dissociative identity disorder ("DID"). The beatings were so severe that my face would be all swollen with black eyes, purple ears, and cut lips. I got a huge hole in my shin from being kicked with a cowboy boot. I was walking behind Bobby asking him who knows what when he turned around and - bam! - kicked me right in the shin with a pointy toe cowboy boot. The gash left a deep hole in my right shin. I had to go to the emergency room to get the hole filled because it would not stop bleeding. No help from anyone, I was a lost soul with no mind of my own. I have three fingers and a thumb with bulging bones from being damaged during beatings from him and my other handlers. I never went to the doctor to have them set.

After California, we return to Michigan and, like I said, I had moved my daughter in with my parents. My parents were so eager to take Amy and send me on my way to find myself. Bobby was about twenty-seven years old and I was twenty years old. Bobby was a steamfitter, and we went what he and his buddies called "booming." Bobby and I end up traveling to Maryland, New Jersey, Delaware, Pennsylvania, and Ohio. All towns with a story.

Lima, Ohio was a very terrible episode. Bobby had beat me hard all across my back while I lay asleep, that is what I woke up to. He was mad because I didn't wake up when he was knocking on the door, and he didn't have his key and had to go get the manager to let him in. He was pounding me in the back and the back of the head when I woke up. The next day I defiantly went out to the bar by myself. Bobby showed up there and attacked me in the public bar. Bobby jumped from behind and started dragging me by my hair out of the bar. The bouncers jumped on him and the cops came and arrested him. He went to jail for a couple days. I was back at my room in a daze after the brutal attacks, and I remember a concerned man knocked on the door. I got up and answered the door without a shirt on. I opened the door, turned around and he gasped when he saw my back. It was so welted with purple, black and blue, and yellow lumps, the poor man almost started crying. But guess who bailed Bobby out. Sandy. What an obsession. I clearly had something done to brainwash me. Now I know he attacked me to get me to leave and go back to Michigan, which I did. As soon as Bobby was out of jail, he started another fight with me and I left and went back to Michigan. Another shipment by the ignorant mule.

Bobby raped and sodomized me as well. There were times that he would get very violent and push me down on the bed face first. He would roughly penetrate me anally and smash my face down hard on the bed. Yet I never left. All the abuse I took and never left him. Bobby and I ended up in New York City. Bobby grew up in the Bronx. After my first two jobs as an executive secretary at Movie Star Lingerie and Royal Prudential Industries, I broke into the legal secretary field. At my first firm, *Stein Davidoff & Malito*, I remember meeting a paralegal who had been hired through a program for reformed prisoners and who fronted me an ounce of cocaine. Bobby and I end up doing over half, and I didn't have the money to pay him. Bobby told me the only option I had was to turn the guy in to my boss, Larry Hutcher. Guess what I did? I turned the guy in. Without even thinking twice about how I was destroying that paralegal's life. I can't even remember his name. I can't remember what happened to him. I remember continuing working there for about six months until I left to work for an attorney specializing in liquor law. The firm didn't even offer to put me in rehab. Just blew it off. How weird. Then the attorney I went to work for, Warren Pesetsky, ended up being a coke head and bought coke from me. Warren would have a mirror, razor blade and coke in his top right hand drawer. I would go into his drawer and do a line or two, thinking he didn't know. Later on, other firms I worked with had to know I was using cocaine, I'm sure, but I thought I was hiding it from them. I've carried the guilt of turning that man in all my life. If there was any way I could apologize personally, I would. It was a selfish, wrong thing to do. I hope that maybe that incident may have gotten him out of the drug business and maybe his life changed for the better. It took me a long, long time to quit drugs. I had absolutely no emphatic emotions for the consequences of my actions to others until my awakening in December 2012.

Throughout my three to four years with Bobby in New York City, he generated a lot of negative energy out of me. Now I know that it was a setup from the beginning. He was with me for those years to generate as much unhappiness for me as possible. He would do such horrible things. He'd say he would be outside my office when I got out of work and there I would wait on 42nd Street. I was so excited when 5:30 p.m. rolled in. Then I went downstairs and no Bobby. There were no cell phones then. I waited an hour outside that office door. I cried most of the way to the train (subway) and on the train ride back to Queens. I clearly know that entities were around me on that train ride to my apartment. I was set up for the loosh harvest. All the beatings in different motels throughout the United States created a lot of low vibrational energy.

Bobby would throw temper tantrums and cut up my work clothes. I came home later than expected and he had proceeded to take scissors and cut slits on the back of my blouses and my skirts. He even backhanded me and cut my lip wide open one morning on the way to work in Wilmington, Delaware. I said something and – bam! – out of the blue a powerful backhand across my mouth. My lower lip was cut wide open and blood immediately squirted out. I doubled up my fist and punched him square on the right cheekbone and of course, broke my knuckle under the pinky finger. It took me two days of agony to finally go to a doctor and have a cast put on my hand. I remember lying to co-workers about what happened to my lip. My brain was so fragmented that I thought somehow I deserved to be beat. Looking back, how was I able to even work with a broken knuckle and huge cut on my lower lip. But I did.

I got temp jobs in Wilmington, Delaware at a bank (big bank, sixth floor desk job) and at a stock broker office, Dean Witter Reynolds. I also bartended in Delaware. I've had temp jobs for bank facilities associated with the Federal Reserve and even worked for engineers in the Monroe, Michigan nuclear power plant. I worked for the vice president of Royal Prudential Industries, many, many law firms, and almost thirty years as a legal secretary (at least twelve law firms throughout those thirty years). I would work three to four years at a law firm and get offered a higher paying job at another law firm then give my two week notice. Never once a drug test at any firm.

Bobby and I finally broke up after about three to four turbulent years. I settled in New York City. About five years after we finally broke up, I ran into Bobby in Grand Central Station in New York City and when I saw him my stomach jumped like a schoolgirl. There was such an unnatural obsession. To still have feelings for someone who humiliated and abused me is not normal. He had to break up with me and I thought I loved him soooo much.

Tommy Killeen
After Bobby and I totally separated our lives, I lived a couple years working, partying, going to see my daughter an average of five times a year. I was this bouncy, highly skilled secretary, with a vivacious sexual appetite, totally programmed slave. I was only snorting cocaine now that Bobby was gone (I could never really give myself my own hit via needle) and mostly only on the weekends. I dated men, called my daughter every week, mailed her stuff all the time, and planned my time off with trips to see her and my parents, of course. It is really hard for me to even believe that in sixteen years of living in New York City and then still being swayed back to New York City to see my longest handler, Tommy Byrnes (I last saw him Thanksgiving weekend of November 2013), I drove well over forty times between Michigan and New York. I always would see my brother Bill, too (a handler and contact in Michigan for the program). He won't admit it, of course, and this can all be considered science fiction, but what do I have to lose? I lived it and can see it all in hindsight now but the truth is still the truth, even if it's the truth of just one. This is my truth. The scenes my brother would pull to keep me in the house while his buddy was removing the goods from my vehicle. One visit at his house, he kept me there all afternoon and kept delaying dinner. Finally around 5:00 p.m., I said I had to leave and his live-in girlfriend Sue told this girl Maggie who was there and acting super weird, "You better call Tommy." Tommy Mollett was my brother's good friend, and I've realized Tommy was around other times I would see my brother. What

did it matter to Tommy Mollett if I was leaving? There were other times my brother acted weird before I left his house or when I would get there.

The next handler that came into my life was Tommy Killeen. He had the usual charm and acted like he was crazy about me. He found me in a bar. I noticed him at the bar I was at earlier. He approached me and charmed the shit out of me. I remember him using the words "rock" a lot. As he was a carpenter and he sheet rocked, he would always say "we rock". I have found that many of my mind control handlers used the word "rock" in their code words for me. Many texts with "Where you at rock?" or "I slept like a rock." Hard to explain but very true. I have men (dudes) come into my life and use the same code words and try to charm me and now I can see through them. One guy even chased me down and said, "Remember, we rock." That was just this January 2016. Tommy's mother, Anne, took me lovingly in, and his sister Barbara and I became immediate friends. Tommy scoped me out to get me to move to Astoria, New York so I could fall into the net of alien/CIA control.

Tommy came on super strong and wined and dined me. He had curly red hair and green eyes, kind of a leprechaun look. Tommy was lots of fun and had lots of friends. His mother owned a bar in Astoria, New York, Matty's Café and we were regulars there. Tommy had season tickets to the Giants and we tailgated the two winters I was with him. Anne, his mom, took me to concerts, on midnight boat cruises in New York City and acted like she really liked me.

Tommy and I were together for about two years. I remember after about a year of dating, Christmas Eve at the Killeens. It was Christmas Eve and everyone was gathered at Tommy's sister Barbara's apartment that afternoon. Tommy had to work a half a day and was supposed to meet me at his sister's apartment. Hour after hour go by and Tommy never called or showed up. Anne, her friends Gladys and Pat all staring at me, watching how sad and stressed I was getting as the hours went by. I am sure that whole scenario was planned. All the energy that was being sucked out of me. I was so disappointed. I should have been with my daughter Amy but instead was upset and discouraged by Tommy Killeen standing me up at his own family's Christmas Eve party.

Tommy would lie to me and then make sure that he got caught in the lie just for my reaction. Like when we had a date for him to come over my house after he finished playing cards, and then he called and said he was tired and was going home. I remember throwing the telephone because I knew he was lying. The next week, sitting at a wedding reception, I overheard his buddy who was playing cards with him that night say, "Boy we sure had fun at that bar we went to after cards. Those girls were really hot." Instant energy reaction.

Tommy's Mom Anne gave us tickets to the musical Broadway play *La Cage aux Folles*. I had absolutely no idea what the story was about. I remember how disassociated I was after watching the first scene with all the beautiful "ladies" (so I thought) dancing and discovered they were actually men. I actually thought the men up there dressed like women were really women. I know now that the transgender scheme has been going on for many more decades behind closed doors.

It was while I was dating Tommy Killeen that I got my daughter Amy back to live with me. Tommy and I drove to Michigan to get Amy. My father and mother gave me a really hard time and my Dad made a huge scene when it was time to leave with Amy. Anne became the babysitter for Amy. Within six months of having Amy back with me, Tommy broke up with me.

Thomas John Byrnes (Second husband)

After Tommy Killeen, Thomas Byrnes came into my life. My second marriage to the father of my two children, who sold cocaine to me before we got married, then did it with me while I was divorcing him. A few years ago, I was talking to him and he said, "Do you know how many rolled up twenties I'd find in your pockets when I'd do the wash?" At the time I thought he was confessing to not giving me my money back, but now I've asked myself, *Why, why didn't he ask me to get help?* Actually those years with Tommy, raising my young daughters, I did have my cocaine use under control. Throughout my years of drug addiction, I thought I was only hurting myself. I didn't realize how it affects your relationship with your children for an entire lifetime. How it opens the doors to what can only be described as a living hell. The embarrassment I feel now. I was like a monkey needing a fix. No one ever offered me help. They must have known I was addicted to drugs. I met Tommy because he was dealing coke. Throughout my marriage I know he must have known I was doing coke, but I think he just shut his eyes to it. When I filed for divorce, he started doing coke with me. Tommy even slipped a small envelope with coke in it under my apartment door to try and get me to be with him. I'm sure his family knew when I would go into the bathroom on Christmas day and do a few lines that I was high. But they never said a word.

I drove to New York over Thanksgiving in December 2013, and I'm sure I have been set up by Tommy and his mother for years. Tommy always has something funny to say and discredits everything I say about the problems of the world. When I was with him he went through many jobs, and now he has a high paying job working on elevators for Con Edison. He says there are sixty elevators. He always acts like he is my friend, yet I now know that he has been the link in the puzzle. He is a great con artist and has been conning me since we met. We all have a percentage of mixed DNA. My goodness, this has been going on for thousands and thousands of years. When I was there for Thanksgiving, Tommy actually bit me in the face. All those years and I never knew. When I stayed at his mother's new apartment, she had a flat screen sitting on the counter directly pointed at the couch that I slept on. How disgusting to know that I was being watched. It never occurred to me. Yes, I did something that is disgusting to me now. I masturbated. I am sure that I was videotaped for years. I am sure that they think I deserve everything I get.

Let me go into some of Tommy's history. Only weeks before our wedding date did I learn that his father had been imprisoned for child pornography of his own daughters. Tommy has three older sisters and one younger brother. Tommy and his brother were taken away from Marie, his mother, because she was investigated as to her involvement in this disgusting pedophilia. Tommy once said to me, "Who knows what was done to me," referring to what his father may have done to him as a toddler. I don't know how many months the boys were taken away but I'm sure programming was being performed. He also said as a young boy he was in the hospital and had a bubble around him for days. He said he remembers his mother hitting him across the back of the legs with a baseball bat when he was standing at the window talking to his friends. She definitely has involvement in implementing Tommy's plan to make my life as miserable as possible and make sure that the proper programming is done to me while with him. It seems looking back at all my handlers, that almost all of them had a mother figure in their life.

During my marriage with Tommy he would deliberately do the most childish things, like not talk to my oldest daughter even if she directly asked him something. I remember complaining to Marie about it and she said, "I don't understand his behavior. He knew you had a daughter when he married you." She probably told him to keep up the good work. He's creating all sorts of turmoil for me and thus keeping the multi-dimensionals happy. It wasn't until this Thanksgiving visit that the puzzle fell together. She always disrupted my life. The day before my wedding day, she gave me a string of pearls to wear, and then they were suddenly gone from the bag I put them in when I went to put them on the next morning. Looking back, Marie held that same bag for me while I went into a dressing room to try something on. Creating negative energy, I felt terrible losing the pearls, never realizing that they had been removed on purpose.

When I married Tommy I was already pregnant and wasn't going to have a big wedding. Marie said and I quote, "I can help you with the wedding costs. He is my first child to get married, and I want to see my son get married." When she said *help*, I didn't know it was a loan. About a week before the wedding, she said ,"You know I am going to need that loan back for the wedding." I felt so used. I actually don't recall the entire amount but it was something like two or three thousand dollars that we had to pay back to her from the wedding gifts. Oh, but she did pay for our honeymoon which I wasn't even thinking about – a package for two to Jamaica for fifteen hundred dollars. Tommy and I were married May 6, 1989.

Tommy would go days without talking to me as well. He became so lazy and wouldn't ever do anything with me that I asked him to do. He wouldn't go to the gym with me. He wouldn't visit with my friends or family if they came to New York to visit. Many trips I took to Michigan alone because he didn't want to go with me. Now I realize that he had a secret life as my personal handler/controller. He made it difficult to want to be with him.

During our marriage, I remember him calling me at work and saying he got third row tickets to the Prince concert that night. I asked him how he got third row and he said they were being held for government officials and he got them. I didn't put it together until about a year ago that that concert was a mind control set up. Of course, Tommy would be getting government tickets since he worked for them. A lot of music is used for programming the mind. I was so naïve, I didn't question anything. I had absolutely no clue about any of this until my awakening in 2012.

I was married to Tommy seven years of the sixteen years I lived in New York City. After our divorce, I decided to move back to Michigan. My parents were getting old, and I wanted to be close to them. I remember Tommy wanting to get back together with me so bad and me telling my mom how he was acting. She suggested I leave the day before planned and not tell Tommy, so I made all the arrangements to leave a day before the departure day I told Tommy. He said when he came over to the condo that night after work and his two daughters and I were gone, cleaned out, it was like getting hit with a two-by-four in the heart. I caused that. That was the most selfish thing I ever could have done. I carried guilt for that a long time. My mother was the instigator for that plan which hurt me for years far more than it hurt Tommy. I am pretty sure he would have known what my plans were to move back to Michigan, as we targeted individuals who have been watched and monitored since our birth. Now I know that Tommy's behavior (which led me to divorce him) was purposely performed.

As of December 1, 2013, however, I know Tommy has been a prime player in manipulating me. Although I can't prove it in court, I know that he has never had my best interest at heart. When I was with him, he wouldn't even speak to Amy, my daughter, from my first marriage.

When our first daughter Kristi was around five years old, he slapped her across the face so hard he left a handprint on her cheek. He said when she woke him up around 10:00 p.m. and I still wasn't home from my doctor appointment, he was angry and slapped her to shut her up. I can tell you that the doctor appointment was at 7:30 p.m. for an hour visit with a psychologist that I had retained as I was going through so much trauma with Tommy. I had filed for divorce but Tommy was still living with me and would not leave for a while. He started doing coke with me. Anyway, at 10 p.m. that evening when he slapped my daughter so hard it left a huge, dark handprint on her cheek and ear, I was having sex with some fellow I had met and started to see. What if, just saying, my every move was observed with sophisticated surveillance technology, and he knew I was with another man? That would trigger such a reaction as violent as Tommy's to his own young daughter.

I reported the incident to the police and he was arrested for it. Actually, all I wanted was for the cops to talk to him but of course, it didn't work out that way. I'm sure he has had it out for me for a very long time. He has played such mind games with me, always pretending to be on my side and actually using me for nefarious forces. The government has people in many places maneuvering the persons they knew were going to wake up from their sleep. I can only try to relay to other individuals the circumstances in my case indicating that I was deliberately mind controlled.

In the early 90's, Tommy, my three daughters, and I went on vacation to California. Tommy's mother, grandmother, and sister also went. We all went to Santa Monica. Because my brother was living in San Francisco, Tommy, my daughters, and I rented a car and drove the Pacific Coast to visit my brother for a couple days in San Francisco.

As soon as we arrived in San Francisco and checked into our hotel, Tommy stated, "My money is missing and I think Amy (my first daughter) stole it." I was appalled that he would think my daughter (around fifteen years old at the time) would steal his money. He was so angry that he didn't want to go to my brother's house that evening and I left with my daughters to visit my brother. The next day Tommy announced that he "found his money." The stress he caused was on purpose. I wonder what he was doing in San Francisco while I was gone.

In 2007, I was working for an attorney, Jack Benefiel, and Jack came out of his office and said he got a telephone call from my ex-husband Tommy. He was kind of laughing when he said it, and he said Tommy told him I was a drug addict. I was so embarrassed and, of course, I didn't admit any of my drug use to him. It didn't dawn on me how devious it was of Tommy to do that. He didn't fire me, and Jack and I even dated for a few months after I went to another firm. Looking back, I am sure he had been offered the opportunity to be a handler for me.

Then just Thanksgiving 2013 Tommy talked me into going to New York for Thanksgiving weekend (driving of course). What a weekend of revelations. He was all over me the first night that I got to New York. He told me to leave my car at his apartment and our second daughter Michelle (now twenty-four years old), who drove with me, could drive it to his mother's in the morning which is where I was staying for that weekend. All my intuition told me that my car was tampered with before I left Michigan. Before he dropped me at his mother's house, he started kissing me and put his hands down my pants. His new wife, pregnant at the time, was in Florida with their son at her parents. Tommy even bit me in the cheek. It was so creepy and I had to remind him that he was married and had a son and another child on the way. I can't prove anything and all that I say will be vehemently denied by Tommy, but I know that he has been the key handler in my life. I just have to realize that I can't change the past and to forgive and remember infinite love is all that matters.

Tommy has been a part of my life since we met in 1988. He would always stay in touch. Numerous times he came to Michigan after our divorce. He flew in for both my parents' funerals. I would go visit him. So many road trips between the sixteen years I lived in New York City and Michigan and all the way up to and until November 2013. From about 1982 to 2013, that is over thirty years of mule service. I know I am the perfect mule. Not having any knowledge of transporting drugs or information makes the best carrier.

During my time with Tommy Byrnes, my vehicles were confiscated. I had a van that was impounded by the New York City Police because Tommy didn't pay tickets on his vehicle…so they impounded my van because his name is on the van also. Ah, that makes no sense, but looking back that would have been the way to put on the gadgets for mule service. I had a Merkur that Tommy had left in a shop claiming it had transmission problems. I took probably twenty trips with the van and three trips with the Merkur Scorpio.

Here is an example of how I believe my vehicles have been tampered with. I got laid off from work and had two vehicles. One was a Grand Cherokee Jeep with a high car payment. Tommy offered to fly from New York to drive the Jeep back to New York and take over my payments. After a few months, I flew to New York to get the Jeep and drive it back to Michigan. At the time, I was with Chris Pachesnik, a crackhead who wouldn't move out of my house. I was with him from about 2002 to 2005. I will share more about Chris below. I told Chris when I came back to Michigan that he should be packed and gone.

He wasn't. As soon as I got back to Michigan, Chris was crying that he needed to get high. He talked me into letting him use the Jeep to go to a usual spot to buy crack. Within fifteen minutes, he was back at my house saying he was carjacked. The Jeep ended up being involved in a car accident, and a man working on his car was crushed between two vehicles. I now am positive, as I have always thought that that carjacking was set up. It was winter time, and Chris wasn't even red or out of breath as he claimed he ran all the way home after the carjacking.

He said, "You don't even care that a gun was held to my head?"

I said, "I would if I believed you."

Only until recently did I link Tommy into that set up as well. It was so very stressful dealing with the insurance company for this. I was interviewed for two hours. I am surprised that the insurance company covered the wrecked vehicle under the circumstances.

The first Christmas that I moved back to Michigan from New York in November 1997, I moved in with my parents, with my young daughters. My oldest daughter stayed in New York. I walked into my parents' house, and there was Tommy sitting in the family room with my parents. I had no clue that they had talked to my parents and that he was coming. After he left the transmission of my van, it blew up at only 60,000 miles. Through an astral dream, I asked my father if he was the one who did that to the van and he said yes. My transmission blew up on my way to work. I asked my dad if I could borrow his car the next day until I got a rental and he said no. When I asked him why I couldn't for one day since he was retired, he said, "Sandy, I love you but I don't like you." In that dream, he said he was assigned to do it and would do whatever he was told to do.

I actually lived with Thomas Byrnes for almost seven years, but he was in my life for about twenty-five years, leaving me alone for a year or two at a time, then becoming my best friend and talking me into going to New York. As I said, he talked me into a road trip in November 2013 that proved to be very insightful. After leaving him in November 1997, I took many trips back to New York. I should add that in all the years I knew Tommy, he never once performed oral sex on me. He always wanted it from me and I don't know why I couldn't ask for it, as sexual as I was. A ritual abuse therapist specialist explained to me that withdrawing from something as pleasurable as oral sex is a form of control. It certainly worked on me. One of the probably ten to fifteen visits I had with Tommy after our divorce, he tried to do it and I said, "Nope, too late now, buddy." I never had sex with him again. On numerous trips to New York after being there a day or two, Tommy would start a fight with me and off I would go back to Michigan.

We booked a charter flight of all New York Yankees fans to Toronto sometime in the early 90's. We got into our hotel room and we had the most violent anal sex. I remember how rough he was. It was more painful than pleasure, and then he fell asleep. I remember walking around Toronto in a daze that afternoon. Knowing what I know now, we were recorded. I had so many incidents, looking back, with many, many men and many, many hotel/motel rooms.

We were in a hotel room in Boston, Massachusetts, and Tommy started a terrible fight with me while we were in the Cheers restaurant. We argued all the way back to the hotel room. Then he wanted to have sex and started getting all sexy. He said, "I'll be right back." I lay there waiting for him to come out and what do you think he came out in? My one-piece lacy lingerie I ordered from Victoria Secret. If a male worker for the cult wants to rise up, a requirement is often dressing and/or acting like a girl. I was totally shocked and certainly didn't expect that. Everything is backwards…keeps the mind confused.

We have to remember we are in 2016, and the technology that is being used and exposed now has been used and exposed for thousands of years. There is nothing new under the sun.

Daniel Farley

Dan was the head of office services and I was a legal secretary at Stroock, Stroock & Lavan in New York City. Dan would come by my desk and chat and because I was divorcing Tommy, we started "dating."

Dan and I would go out to restaurants for drinks and dinner and often times go back to his office and have sex. How convenient that he had a couch in the file storage area. I am sure there were cameras set up filming all this wild, passionate sex.

While dating Dan, Tommy showed up one night at Dan's house. The scene was so stressful. Tommy was outside Dan's house screaming at us. I had been at Dan's house for hours before Tommy showed up. How did he know where I was? There had to be tracking devices on my van. I was so embarrassed that I never thought to ask Tommy how he found Dan's house.

Another time Dan was at my house and Tommy showed up the next morning banging on my door. I opened the door and Tommy barged in and punched Dan in the face. I was between them but Tommy reached over me and clocked Dan. Down Dan went. It was pitiful and very traumatic. The police came but I don't understand why Tommy wasn't charged with assault. Looking back, many incidents had to be a set up.

Dan also had his mother he lived with and she hated me. Dan and I dated for about two years.

An incident I asked Dan about in 2015 when I called him (he won't return my phone calls now that I confronted him as to being a handler) involves lost time. Dan invited me to a black tie wedding in New Jersey probably around 1995 or 1996. He took me shopping and bought me a beautiful dress for the event. Dan, his mom, and I drove to New Jersey for the wedding. The wedding was beautiful with a cocktail hour, beautiful ice sculptors, excellent food, etc. I remember being in the backseat driving back to the motel, and I couldn't keep my eyes open. I felt drugged up and then passed out. I woke up the next day in the motel room with no memory of most of the drive to the motel or going into the motel, etc. A complete loss of time. I asked him what he did to me and he, of course, said he did nothing. I had so many incidents with lost time and this one always has left me with an uncomfortable feeling.

Dan and I even hooked up after I moved back to Michigan. I remember meeting him in New York City two times during my many visits after I had moved back to Michigan. Dan came to Michigan to visit me a couple years after I was back in Michigan.

Robert Lee Darling (Third husband)

I was married in New York City for seven years to my second husband. I lived in New York City for sixteen years. I left New York City and moved back to Michigan in November 1997. Shortly thereafter, I was reintroduced to my third husband, Robert Lee Darling. I am sure he is a Freemason or controlled by a Freemason entity. Bob Darling was my sister JoAnn's husband, Wade Vires' nephew. Wade's dad's first name was even Mason. Looking back, I remember being attracted to Bob Darling as a little girl. He had blonde/red hair and those same blue eyes that I've always been attracted to. I met up with Bob through my nephew Michael Vires (my sister JoAnn's and Wade's son). All the time with the men I did crack with, my nephew Michael was around pretending to love me, but doing crack with me nonetheless. He was in my life, doing crack with boyfriends, Chris Pachesnik, Jerry Watson, and George Huskey (you will read about these men below). He would contact me and get high with me and each of these men. Now he won't even talk to me. I haven't spoken to him in over eight years.

I knew Bob a year, was a married a year, and then divorced. What a bizarre time that was. He gave every indication of being an alcoholic and I still overlooked it. He reminded me so much of Bobby Craven, who I now know was a handler of mine. I already described some of Bobby Craven's traits. Let me tell you how stupid I was with Bob Darling. I caught him dead naked going down a woman. With the same "friend" he introduced to me when we first met. Of course, when I met her I asked him if there was still anything going on between them. He said they went out a couple times but nothing sparked and that they remain friends. The night I caught Bob dead naked with that woman was when we both had two residences. I was just sitting watching T.V. and something told me to go over to Bob's house. Bob was a mechanic and it wasn't unusual to have a few vehicles parked outside his house. I never noticed the woman Kathy's car. I walked through the garage, into the kitchen, noticed a bunch of beer bottles on the table and expected when I rounded the corner to his bedroom to see him lying there passed out. Nope. Kathy was lying on her back naked, and Bob was between her legs munching away. My stomach fell to the floor. They never heard me come into the house and I walked right into the bedroom on them. What energy that created.

Let me also share that I was pregnant at the time. I had already gone to an abortion clinic with my Aunt Mary Ann to abort the baby, but after I was on the table, I changed my mind and decided I was going to keep the baby. Then about a week later, I walked in on him straight up having sex with someone else. All my heart said was that I couldn't be attached to such an evil man and give a child a life of turmoil. My deepest regrets for making that decision. That decision wasn't mine to make. I had life in my womb, a son I think. Of course, I called Tommy and he flew in to Michigan to make sure I got the abortion. Looking back, it was very creepy Tommy coming all the way to Michigan to make sure I got that abortion. I was an emotional wreck so easily persuaded that getting the abortion was the right thing to do. Learning now about planned parenthood and what is done with the fetuses, I can only imagine what was done with that baby. That child would be about 18 years old now. I also had 3 other abortions. My bloodline is very powerful and since I am Rh negative (as told by mother, who should know) I am sure my fetuses were experimented on and perhaps even some type of cloning.

Tommy came to Michigan for several days while I got the abortion and then was back to New York. I was passed back to Bob and even after that incident, I forgave Bob and had sex with Bob as soon as Tommy left. Bob accused me of having the abortion because it was really Tommy's child. I had gone to New York City to see Tommy while I was living with Bob and Bob accused me of having sex with Tommy while I was in New York. Tommy and I messed around but he never penetrated me. I ended up pregnant with Bob's child. I knew it was Bob's child. Bob played sooooo many head games, but I stayed, I took it. I thought I was in love with him. He was so mean and angry. Always verbally assaulting me, accusing me of being with other men but I stayed. A few months after the abortion we bought the Ferndale house. The house I was at with all the terrible men after Bob moved out. We decided to remodel the kitchen and he suggested black and white checkered tiles. The kitchen in this house was so huge it had four ceiling fans. The floor ended up looking exactly like the floors in the Freemason lodges. The Masonic checkerboard is one of the most important symbols to the Illuminati, for it is used in ritualistic ceremonies. This is used because black and white is a symbol for duality or the base of consciousness. Duality patterns, such as checkerboards, stripes or zebras, are also commonly used as triggers for mind control slaves in order to reach specific alters. I lived in that house for about nine years with that checkered floor. Bob also collected owls. In particular, he had a large ceramic lamp with three owls on it. The owl is a long-time symbol of the Illuminati and Freemasons. For them, the owl symbolizes mourning and desolation because it is a bird that lives for the darkness. Thus, it represents sinners who have given up living in the light and have chosen the darkness of sin. Since it hides in darkness and avoids the light, the owl also came to symbolize Satan, the Prince of Darkness. "I am a brother to dragons, and a companion to owls." (Job 30:29) Of course I knew none of this at the time.

About a year after we were in the Ferndale house, I came home from work and there was a baby diaper bag on the couch. Bob's "girlfriend" had left behind her diaper bag. I found a dirty diaper in the garbage. He was home from work that afternoon but claimed to have no clue where the diaper bag came from. When I walked into the house that day, Bob was coming down the stairs to the bedrooms with his arms full of the sheets and pillow cases that were on the bed. I turned the corner to the living room and there on the couch is a diaper bag…not a toy diaper bag but real human baby's diaper bag. That was the last straw. About the time I filed for divorce, he stole my van. He went into my briefcase under my bed and took the title out, forged my name, and signed the title at the Secretary of State to himself. He would leave lengthy voicemails describing how he was going to cut the van up if I didn't buy it back from him. He was holding my van for ransom. I told him it was just a van, not a family member being held hostage. I expected a bumper to be laying on my front porch or to get a mirror mailed to me. It was all so ridiculous. All the negative energy I dispersed during the time with him. There are many other terrible arguments that he would start and, of course, I was drinking, too, and would argue right back. During two of the at least three or four times the police were at my house, Bob had me arrested for domestic violence. He lied to the officer and said the cut that was on his face was from me. They actually believed him because I admitted that I had shoved him. That was so bizarre. The police arrested me and the next morning, the police drove me home saying there was no case.

The officer who drove me home that morning asked me, "What were you arrested for?"

I said, "My husband told the cops I cut him and they arrested me for domestic violence."

He said, "My goodness, how big is he? You're barely over five feet tall."

I said, "He's about six feet tall."

Officer: "Boy you must be a scruffy thing. A six foot man and YOU get arrested."

The second time I had to be bailed out, but Bob didn't show up to court to press charges and the state dropped it.

He brought a very large picture of a leopard home one day, a big picture with a huge dark frame. One day I took a picture of that side of the room and in the picture was clearly a demon's face. The leopard is in the middle on the branch and in the bottom right of the picture is clearly a demon's face, with fiery eyes and a creepy smile. I showed it to my family and they saw the face as well.

Bobby Darling definitely had two personalities. Even his handwriting would change. I looked up Freemason masonic lodges in Michigan and found at least one hundred. Not surprisingly, Bob Darling was from Pontiac, and there were three lodges there. The city of Ferndale and the next nearest city, Hazel Park, both have lodges. There are lodges listed in up north cities where cousins of mine have retired. The town where I bought my home and twenty acres is surrounded by cities with Freemason lodges. Very well may be a coincidence but since secrecy is so important to keeping the Freemason activities thriving, who would know. I found my twenty acres and home on Craigslist. Beautiful twenty acres with a nice pond. Nice landscaping. However, what I didn't think about when I excitedly said I would buy it was that there are strategically located homes and buildings all about the property. I am sure since so much effort has gone into following and disturbing my life thus far, this surveillance won't end until I depart this earthly journey. I mean really, they built a hut-type building directly across from my house in the front of a ten-acre plot that looks directly into my dining room window. I have twenty acres, and there is a neighbor on the near side of my house with many buildings. Very suspicious. Knowing that my whole life has been planned and set up to be destroyed has made me paranoid, to say the least. Since everything in the world is recorded, the truth about all these supposedly loving friends and family will be known. I definitely am looking forward to getting out of this container and getting to real truth. With all the mind control I have had in this lifetime, I question any information or ideas that comes to my mind. Are these my thoughts? Are these the thoughts they want me to think? Very exhausting. Have I had any truly original thoughts of my own?

There has to be more people out there with this same enlightenment. They're probably called crazy, too. It's sad that this had to be this way. They could've done it so much differently. They're just so out of control with lust and greed. It's so wrong. It's cruel, actually. Most "common folks" know nothing about what has been going on behind closed doors.

People are put into our lives to play a part in the mind control. My parents were able to control me and put me into vulnerable positions as far as my well-being and education were concerned. Now I understand the mind control that was already being put to use in my decision-making. Even while with Bob, I remember going back to New York several times. My youngest daughter, Michelle, had wanted to stay with her Dad in New York. After being there less than a year, Tommy stopped letting me talk to Michelle on the telephone. So there was Bob chirping in my ear, "Come on. Let's go to New York and get her." So we did. What drama that was. I am sure that entire scheme was planned out to get me to go to New York yet again.

Christopher John Pachesnik

After Bob Darling and I broke up, Christopher Pachesnik came into my life and moved right into my home within a couple months. I was introduced to Chris by my brother Bill. He was on my brother's bowling team, and I would go up and watch my brother and his team bowl on Friday nights. My brother and his buddy Ted encouraged me to go out with Chris. Numerous times have I heard my brother say, "Teddy still feels bad for setting you up with Chris." Never once have I heard my brother have any remorse for the things he did to me. Chris is the one who got me smoking crack. This was probably in about the spring of 2000. He would take money out of my purse and go buy drugs. I'd say to myself, *Well, I bought them. I might as well do them.* What a sick mind I had. He stole from me, punched me square in the forehead one night, made me feel terrible about myself. Two times in the two years he cold-cocked punched me when I wasn't looking. He punched me so hard I fell to the ground, caught myself and fractured my thumb. The dislocated bone protrudes on the side of my thumb today. He would come off so fun loving and kind, but underneath he was devious and calculating. He used me completely. Chris ran up porno bills, stole money from my bank account, used phone sex, all components of an evil possessed person. He would hide under my basement stairs. I found makeshift beds under the basement stairs where storage doors opened on either side to beneath the stairs. He had blankets, a pillow, a watch, and a crack pipe in the loft in the garage. Even in the crawl space under the house there was a cubby where he built a nest. He would pretend he was going to work and come back to the house and sleep all day. In front of the washer and dryer in the basement, there was sometimes a pile of dirty laundry. He said he even hid under the clothes with a hose to breathe through. I had to file eviction papers to get him out of my house.

In December 2004, Chris' best friends invited us to a condo resort in Cancun, Mexico. I paid for the trip for Chris, my two youngest daughters, and I. The second day we were there Chris started a fight with me, pushed me down on the beach and shoved my face in the sand. I was so upset that I packed my daughters and my bags and went to a resort down the street. What stress this had to cause my daughters. Within a day or two, we were back at the resort with Chris and his friends. Looking back, with the predictive behavior patterns I have, I am sure it was planned for me to leave and then return.

One New Year's Eve, around 2005 I think, I went with Chris to his ex-girlfriend Dede and her husband Rick's house. I decided I wanted to go home. It was early in the morning New Year's Day.

Rick said, "I'll take you home."

Chris said, "I'm staying here."

I said, "Okay, I just want to go home."

Rick offered me a drink, last one for the road. I drank it. I remember walking out of the garage and don't remember the ride home at all. The ride was only fifteen minutes. I woke up in the hospital at three in the afternoon. Rick had left me in the driveway with my pants down and my shirt up. I lay in the driveway two hours before a neighbor called the police. My hands had frostbite, and the neighbor saw Rick drag me from his car and lay me in the driveway in what was described as a fireman's hold. I didn't put it together that Chris was probably doing Dede that morning while I lay in my driveway freezing to death. I feel that was a deliberate act to try and kill me.

A week or two later I saw the neighbor and thanked him for calling for help. He said, "I saw you laying out there for a long time and thought you'd freeze to death if I didn't do something. I'm sorry I waited so long to call the authorities. I kept waiting for you to get up."

I would complain to Chris that I can't afford everything. I was supporting my daughters, a mortgage payment, car payment, insurance, etc. and two people's crack habits. He would not go to work. I sold the camper I had, a boat I had, and I remember telling him, "Since I met you, I bought a boat and a camper and now have sold them." His reply was, "And you have a crack habit." I remember saying to Chris, "Just bring in a couple hundred a week, something." He replied, "I drive your kids to school every morning." I responded, "You have to be the best paid chauffeur in the world."

I was with Chris for over four years. Smoking crack night after night. Spending tens of thousands of dollars. I get sick when I think of all the money I spent on drugs most of my life. So much more I could have done with my daughters and for humanity. Chris rode my brand new bike to the party store one afternoon when he was supposed to be watching my girls while I was out with my girlfriend. He said he went into the store to buy cheese and when he came out the brand new bike was replaced with a broken down beat up bike. As I shared about the Jeep, Chris was an accomplice in that "carjacking".

During my time with Chris, there were several times he hit me. Chris and I were arguing over crack, and he just punched me hard straight in the forehead. He punched me in the forehead, and a huge black and blue lump the size of an egg was on my forehead. Another time we had left a restaurant and were arguing. Chris was driving my car and I told him to pull the car over and for him to get out. As I walked around to the driver's side of the car, he punched me square in the face and I went down. As I tried to catch myself, when I hit the ground my thumb was fractured.

I met Chris' Mom only a couple times for breakfast. She was so nice to me and complimented me on how pretty my smile is. Many times she mentioned my nice white teeth. She wasn't the busybody like all the other handlers' mothers.

Gerald Allen (Flip) Watson

After Chris and I broke up, Gerald Allen Watson (a/k/a Flip) came into my life. I met Flip at a mandatory, once-a-week class I was court ordered to attend for alcohol and drug rehab. "Somehow" Flip got my telephone number from the workers and called me on a Saturday a few weeks into the classes. Anyone in their right mind would have had a lightbulb go off and ask why my number would be given out. Instead, I was so flattered, and he was so cute I fell for him immediately. He acted like he was so in love with me. During the first few months of the relationship there were no drugs involved. Then slowly we started smoking crack until it became a habit. He had a really nice apartment and would cook for me, but when we were out, for instance at a party (he would invite me to a friend's house), I would find a note written to Flip on the seat from a woman saying something like, "Why did you bring her here?" or his first wife would call and leave messages on his answering machine about Flip not calling her back.

He actually set me up to get busted on a drug run he asked me to do for him. These were all diversions to keep me from feeling and understanding the truth. Yes, I spent twenty-three days in Oakland County Jail, Pontiac, Michigan over that bust. Because of that bust, I violated my probation. Yes, drugs are illegal, and there is always the possibility that it just happened that way, but I know by the way it happened that he set me up.

This particular Friday night I was repeatedly calling Flip and he wouldn't answer. Then around 11:00 p.m., when he finally answered he said, "You fly, I'll buy," and of course I jumped on it. I was so excited that he answered that I didn't hesitate to do it. Three cops, including two males, one female, just happened to pull me over. They witnessed nothing. I so wish my intuition had kicked in when I was on the telephone with him. I ended up spending Friday night, all day Saturday and Saturday night in jail and finally saw a judge on Sunday via telecom. However, by the time I went in front of the judge and the time came for me to get bailed out, I was transferred to Wayne County Jail, Detroit, Michigan because I wasn't bailed out before the transfer time. When I finally got out of jail, I went rushing right back into Flip's arms. I remember thinking, *Yes, he does want to be with me.* What a fool I was. I had zero self-esteem. It never occurred to me at the time that Flip had set me up. Although I can't legally prove it, I now know that he did. It was shown to me in revelations while meditating.

There is a particular incident that occurred one Saturday night during my time with Flip that I have to share. The thought of it disgusts me but it has much relevance. We had gone to a party and went back to my house. We decided to get high. I watched him pull out of the driveway to go across 8 Mile Road to get crack and I was standing on the side porch. The porch had four steps to the landing. While I was standing there, "something" pushed me straight off the porch. I landed flat on my face. I looked horrible, but all I cared about was getting high. How disgusting I must have looked with gravel and blood all over my face and hitting that pipe. I felt something push me from behind. To this day, I know I didn't just fall. I wasn't walking or planning on moving, but I didn't even bother to clean up my face. I was so happy when Flip pulled in with that crack. It wasn't until the next day that I even looked in the mirror. I looked horrible. The following Monday I went to the doctor and my oldest daughter, Amy, walked into the waiting room, took one look at me, and said, "Happy Halloween." I looked that gruesome. How embarrassing going to work with my face all broken up.

I used crack off and on for seven years. I did disgusting things. Crawling on my hands and knees looking for pieces of crack that may have fallen off the table. Digging through the carpet for little white pieces. Smoking potato chips and fingernails. Gross, I know, but I am sure that I did. Crying because there was no more. I have so much absolutely indescribable regret that I can barely hold my head up at times. If a gun was put to my head and a pipe forced in my mouth, I would take the gunshot. There is absolutely nothing good about drugs, and I have absolutely no desire to be in that state of mind ever again. If only I had realized sooner, I wouldn't have wasted all that time and money and, most importantly, all the time with my children. Smoking crack seemed to enhance my already highly charged sexual appetite. I was masturbating all the time. I even masturbated with a crack socket. Tell me someone like that is not being watched and recorded. Remember folks, they fragmented my mind when I was three years old.

Another strange incident in that house was when I had a friend, John, over and we were in the kitchen. I was watching when John was walking in front of the stove. Then – bam! He looked like he was shoved or pushed and his head hit the fan over the stove. He said, "What the hell was that?" I said I didn't know but it looked like he got pushed. He said he felt something punch him hard in the side of his body.

Robert Monroe, the author and out-of-body expert, while on an out-of-body experience was able to pinch someone. It was verified by the person he visited. He said he went out-of-body and went to his friend's house. There was a group of people and he pinched his friend in her side. When he told her about it, she said, "That was you? I felt a pinch and a huge bruise was on my side." If he could do that, just think what the multi-dimensional beings can do.

One night in that same Ferndale house while lying in bed, I felt something sitting on my chest and I could barely breathe. I pushed myself up and saw little footprints running across the comforter.

There were little indents clearly running across the bed but I couldn't see anybody. I have no reason to make this up. Believe me, this is far too embarrassing for me to be making it all up.

Flip, I suspect, is a Freemason. He was from Berkley, and there are two lodges there. Flip's father was from Berkley and had three sons. Flip is the youngest.

Flip would tell me about the sexual abuse he endured from his Father during his young years. Flip drank excessively and was in a lot of pain from his Father's abuse. One night when he was drunk, he confessed the abuse he endured at his Father's hands. His mother, Gene, would go bowling and his Dad would have anal sex with him. I pictured graphically the scene as Flip described it.

He said, "My dad would be in the living room and would call me out to him. He'd say, 'Pull your pants down and bend over, boy.'" I pictured it in my mind. His Mom walking out the door every week for bowling, as my parents both did on bowling nights. His Dad sitting in the living room playing with himself, calling Flip out of his bedroom. Flip obediently bending over. The whole scene is what I was taught was normal from the huge, thick, graphic cartoon book I was given as a play toy at a very young age.

Flip didn't fight it and didn't tell. His Dad would take him on camping trips and take him aside into the outhouse and have sex with him. That went on for years. I'm sorry if this offends you, Flip, sharing your cruel Father's upbringing for you, but all points indicate that this is generational type Freemason abuse. The sad thing is that this actually sexually aroused me at the time when he described it. I even masturbated to that fantasy with his Dad pounding his ass (Flip has a very nice ass), the Dad's hand pulling on Flip's little dingy, and Jerry's face buried in his Mom's vagina, pulling on her nipples long and hard. I noticed Flip's Mom always sat with her legs wide apart and her feet up on the chair. If that sexually arouses me, an advocate against hurting children and someone who could never actually do harm to a child, what are the lusts, needs, and cravings of those who do these things to children on a daily basis? How many men masturbated to watching me and my cousin performing our sexual acts? All the while their daughters and sons are living "normal". It is multi-generational incest and child mind control through sexual perversion and deception. These old-timers have been watching us our entire lives through "top secret" porn rings. The Masons are a very old society and there are multi-generations of them that we are dealing with now. The families are very secretive and now have grandfathers, fathers, sons and grandsons all working for the organization. Anything for a paycheck and a pension.

Flip and I were together on and off for about three years. It was rocky road and he did a lot of things to me to cause the anxious, distrustful feelings - energy the inter-dimensionals love to suck off of. He went for a job to paint a home with his friend for a week. The job was far enough away that they were going to stay up there for the week. Two to three nights and days he did not answer his telephone or call me. This was the man who was living with me at the time. The anxiety I experienced. Once Flip, out of the blue, picked up my car keys and drove my car and left me at the bar with his friend. He would pull stunts like that all the time.

Flip and I were not together during the entire three years. Sometime in between I dated a guy, John McFaul, for a few months. He came on real strong, too. He had a nice house, fishing boat and was an Allen Jackson look alike. Really, until he took his hat off (LOL) the top of his head was all bald, but with his hat on he had his ponytail so there was the illusion of a full head of hair. At an Allen Jackson concert we attended at DTE (Pine Knob, Michigan), people were taking pictures with him and saying, "Now I can tell my mom I met Allen Jackson." He had his wife beater, cowboy boots, hat, and was loving all the attention. It was actually great fun. John and I went on a weekend fishing trip to Ludington, Michigan to salmon fish on Lake Michigan. On that weekend John wigged out and I remember looking across the water at the shore, way out on Lake Michigan, thinking, I *wonder if I can swim that far to shore.* Thank God he took a nap and went to sleep. I mean just a few hours before I was dancing on the pole on his boat, having a cocktail and bam! Whoop! There he goes bi-polar. The tension caused fuels the negativity that the archons love to suck on.

Country music is also a big part of the mind control program. I had no clue about the country music connection with the mind control programs. During an argument in the few short months we dated, he took my cell phone and threw it against the wall. Flip started calling me again when he found out I was dating John and since John was also not stable, I went back to Flip.

Flip bought me a wedding ring set. An engagement ring and wedding band. The wedding band mysteriously disappeared one day. I thought at the time I had lost it, but now, knowing all the games being played with my head, I am sure Flip took the ring and sold it or pawned it.

George Melvin Huskey

Reflecting on the people in my life, I met Kim, who introduced me to Ray, my fourth husband, through the boyfriend I had before I met Ray, George Huskey. George tracked me down in a local bar. I was still being stupid and going to bars, trying to find my life partner. George charmed me in the beginning. He has intense green eyes and knows exactly the right things to say. When I met George, I hadn't smoked crack for maybe six months. Of course, he got me hooked right back on it. With George, though, I lost everything in less than a year. I got fired from my job and was behind on my mortgage payments by two months. I clearly recall one time George, my nephew Michael, and I were on a binge. Michael had the money, George had the balls to go get the stuff, and I was the middle man between them. Three days we were in motels. George would get violent, and Michael and I would cower while George wielded a knife at us. One night George was lying in bed with his shirt off. I looked at his spine and it was like a lizard. I'm sure he was not entirely human either. George had the ability to control me, too. All the times of smoking crack, I would feel demons around me. It wasn't my imagination. They were there sucking up the energy I expended.

I lived in the same house in Ferndale, Michigan for ten years. Within six months of hooking up with George, I lost my job in 2008. I fell behind on mortgage payments and let it go back to the bank. George talked me into moving to South Carolina with him. I blindly agree, leaving my daughters behind. Michelle was only sixteen years old and Kristi was eighteen years old. No wonder they want nothing to do with me. I was there for eight horrible months. He was always violent and I just pushed it off, being so used to being abused from my earliest relationship. I am so blessed to see it clearly now. He would grab my face and squeeze very hard or backhand me if I said something he didn't like. It took him violently beating me with his fists to finally leave him.

Between South Carolina and Michigan I drove probably five times. I also drove between New York City and South Carolina two times. While in South Carolina, George started getting very violent. He smacked me so hard across the head I thought my eardrum had ruptured. One evening, everything was fine, we were having a fire, and I walked into the house. George and another girl walked out of the bathroom together. I said something and he pushed me back and I cut my head open on the molding of the door. I had to go to the hospital for stitches. In the meantime, Tommy Byrnes started calling me again. He talked me into going to New York to stay with him. I left George in South Carolina and went to New York City. George kept calling me and harassed Tommy. George talked me into going to South Carolina for a visit. As soon as I left New York, Tommy changed the locks and said I wasn't welcome in New York again. After just being in South Carolina again for a couple weeks or so, George beat me up so bad I finally left him, but let me tell you, just before he flipped out and started beating on me, we were talking about getting married. That is how mind controlled I am that I actually would have married such a horrible person. We were out on the front porch and George accused me of having sex with Tommy when I was staying with Tommy in New York. When I said Tommy wanted to and we kissed and hugged one night but we did not have sex, George leaped out of the chair and punched me square in the face. I kicked him hard in the belly and he went back. I jumped out of the chair and ran into the house. I was screaming but no neighbors called the police. He came into the house, grabbed me by the hair and punched me again in the head. I remember him hitting me so hard I saw stars in my head just like in the cartoons. It only stopped when I kicked him square in the balls and he fell to his knees. My face was so mangled and bruised. I had to go back to New York to get my stuff before I returned to Michigan because I wasn't welcome in New York anymore. I drove from South Carolina to New York to Michigan within twenty-four hours. I know this is confusing, but I just need to share all the road trips I took.

Interestingly, I have total recall of being with Tommy Byrnes during all the relationships above. Tommy was visiting me in Michigan but I was already seeing Bob. I accidentally called Tommy "Bob" and that caused a huge argument. As I mentioned, Tommy flew in to make sure I went through the abortion with Bob's baby. Another instance, I was in New York, at Tommy's apartment, in his bed and we started fooling around. I ended up saying, "Oh, Chris." Bam! That ruined that. I was thrown out of Tommy's apartment and went to a motel. Then back to Michigan. I know Chris had to leave my house and stay at a motel at least three times while Chris lived in my house because Tommy was coming to Michigan.

Tommy came in for my dad's funeral, the morning of September 11, 2001. My dad had died on September 9th and that is Tommy's birthday. Tommy was born in 1966. That was scary knowing Tommy was on a flight departing about the same time as the plane crashed into the tower. There was no information on where/how the plane had crashed.

Then my mother died five months later (March 2002), and Tommy came in for that funeral. Another time, before my parents' death, Michelle, our youngest daughter, had a dance competition. Tommy and his mother came to Michigan for that and stayed at my house. Chris stayed at a motel and smoked crack. What bizarre living.

While with George, he would frequently get violent. Once George actually took his belt off and started beating me. He also went on a rampage when there was no more crack and started foaming at the mouth and threw a knife at me. The knife barely missed me.

Rayford Levoy Goodridge (4th husband)

I married Ray Goodridge in 2010. All the incidents I explain that happened while with Ray happened in a little over one year. I met Ray in November 2009 and married him in February 2010. I left him April 1, 2011. Before I met him, I had filed for social security disability. It had never occurred to me to file for social security benefits until a therapist suggested I file. At the bottom of a particularly long questionnaire, there is a blank to be filled in with the name and telephone number of the person who helped you with understanding the questionnaire. Not questioning how that could later be used against me, I filled in this supposed friend name, Kim Huskey, and included her phone number and name. A month after that Kim called me and invited me to participate in a radio survey. All I had to do was listen to three hours of tunes for one hundred dollars. I was like, sure, yeah, no problem, easy money. I did ask Kim where she found out about this survey, and she said it was through a lady she knew. I'm so darn trusting. Of course, I would never have participated now that I'm aware of the mind control with subliminal messages that can be generated. Why hadn't I heard of these surveys advertised on radio stations? It was a set up. I sat there with earphones on my head being fed subliminal messages. The survey was being held at a fancy hotel in Dearborn, Michigan. There were long tables with chairs and headphones and name tags where to sit.

The songs the slave hears on the radio, will for instance have code words. The Programmers due to the corruption of the music industry knows what hit songs are coming out, and they will haul their slaves in and program them according to the lyrics of the soon-to-be hits. The lyrics will be written so that programmed meanings can be attached to certain words and lines.[22]

So right after that particular one hundred dollar survey I participated in, Kim had her boyfriend's cousin visiting from Alabama and wanted me to meet him. It was Ray Goodridge, a chicken farmer from Henagar, Alabama. It was an unexplained attraction. Not surprisingly, Ray could sing and play country songs on his guitar. I fell in love with him and moved to Henagar, Alabama. I later found out that the mountain is appropriately nicknamed "meth mountain." I believed everything he told me. Looking back I know he has contacts with different species, whether they be celestial or terrestrial, I can't say. He was full of lies and deceit from the beginning. Grand dummy I was. And the story I will share with you as to what happened to me in Alabama leads me to believe that the government and satanic followers are a part of this evil game that I've been a participant in. I can't prove anything with printed out hard evidence, but I know because I lived it, that it was definitely a planned experience my being with Ray. I witnessed him change his face so peculiarly. He could change it into an old man and his facial features often seemed different to me. I remember sometimes thinking that there were two of him.

There was a man whose face shapeshifted in front of my eyes into an evil demon face at a Flea Market in Fort Payne, Alabama. The flea market incident was clearly a set up, too. Ray had taken me to the flea market two times before the horrifying third time when the incident occurred.

He said on Saturday, "Hey, we're going to the flea market tomorrow morning."

I said, "Sure, it has cool stuff."

---

[22] Fritz Springmeier & Cisco Wheeler. *The Illuminate Formula Used To Create An Undetectable Mind Control Slave, Science 5. The Skill of Lying, The Art of Deceit.*

This time we got there and I immediately noticed there were only men in the market. Groups of tall, dark-haired, men with dark complexions standing around in groups of two and three in different corners of the market. The men seemed to be looking at me and whispering between themselves. As Ray and I were walking through the market we split up. When I got to the end of the main walkway of the market, I noticed a man following me. I turned around and there was an older man following me. As he got closer I turned around again to look and he was an older man. The third time I turned around, his face shapeshifted into a demon face right in front of my eyes. His eyes turned yellow and slanted wide across his face. His hair flared out and two horns came up. Ugly fangs came out. I immediately went around the corner and back to where Ray was standing, probably watching. I remember he was giggling. I grabbed his hand and then directly behind me were four or five men standing very, very close to what I called at the time *breathing down my neck*. Now I know they were sucking the energy I released from the startling appearance of the demon face.

I told Ray, "Let's go. I want to go home." He took me the long way through the flea market, and there was an old lady following us in a wheelchair. She was so creepy, slowly following us in her wheelchair with a respirator attached to her. She was the only lady I saw there except for the husband/wife behind one particular counter. All I wanted was out of that flea market but Ray was taking his time, stopping to look at stuff to buy.

At a CD counter, the lady behind the counter commented to Ray, "She's not doing too well today, is she?" All too weird to be coincidence. That man shapeshifted right in front of my eyes. By the time we got out of the flea market and into Ray's truck, I was crying. When I told a local resident about the incident at the flea market, she said there have been stories about witchcraft at that flea market.

Aliens [fallen angels] are known as face changers. They're walking around with us all the time. The people who believe in God and feel the demonic presence call them fallen angels. Whether they are fallen angels of an all-powerful, all knowing God or just evil Reptilians, doesn't matter. We are definitely not alone. They've instilled fear into us. Too much has happened to me to be a coincidence. I've been brain controlled to try to kill myself two times. I've had to fight depressing thoughts, knowing they are not mine, of killing myself as the only way to hurry up and get out of this biological body. I know that infinite awareness is everywhere and I want to be a part of it again. I meditate daily and have received much knowledge with the infinite truth awareness.

We would leave the house, neither of us having taken a shower, and when we returned there would be wet towels on the bathroom floor. Food would end up disappearing. I knew someone was coming in and out of the house while we were gone. I even put tape on three doors in the house before we left. When we returned two of the three doors had the tape knocked off. I became so paranoid, but all the while Ray debunked me and denied any wrongdoing.

In April or so, about a month or two after we got married, I took a trip to Michigan to visit my daughters. When I came back certain things were not right. I came back and the spare bedroom in his house that I had put all my personal belongings into was all pulled apart. All my belongings were scattered and all my paperwork had all been gone through. Within a couple weeks of coming back from Michigan a favorite Aunt of mine had died. Because I had just returned from Michigan I couldn't afford to drive back for her funeral. I got so depressed or so mind controlled, I took a bunch of Xanax. There were no more than twenty-five low dosage Xanax. I didn't even pass out from them. I told Ray a couple hours after taking the pills and he called poison control and an ambulance. I said I don't want to go to hospital, that I am fine. The police came and said if I didn't go to the hospital they would arrest me. I dared the police to arrest me and when they went to put the handcuffs on me, I remembered my jail time and backed down. Like a dummy. I got in the ambulance. I was admitted on a

Thursday, early evening. In the emergency room, they started sticking stuff down my nose and blood started spewing out everywhere. I remember being shoved back onto the table. The next morning I woke up in ICU with a guard. Yes, with a guard. Then they have someone from the local mental clinic come to evaluate me that Friday afternoon, and he gave recommendation that I to go to a mental hospital. Decatur Mental Hospital is three hours from Fort Payne, Alabama in Decatur, Alabama. After getting out of the mental hospital, I read the court order that was faxed from the judge on the same Thursday evening that I was admitted into the Fort Payne, Alabama hospital. That was even before I was evaluated by the local mental clinic therapist, so it is apparent that the move to the mental hospital was all prearranged from the time I was admitted into the emergency room. On the following day, Saturday, I was escorted in handcuffs through the hospital, put into a police car and driven to a mental hospital three hours away where I was kept for five more days. The order was signed by a judge the same evening I was admitted into the emergency room, even before I was evaluated by the mental therapist the next afternoon. A clear set up. Boy, did that create a lot of confusion for me! Such sadness. I didn't understand the significance of this incident. I find myself even today being tracked and mind controlled. I was a victim and so innocently fell into the plan. That isn't a usual incident in someone's life. The first forty-eight hours in the mental hospital I was not even allowed a telephone call. Coincidentally, I never received a bill for that five-day, three-meals-a-day mental hospital stay. I'm sure I was under evaluation for whatever was done to me in the first Fort Payne hospital. Incidentally, I never got my clothes back or the money that was in my jeans pocket from the Fort Payne Hospital.

The staff was always asking, "What's your name?" and "What's the date?" Dates can trigger us slaves as well. I notice myself repeating numbers like today is February 6, 2016 and so in my head I see 262016 and then 02062016. Like there is something to numbers. Of course, while there, I was forced to take their drugs. I even took them afterward for a few months with Ray, as I actually believed there was something wrong with me and that maybe the pills would help. One pill even had a side effect of making my breasts lactate. It was horrible. A fifty-year woman with lactating breasts. Imagine what all the big pharma drugs are doing to the millions of people on them.

There is strange writing/formulas on a wall in a room in Ray's house. I would see these weird formulas on the wall and say. "What's that?" and he'd say it was nothing and shuffle me out of the room. When we would come back to the house, the writing would be gone. They looked like algebra equations.

There were numerous times I was given roofies (drugged) and bodily attacks performed on me. I suspected something happening after a particular party he took me to where I blacked out and had no recollection of even driving home. The last memory I had was listening to Ray and his friend playing their guitars and singing around 11:00 p.m. The next morning my necklace was missing and I felt uncomfortable the entire next day. About two weeks after that date, I was going through pictures on a cell phone that wasn't being actively used, and there was a picture of me, laying in the moonlight with something wrapped around my neck. I look beautiful in a creepy eerie way under the moonlight. The date of the picture was the same date as that particular party, taken at 3:00 a.m., the same morning that I have no recollection of leaving the party in May 2010. I asked Ray about who took the picture and where was I. He denied knowing anything about it and even said, "Where did you go that night?" changing the blame onto me.

I said, "You know, I'm always up your ass. You tell me who took this picture." To this day, I can only imagine what was done to me during those lost hours. Looking back, I'm sure finding that picture was purposely planned to get a reaction out of me. Imagine how you would feel finding a picture someone took of you during an early morning of which you have no recollection.

Also, Ray did a very hurtful and sneaky deed about a month or two after Ray and I got married. A girl knocked on the door. She said her name was Mindy and that she was a friend of Ray's. I told Ray and he said to let her in. She proceeded to stay for several hours, and we shared telephone numbers. She immediately started texting to me every day. I point blank asked her straight to her face and Ray straight to his face if there had ever been anything more than a friendship between them. They both said they had always just been friends. There was one or two more times that Mindy came over to Ray's. We would all three shoot darts. Then about six months into our marriage he blurted out, "Well, you know, Mindy and I were engaged." What a slap in the face. Think of the pure negative energy that expelled with that kind of a deceit. I verified the engagement with Ray's first wife. When I called and asked his first wife if Ray and Mindy had been engaged, she said, "Oh, they were engaged, alright. They were attached at the hip." Deceit and lies are the most profitable forms of loosh to harvest from people by setting them up to be disappointed and crushed. The loneliness, disappointment and sadness are so profitable.

Ray and I were driving in the car one Saturday afternoon, and we drove by people riding horses. Ray was a friend of one of them and the guy invited us to a party. While at the party, I asked Ray's friend if we could smoke a joint. He said no but that we could take a horseback ride and smoke on the trail. I say I wasn't sure about it since I knew it was late. The friend talked me into going for a horseback ride. Even while he was getting the horse, I was having second thoughts.

I walked up to Ray and said, "Ray, your friend wants me to go for a horseback ride and I really don't want to go. Why don't you tell him it's late and that I'll go for a ride some other time?"

He said, "Oh baby, he's already got the horse saddled." Here he came with one horse. I thought I was getting my own horse, but instead I ended up on the back of his horse. Right in the middle of the ride he got off the saddle and stepped down off the horse. There I was on the back of the horse with nothing to hold on to and the horse bucked me off. I ended up breaking three ribs. Tell me that wasn't a set up. I'm sure they were hoping I'd fall off the horse and hit my head and maybe die.

After I got up off the ground, the first thing this guy said was, "Hey, do you want to smoke that joint?" He proceeded to try to get me to take my top off and show him my breasts. When I told Ray about it, he said, "I knew he would hit on you."

While with Ray, I would often wake up with anal pain. I even went to a doctor to ask him if it looked like anything was abnormal since right after Ray and I got married, he refused to have sex with me, but my vaginal and anal area felt like I had been having sex all night. The doctor said he could see anal tears. I woke up one morning with my jaw in terrible pain. I went out into the living room and there was Ray and a friend of his who apparently arrived while I was sleeping. All my instincts told me they had done something to me to cause my jaw to feel dislocated. So many unexplained incidents that made me realize that he was evil and I had to get away.

While with Ray, he also had my dog Samson killed. I had the dog for ten years and brought him with me to live with Ray in Alabama. Killing Samson was necessary because he hindered all the coming and goings in Ray's house while we were not there. Samson never went by the road. Then one afternoon we were outside and I went inside to get Sam some water. I went back outside and asked Ray where the dog was. He said, "I don't know. Maybe he followed you into the house."

I looked inside the house and he was not there. I went back outside and started calling him, walking around to the back of the house where Sam usually would wander. I came back from around the house and I spotted Sam across the highway. I started yelling for him to stay where he was. Too late, he stepped right out in front of a pickup truck going at high speed. He was killed right there in front of my eyes. I threw myself on the ground screaming, "No!"

That evening I was in the living room crying in a corner. I looked across the room at Ray and he was snickering. I bet that incident brought him much joy from the amount of energy that was harvested from that incident. Weird how he went through all this trouble to engrave a headstone and bury him and place the bowling ball the dog liked to play with on his grave.

I remember him saying, "Oh, that dog was getting old anyways. His breathing was getting heavy." There was nothing wrong with my dog's breathing.

Ray would do all sorts of mean things to me. We got into an argument one evening over something I said wrong and Ray went out the back door and brought in a sledge hammer. He proceeded to destroy the pool table I had bought (I loved shooting pool), smashing it over and over again with a delirious, deranged face. Imagine the scene from *The Shining* and the deranged face of Jack Nicholson. I sat on the couch in disbelief and shock. He then went into the kitchen, came back into the living room, poured syrup all over my head and dumped flour on me. I cried myself to sleep and woke up with all the mirrors in the house spray painted black.

What a year of hell. Thank God I got myself off the drugs and out of that mess. In late December 2012, he tapped into my telephone and altered pictures I had stored on that telephone. I have witnesses to it. When I was with him, he would tap into my computer and alter pictures as well. His mother had given me a picture of Ray and I and my eyes were clearly blacked out. All the lies he told me to get him to marry him! He would go through all my belongings and alter my clothes. His mother was an expert seamstress and had access to the house we lived in. Belt loops would be added, then later removed. Jeans pockets would be altered. Sleeves on my jackets lengthened. A woman knows her clothes and I knew they were different. The energy I created that was harvested with all these happenings! It was sheer evil at work, working hard on me. I would be so flustered and I would say to Ray, "It's not supposed to be like this." Ray would laugh and say, "You said its snot." What a waste of energy and time.

Mental hospital, broken ribs, trying to get me addicted to meth, altering my clothes, killing my dog. What a miserable circus. The Reptilian race is known to induce drugs and to be particularly involved with crystal meth and crack cocaine. I'm so ashamed to say that I've participated in both. Throughout my life I have tried to stop using drugs and now today I know that I would never do that to my mind again.

Interestingly, the following address is one listed in a short list of some addresses of abusers who are part of the Network, a/k/a New World Order shared by Fritz Springmeier: *"Alabama Country Music Group, Satanists and Monarch slave handlers, Box 529, Ft. Payne, Alabama 35967."* According to the source, this information is shared to display to readers that the veil of secrecy is no longer holding up for the Mind Control Programmers.

When I left Ray on April 1, 2011, I returned to Michigan and was even talked into going back to Alabama to see Ray a couple months later. Of course, once I got to Alabama, Ray started a fight with me and I left after only a couple days in Alabama back to Michigan. The total times I drove between Alabama and Michigan in about a year and a half was seven times. Again, I'll repeat, the perfect mule doesn't get paid, pays for the trip, and doesn't even know anything is being transported.

Brian Rowe

Brian was my last handler. I met Brian in January 2012. It was so weird how we met. I had been on Craigslist looking at dressers for sale. I had never ever gone to any personals or dating websites before. Something told me to go to the personals on Craigslist. After reading about twenty ads, there was "Mr. Nice Guy." I respond to his ad and within a week we were dating. Within a month, he gave me keys to his apartment. Within two months, I was buying a home and twenty acres in northern Michigan for Brian and me to move to.

After a couple months into the relationship, I received a text from Brian that he was leaving work to have his knee checked. I texted him back and asked him if he wanted me to meet him at the doctor's office.

He responded back about two hours later with, "Sorry, I was in x-ray."

Then I didn't hear from him all afternoon. The next day I was at his apartment and he was showing me where his knee had been drained. I couldn't see any indication of anything being put into his knee for drainage. I asked him for the doctor receipt and he said he didn't get one. My gut was telling me he was lying. It ate at me for about a month until I finally backed him into a corner and said we were calling the doctor to get a receipt for the doctor visit. He finally admitted that he didn't go to the doctor that day much less go to work. I was like, "Well, what were you doing in x-ray then? Nurse Good-body was taking care of you?"

I broke up with him and moved up north by myself, but, of course, Brian texted me and emailed me every day. He said he was so sorry and would never lie to me again so I let him move up north with me.

He proceeded to lie to me numerous times during the two years we were together. Brian finally moved out in July 2014. During that time, Brian and I drove to Illinois to pick up his grandsons to stay with us for a month during the summer of 2013. These two boys were so odd. The youngest, about nine years old, still sucked his thumb and talked baby talk. Yet, he would ask me questions like, "So Sandy, how much did you pay for this house?" He would follow me wherever I went. When Brian's daughter Sarah came to pick up her sons, I remember the youngest boy saying to his mother, "I'm a man." I swear, I think he was actually older than he acted.

Once when we were out to dinner the two boys were talking. The youngest said, "Grandma is cray cray." The older boy said, "The doctor said we can't say cray cray." Then the younger boy said, "I'm going up in a spaceship." I had never heard of the term cray cray and then while still watching television sometime in 2013, a major media outlet shares about new words in the dictionary. One of them was cray cray. Just like Orwell's 1984 control the language and meaning of words, control the herd. In May 2017 I was in a store looking at the candy. I had noticed earlier in the year that Snickers now puts words on their candy bars rather than their name Snickers. One box of candy bars had in big letters the words Cray, Cray. Interesting to say the least.

The older boy had very feminine mannerisms. Both boys had many scars on their legs. Brian pinched the younger grandson on his ass so hard that the boy started crying. I thought it very inappropriate for Brian to be pinching his grandson's ass. The boys had left their controllers for their video games and Sarah promised to mail them right after we left for Michigan. She claimed she mailed them and then they were returned to her so she was re-mailing them. Every day we would check the mail. The controllers never came. Sarah has the butterfly tattoo on her wrist and had butterfly decals in her car window.

A mysterious incident happened with Brian during the full moon in December 2012. There was a terrible storm and the electricity went out in the house. Brian came home from work and suggested we go to a motel. He told me to call the Surrey Motel in Farwell, Michigan and see if they had a room. They, of course, had vacancies. We pulled into the motel and we were the only people there. I mean the entire parking lot was empty. We were given a room in the middle of the motel. I remember thinking as I relaxed on the bed around 7:00 p.m. that I will just watch this show, then get up and take a shower. The show WipeOut was on. Within ten minutes of watching that show I passed out (probably hypnotized) while sitting up with a beer still in my hand. I woke up at 11:00 p.m. with the worst headache of my life. I woke Brian up and asked him what happened. He said I fell asleep and he removed the drink from my hand and he fell asleep, too. I was so shaken up, feeling like something happened to me that I went out of the motel room. All the rooms were full and people were walking around outside, some with no shirts on, in the dead of winter. It was all so weird that I walked home. To this day I feel like some satanic ritual was performed on me at that motel.

On Wednesday, February 20, 2013, Brian made me dinner and served me. I took a bath while he made dinner. It was all his idea. I did not watch him at all while he prepared the food. The food seemed to have an aftertaste. I just figured it was a frozen bagged dinner. Then I lay down to watch TV and within ten minutes, a little after six, I just wanted to shut my eyes. That is all I wanted to do. I woke up at 11:00 p.m. with an extreme headache. I couldn't really fall back to sleep for hours, feeling something wasn't right. The next morning I looked in the bathroom mirror and my nose was swollen. I looked further and there was a red mark on my forehead, an indent, and marks and wrinkles all over my forehead above my eyebrows. The skin was all puffed and my nasal passages felt painful. On the sides of my nose, there were clear markings where something had pinched off my nose. Throughout the day I felt such nasal pain and a clicking sound coming from my nasal passages. I periodically looked in the mirror and noticed my eyes were black and blue and swelling. I felt so strongly that I had been drugged and my face pushed on that I went to the hospital for an x-ray of my face, and it confirmed that my forehead was swollen and my nasal passages damaged. I have it on record. For what? The possibility of a demon ritual? The possibility of trying to suppress my third eye chakra? Now I can look back at all the horrible boyfriends I've had that scouted me out, all the beaters, and see that they made sure to hit me in my head and especially forehead. There were times during the two years I was with Brian that I would wake up and find Brian standing over me glaring at me with a very evil look on his face.

The men described above are just a handful of the handlers I was passed around to. I counted at least sixteen men in my life that I consider to have been handlers. I had sex with over a hundred men in my lifetime. It has now been almost two years since I have lived with anyone.

I remember waking up on the couch and Brian standing over me with an evil, ugly snarl on his face. Many times I tell Brian I think he is an alien. One would think he would leave a person saying such a thing. No, Brian stayed with me until I finally had enough and insisted he move out. Brian had saved in a box a Playboy magazine with Jayne Mansfield on the cover. She was a known Satanist. He also had several crosses with Jesus hanging on them. My understanding is that Satanist love seeing Jesus (Yahushua) hanging on the cross in agony.

Brian and I met in January 2012 and he finally moved completely out of my life in July 2014. During our time together Brian and I split up about three times. I know he went to his brother's for a week and then to stay with his daughter for about month and a half. He always talked his way back and when he left for his daughter's he left every-thing behind so he had to come back.

In between these men were many other men that came and went from my life. I have two instances that I want to share about rapes that were never prosecuted and that I will never get justice for.

There was a rape by a bunch of motorcycle members. I met Ron-nie (Crush) biker name through a "friend", Elise. I use that term lightly for this particular gal as she betrayed me a few times. Anyway, Ronnie and I were out at a couple bars and it got to be around 11:00 and Ronnie suggested with go to his club house, The Highway Men. Yes, I had drank a few beers before we got there but not enough to make me black out. We went into the club house and about 6 of Ron-nie's buddies invited me to join them for a shot of Jaggeur. I clearly remember Ronnie on my left and basically being surrounded by all these big biker dudes. The next thing I remember is waking up in my vehicle about 3 hours later and my ass being sore. I went into the bar and confronted Ronnie. I said "What happened? How did I get out-side?" "What did you do to me?" He laughed and said I passed out and he had to carry me outside. I was so disoriented, all I wanted to do is go home. The next morning I woke up with terrible pain in my anal area. My body was shakey and I felt disoriented all day. I was on probation at the time and couldn't file a report as I was not supposed to be drinking. I will never be able to prove anything but all my heart tells me that something happened to me.

Another time I totally put my guard down with two guys, Ron and James, that were supposed to be friends of mine. I had gone to their house in the afternoon and they suggested we go out and shoot a couple games of pool. I had been staying by myself a lot and really thought it would be fun to listen to some music and shoot a few games of pool. I left my vehicle at their house and us three drove to the nearest town (about 5 miles away) to a bar with a pool table. Well while still at the bar, I noticed myself feeling loopy. I told them I was ready to go home and to take me to their house so I can get my vehicle and go home. By the time we got to their house, I knew I couldn't drive. My head was spinning and I was having a hard time focusing. They wanted me to stay at their house and I insisted they drive me home. They both got into the vehicle and drove me home.

I would say it was somewhere between 11:00 pm and midnight when James took my keys from my hand and opened my house door for me. The next thing I remember was James kissing all over my face, practically licking my face and pushing me down on the couch—then it was lights out. I woke up several hours later on the couch. My pants were on, very wet and as I walked to go the bathroom, I noticed my panties lying on the floor. I went into the bathroom and noticed my hairbrush full of hair. I mean a lot of hair but dismissed it. I went back to sleep and woke up all shakey and disoriented. I tried to find my keys and they were gone. I called Ron's house and he answered. I said "Ron, where are my keys?" You guys drove me home last night and now my car keys are gone. Ron said "Only Jimbo (nickname for James) drove you home. I stayed at my house. Jimbo isn't here right now, when he gets back I will ask him if he has your keys." He said "Oh, Sandy, don't you remember how loving you were last night, you even kissed me. Do you remember me brushing your hair?" We ended that conversation. As an hour went by I put more of the pieces together. If Ron hadn't driven with Jimbo to take me home, how could there be excessive hair in my brush. I noticed bruises on my wrists and actual finger marks inside my thighs. I grabbed a mirror and checked what I looked like "down there." Very humiliating to say the least. I was all red and swollen and it looked like I had been having brutal sex. There was a bruise on the lower side of my stomach. I called Ron's house again. I said "Ron, I know you guys did something to me." He proceeded to call me crazy and to get a hold of myself. We hung up again and for some reason I called my ex-handler Brian. I was crying and told him I knew something happened to me. He just kept telling me to calm down and take a shower. He talked to me for about half hour and during that conversation told me to take a shower more than a few times.

I took a quick shower and as several hours went by and the more I knew what happened to me, I decided to call the police. I called Clare County Sheriff's Department as I lived in Clare County. Instead of a local sheriff coming to my house, a Michigan State trooper came. Trooper Tayler came in and actually talked me out of doing a rape kit. He wouldn't look at any of the bruises on my legs and said he didn't see the bruises on my wrists. There were clear grip marks on my wrists. Trooper Tayler took a statement but refused to drive me for a rape kit. He told me I don't have a case. He didn't care about the hairbrush or the panties in another room. He accused me of having consensual sex with the men and that maybe I forgot. It is laughable how many of these people get away with giving people roofies (blackout pills). There is normally no recollection of what happened, just a feeling of being violated and mentally unbalanced the next day.

Chapter 6

The Spiritual Body

This last trigger apparently was supposed to keep me stuck in my religious beliefs, but I am so grateful to have been led to the truth about religions. Religions teach nothing about a true relationship with Yahuwah and caring about our planet and fellow human beings. Nothing about the energy we carry in our bodies through our souls or about the importance of deep breathing. Just remembering to breath a few times a day for yourself makes a big difference. The brain has a pineal gland that must be stimulated. Our spirits are energy and that energy soars through our bodies.

What I've learned is that many Christians feel that yoga and energy therapy are against God and the church. When I told a Jehovah Witness that I practice yoga she said, "Oh, you're opening the door to Satan." I told her that Satan has been after me my whole life and yoga is not the cause of that. Satan attacks those who love Yahuwah.

While walking for a Hunger Walk sponsored by a Catholic Church, I met a gal and we were having a great time exchanging scriptures and chatting. Once I mentioned I practice yoga, she immediately stopped talking to me and said I was worshipping another God. A healthy spine is a healthy mind. Yoga adjusts the body's natural energy vortexes and stimulates health and youthfulness.

There are seven main Chakras and also Chakras in the hands and feet

There are seven main chakras from the base of the spine to the crown of the head and energy flows through them. There are also chakras in the feet and the hands. These chakras are also called wheels of light, as they are energy vortexes that oscillate in our bodies. The seven main chakras. The first chakra, the Root or Base chakra, is located at the base of the spine is red. Its lesson is survival - the right to exist. It deals with tasks related to the material and physical world like the ability to stand up for oneself and security issues. The second chakra, the Spleen chakra, is orange and is located below the navel, the lower abdomen. Its lesson is feelings and the right to feel. It is connected to our sensing abilities and issues related to feelings and sexuality. It relates to the ability to be social and to intimacy issues. The third chakra is Solar Plexus chakra and is yellow, located above the naval in the stomach area. Its lesson is personal power, intuition, and the right to think. It includes the balance of intellect, self-confidence and ego power as well as the ability to have self-control and humor. The fourth chakra is the Heart chakra. It is the color green and is located in the center of the chest. Its lesson is relationships, the right to love, forgiveness, compassion, empathy, the ability to have self-control, and the ability to have acceptance of oneself. The fifth chakra is the Throat chakra and is blue. It is located in the throat region and its lesson is the right to speak. It relates to learning to express one-self and one's beliefs (truthful expression), the ability to trust, loyalty, organization and planning. The sixth chakra is the Brow or Third Eye chakra. Its color is indigo and is located in the forehead, in between the eyes. Its lesson is intuition - the right to "see", trusting one's intuition and insights, developing one's psychic abilities, self-realization, and re-leasing hidden and repressed negative thoughts. The seventh chakra is the Crown chakra. Its color is violet and it is located at the top of the head. Its lesson is knowingness – the right to aspire, dedication to the divine consciousness and trusting the universe. It also includes learning about one's spirituality, our connection to the concept of "God" or a higher intelligence, and integrating one's consciousness and subcon-sciousness into the superconsciousness or God-consciousness.

Interestingly, it was brought to my attention that when the chakras are aligned and oscillating to optimal frequency the total count for the wheels to be oscillating is 144,000. Then I read this scripture and it was another "ah ha" moment. "And he measured the wall thereof, an hundred and forty and four cubits, according to the measure of a man, that is, of the angel." (Revelation 21:17) We are spiritual beings, energetic beings being human.

The pineal gland was once dubbed the "third eye." This originated for many reasons, ranging from its location deep in the center of the brain to its connection to light. Some regard it as the principal seat of the soul, and the place in which all our thoughts are formed. Located between the brain's two hemispheres, the pineal gland is a very small organ shaped like a pine cone (which is where it gets its name) and is a small part of the body's endocrine system. It is reddish-gray and about 1/3-inch long. It is responsible for the synthesis and secretion of the hormone melatonin. Melatonin maintains the body's circadian rhythm (sleep-wake cycle), regulates the onset of puberty in females, helps pro-tect the body from cell damage caused by free radicals and much, much more. Besides regulating sleep patterns and sexual development, many researchers believe that it has the ability to connect us to other dimen-sions like dream world, spiritual realms such as deep meditation and astral travel and during near death experiences through the release of dimethyltryptamine (DMT). The gland is thought to be highly active during dreaming, meditation and spiritual experiences.

The pineal gland often appears calcified in x-rays, which is usually due to fluoride, calcium, and phosphorous deposits that build up with age. Hence, all the fluoride added to drinking water. In the 1990s, a British scientist, Jennifer Luke, discovered that fluoride accumulates to strikingly high levels in the pineal gland. As a calcifying tissue that is exposed to a high volume of blood flow, the pineal gland is a major target for fluoride accumulation in humans. Studies have found that calcified deposits in the pineal are associated with reduced melatonin production as well as impairments in the sleep-wake cycle as well as potentially disrupting normal puberty function.

Sodium fluoride is the number one enemy of a healthy pineal gland. Before World War II, the Germans fluoridated the water sup-ply in Germany before rounding up the Jews. The Nazis reputedly believed it makes people easier to control. There was a study, I believe, in China of two groups of children. One group was given fluoride in their water and the other group was not. After two years, the children were tested and the children with the fluoridated water were seven to ten points dumber than the children without the fluoride added to the water. Just food for thought…in the Vatican there is a huge eleven foot statute of a bronze pine cone. "The light of the body is the eye: if therefore thine eye be single, thy whole body shall be full of light." (Matthew 6:22) I feel Jesus (Yahushua) is speaking of the single eye as the "third eye" or inner eye of enlightenment. It is said that humans were first created perfect, they were enlightened by the third eye, but after the fall, it is now only reached through meditation.

Recent studies have proven that EMFs, electro-magnetic frequencies, have a negative effect on the pineal gland. Most recently, Malka N. Halgamuge of the University of Melbourne in Australia further examined the effect of manmade EMF on the pineal gland. Halgamuge states in his research that the pineal gland likely recognizes EMF as light, which consequently would result in reduced melatonin production. "...the results show the significance of disruption of melatonin due to exposure to weak EMFs, which may possibly lead to long-term health effects in humans."[23]

However, as I know in my lifetime and as is apparent by others, multidimensional beings are parasites to us humans. They feed off our energy. They are all around us and most cannot perceive their presence. I see prison bars all the time in my third eye. The aliens are our prison wardens. By concentrating on remembering who you are, past lives will be revealed to you. The original Holy Bible was written for mankind to learn truths, not to be entrapped in beliefs. It has been altered and watered down. Then only 2,000 years ago, the New Testament was written. Remarkably, almost all Christianity is based on the New Testament. God-consciousness has been around for many, many thousands of years. Mankind has been entrapped in religious beliefs many, many thousands of years. In the original Hebrew Bible, God reveals his name as Yahuwah. He is a superior being, but has manipulated man for a very long time. Yahuwah is a superior of the God-consciousness, and we all are a part of the infinite awareness and love consciousness. Yahushua speaks about how every person who loves the Father is to him a mother, brother, sister. We are all one.

> While he yet talked to the people, behold, his
> mother and his brethren stood without, desiring to
> speak with him. Then one said unto him, Behold,
> thy mother and thy brethren stand without, desiring
> to speak with thee. But he answered and said unto

---

[23] Malka N. Halgamuge. Oxford Journals.

him that told him, Who is my mother? And who are
my brethren? And he stretched forth his hand toward his disciples, and said, Behold my mother and
my brethren! For whosoever shall do the will of my
Father which is in heaven, the same is my brother,
and sister, and mother.[24]

We are all specks of the universe, parts of infinite consciousness experiencing ourselves individually being human. Spiritual beings experiencing being human. We are all One from the great Source, the
God Pleroma of the universe, the electric universe. Nikola Tesla
(1856-1943), probably the greatest inventor and scientist of the twentieth century said in 1942 regarding the UNIverse (Us), "If you want
to find the secrets of the universe, think in terms of energy, frequency
and vibration." We are all energy vibrating in a frequency range here
on planet Earth.

I never even heard about Nikola Tesla until a few years ago. I
asked my daughters if they learned about Nikola Tesla in school and
they said, "Who?" I've since read an autobiography on Tesla and saw
a great video called "The Secrets of Tesla." Of course, the PTB didn't
want the general public to know about all the technology created at
the turn of the twentieth century. Tesla was born July 10, 1856 and
died January 7, 1943 at the age of eighty-six. The fact that his far-
reaching, advanced inventions were omitted from the history and science books speaks for itself as to the government's capabilities to
control the history and, thus, control the present and future. In a 1926
interview with Tesla, he historically predicted the smartphone:

> When wireless is perfectly applied the whole earth
> will be converted into a huge brain, which in fact it
> is, all things being particles of a real and rhythmic
> whole. We shall be able to communicate with one

[24] Matthew 12:46-50

another instantly, irrespective of distance. Not only this, but through television and telephony we shall see and hear one another as perfectly as though we were face to face, despite intervening distances of thousands of miles; and the instruments through which we shall be able to do this will be amazingly simple compared with our present telephone. A man will be able to carry one in his vest pocket.[25]

The els, the Elohim, is the Hebrew word for gods as in the ang*els* Gabriel, Michael, Raphael, Uriel, and so on. Yahushua's words are, "And now I am no more in the world, but these are in the world, and I come to thee, Holy Father, keep through thine *own name* those whom thou has given me, that they may be *one, as we are.*" (John 17:11, emphasis added). Yahushua also said, "That they all may be one; as thou, Father, art in me, and I in thee, that they also may be one in us; that the world may believe that thou hast sent me. And the glory which thou gavest me I have given them; that they may be ONE, even as we are ONE." (John 17:21-22, emphasis added)

We are all one in an electric universe. The El is all powerful, the [El]ectric universe, all energy vibrating in frequencies.

Even as a young child, I always knew that our souls are energy and energy can't be destroyed, only transferred. Our spirits are energy, consciousness. Yahuwah is a spiritual being. When Jesus (Yahushua) responded to a woman's comment about where people ought to worship, Jesus replied:

> Woman, believe me, the hour cometh, when ye shall neither in this mountain, nor yet at Jerusalem, worship the Father. Ye worship ye know not what; we know what we worship: for salvation is of the Jews.

---

[25] Collier's magazine reproduced by Twenty-First Century Books, titled "When Woman Is Boss"

> But the hour cometh, and now is, when the true
> worshippers shall worship the Father in spirit and in
> truth: for the Father seeketh such to worship him.
> God is a Spirit; and they that worship him must wor-
> ship him in spirit and in truth.[26]

That pretty much sums up the power of the Spirit and his knowing who really comes to him in truth and who really wants to know the truth. Right from the beginning, the bible says, "And the earth was without form, and void; and the darkness was upon the face of the deep. And the Spirit of God moved upon the face of the waters" (Genesis 1:2), and "My soul longeth, yea, even fainteth for the courts of the LORD [Yahuwah]; my heart and my flesh crieth out for the living God. (Psalms 84:2) He is a living, spiritual god amongst other gods and fallen angels. There are many deceivers and archons out there.

If we just remember that we are energy vibrating and that we don't die, all is accountable for much of the confusion and fear would dissipate. Bill Hicks quote comically describes what I mean:

> Wouldn't you like to see a positive LSD story on the
> news? To base your decision on information rather
> than scare tactics and superstition? Perhaps? Would-
> n't that be interesting? Just for once? "Today, a young
> man on acid realized that all matter is merely energy
> condensed to a slow vibration – that we are all one
> consciousness experiencing itself subjectively.
> There's no such thing as death, life is only a dream,
> and we're the imagination of ourselves. Here's Tom
> with the weather. .Hicks, Bill, www.brainyquote.com.

Bill Hicks, an American comedian, was way before his time. Very few Americans ever heard of him. Bill was born December 16, 1961

---

[26] John 4:21-24

and died February 26, 1994 from cancer. David Letterman even taped a show and then the media decided not to air Bill's episode. It can now be found on YouTube with Letterman saying he doesn't know why he didn't air Bill's show then. Well, the American people were deliberately kept in the dark about such an enlightened, truthful, comical person.

> This is the material, by the way, that has kept me virtually anonymous in America for the past 15 years. Gee, I wonder why we're hated the world over? Look at these fat Americans in the front row – "Why doesn't he just hit fruit with a hammer?" Folks, I could have done that, walked around being a millionaire and franchising myself but no, I had to have this weird thing about trying to illuminate the collective unconscious and help humanity. Fucking moron.[27]

The Bible does have truths in it and is the Word of Yahuwah. "Sanctify them through thy truth; thy word is truth." (John 17:17) But it takes many hours of many days to dig to the truth. It was complained about thousands of years before the New Testament that this planet is prison.

> I cried unto the LORD [Yahuwah] with my voice; with my voice unto the LORD [Yahuwah] did I make my supplication. I poured out my complaint before him; I shewed before him my trouble. When my spirit overwhelmed within me, then thou knewest my path. In the way wherein I walked have they privily laid a snare for me. I looked on *my* right hand, and beheld, but *there was* no man that would know me; refuge failed me; no man cared for my

---

[27] Bill Hicks, Sane Man (1989).

soul. I cried unto thee, O LORD [Yahuwah]: I said, Thou *art* my refuge *and* my portion in the land of the living. Attend unto my cry; for I am brought very low; deliver me from my persecutors; for they are stronger than I. Bring my soul out of prison, that I may praise thy name; the righteous shall compass me about; for thou shalt deal boun- tifully with me.[28]

In the King James version, translated and interpreted in the 1500s by a Freemason (also said to be a homosexual and/or pedophile), GOD or LORD in all caps was written instead of the name Yahuwah as writ- ten in the original scriptures. He revealed his name but the higher powers of mankind manipulated the wording to keep the personal ex- perience separated. I'm sure in an original Bible written many thou- sands of years ago, Yahuwah revealed himself as a being having super intelligence known to man of today as an "alien." God and his helpers live through us parasitically. What a boring life the superior beings would have without mankind. There is a God-consciousness and it has been tapped into for thousands of years. That's why God stirred up Saul's heart against David. They both worshiped the same God. The energy ("loosh") that was harvested from David alone had to be staggering. We are puppets, sheeple, following what is taught to us. Why, only at fifty-three years old, did I find out the name of God as Yahuwah? Never was it spoken in the many, many church services I attended. Christians are not supposed to know the true essence of Yahuwah. It was always taught the Father, Son and Holy Ghost. Yet here is scripture that attests to the importance of the Word. "For there are three that bear record in heaven, the Father, the Word, and the Holy Ghost: and these three are one. And there are three that bear witness in earth, the spirit, and the water, and the blood: and these three agree in one." (I John 4:7-8)

---

[28] Psalm142:1

Yahushua (Jesus Christ) said:

> And there was delivered unto him the book of the
> prophet Isaiah. And when he opened the book, he
> found the place where it was written. The Spirit of
> the Lord is upon me, because he hath anointed me
> to preach the gospel to the poor; he hath sent me to
> heal the broken-hearted, to preach deliverance to
> the captives, and recovering of sight to the blind, to
> set at liberty them that are bruised. To preach the
> acceptable year of the Lord.[29]

Here is the exact scripture that was quoted by our holy redeemer and
teacher:

> The Spirit of the Lord GOD [Yahuwah] is upon me;
> because the LORD [Yahuwah] hath anointed me to
> preach good tidings unto the meek; he hath sent me
> to bind up the brokenhearted, to proclaim liberty to
> the captives, and the opening of the prison to them
> that are bound; To proclaim the acceptable year of
> the LORD [Yahuwah] and the day of vengeance of
> our God; to comfort all that mourn; To appoint unto
> them that mourn in Zion, to give unto them beauty
> for ashes, the oil of joy for mourning, the garment
> of praise for the spirit of heaviness; that they might
> be called trees of righteousness, the planting of the
> LORD [Yahuwah], that he might be glorified. And
> they shall build the old wastes, they shall raise up the
> former desolations, and they shall repair the waste
> cities, the desolations of many generations.[30]

---

[29] Luke 4:17-19
[30] Isaiah 61:1-4

To proclaim liberty to the captives, and the opening of the prison to them that are bound. There is something to this being called a prison planet. It is definitely worse for some than others. Until humanity on a whole figures out that it is not "survival of the fittest" but mercy and charity to others, this will be an ongoing battle for thousands more years. This fight has been ongoing for thousands and thousands of years. This is nothing new. There is nothing new under the sun. For the LORD (Yahuwah) heareth the poor, and despiseth not his prisoners. (Psalms 69:33) Its right there in Bible.

I also want to mention crystals. Crystals are very powerful energy minerals and were used by the ancients thousands of years ago. Crystals come in many varieties, shapes and sizes. The pyramids were built with crystals inside them. Kiesha Crowther teaches about the power of crystals. Her shaman name is Little Grandmother. In one of her videos, she explains that she put a crystal into radiated water and the radiation dissipated within two minutes. Her work as a Wisdom Keeper also includes the planting of sacred crystals in very specific locations around the world for the renewal and strengthening of Mother Earth's precious ley lines. She has also been going around the world putting crystals into oceans, seas and lakes. Our bodies have crystal inside and our energy is stimulated and repaired when we hold crystals in our hand. There are crystal healers.

I had a "friend" put bedbugs on my bedding before I went to sleep on his couch at his house. I know it was done on purpose because he and his brother practically begged me to stay over, saying I should save the money for a motel and they didn't want me to get pulled over since I had been drinking. That was in July 2015 and I was still drinking several times a week to take the edge off, so I thought. (Now I realize it is poison). I woke up all eaten up. I mean my arms were welted from itching and my ankles and legs had numerous bites. I even went to the doctor for relief from the pain. I thought it might be shingles. She confirmed it was bed bugs. Then I remembered hearing crunching sounds right before I fell asleep. The dam bugs were chewing on me. Bedbugs can live for months in a jar without feeding. Anyway, the bites were taking a while to heal and after about a week and a half I started rubbing crystals on my ankles and wrists where the nasty ones wouldn't seem to heal. Within hours I noticed a difference and the bites were almost completely gone in about two days. I envisioned the energy of the crystal working with the crystals in the water of my body (our bodies are something like 80% water) to repair and heal my skin. It worked. I wonder how much they got paid. I hadn't even talked to that person in months and then he just called and now I realize anyone in my telephone can be contacted and bribed.

Orgonite, first discovered by Wilhem Reich in the 1930's and 1940's as a positive energy booster, is now made with quartz crystals inside. There are testimonies attributing adding orgonite to your environment induces positive energy and negates negative energy. Sherry Shriner sells orgonite on her website (sherryshriner.com). She said she found orgonite in the Bible codes that she uses to decipher the Bible. She claims it keeps aliens away and she claims by placing her orgonite blasters outside she has crashed thousands of alien spaceships. She has over 130 nations listening to her weekly radio show. I went to see her and to make a long story short, she refused to see me the next day after speaking with me for a couple hours the night before. She told me an insider government friend had warned her a year before that someone from the Program named Sandy would be coming to see her and she didn't want to meet with me because of the possibility I could be a sleeper assassin and kill her. I told her I don't even own a gun. She is the one who wants to kill all the aliens. An evil consciousness cannot be overcome with the same level of consciousness. We need to all get along. I don't know if the orgonite can crash spaceships but it is definitely worth looking into if you are interested. There are others who are selling orgonite for its positive energy properties.

There are stones mentioned in Revelation. In Revelation 21, the foundations of the wall in the new city are garnished with jasper, sapphire, chalcedony, emerald, sardonyx, sardius, chrysolyte, beryl, topaz, chrysoprasus, jacinth and amethyst. Twelve stones are described. I personally keep a crystal around my neck, next to my heart. I have many crystals that I carry and keep around me.

Chapter 7

The Heart and Wisdom

Wisdom is so very important and the lack of wisdom is what TPB are counting on to keep the herd in line. Ignorance is power to the controllers. Knowledge is strength for the awakened. All we take with us after this experience is complete and we get over the finish line is our wisdom, knowledge, understanding and experience. Seeking wisdom by reading the Bible and other literature YOURSELF and opening your mind to all possibilities and realizing this has been going on for thousands and thousands and thousands of years is the only way to get off this hamster wheel of soul recycling. "Bind them upon thy fingers, write them upon the table of thine heart. Say unto wisdom, Thou art my sister; and call understanding thy kinswoman." (Proverbs 7:3-4)

I love this scripture:

> Thus saith the LORD [Yahuwah], Let not the wise man glory in his wisdom, neither let the mighty man glory in his might, let not the rich man glory in his riches; But let him that glorieth, glory in this, that he understandeth and knoweth me, that I am the LORD [Yahuwah] which exercise lovingkindness, judgment, and righteousness, in the

earth; for in these things I delight, saith the LORD [Yahuwah].[31]

Set your intentions for truth and love and your treasure chests will be filled and cups will runneth over with wisdom, truth and righteousness. It's all in your heart. The kingdom of God is in your heart. Yahuwah speaks to your heart and refers to the heart in many in many, many scriptures. "The firing pot is for silver, and the furnace for gold; but the LORD [Yahuwah] trieth the hearts." (Proverbs 17:3)

The heart is the main energy source of this biological computer suit we call a body. It is scientifically proven that there are more neurons and electrical signals leading from the heart to the brain than from the brain to the heart. Scientist Rollin McCraty writes:

> Compared to the electromagnetic field produced by the brain, the electrical component of the heart's field is about 60 times greater in amplitude, and permeates every cell in the body. The magnetic component is approximately 5000 times stronger than the brain's magnetic field and can be detected several feet away from the body with sensitive magnetometers.

The heart is the fourth chakra, the color green. The heart is the center of our beings, the place from which our energetic auras, light bodies, electromagnetic fields and torus fields spring. It is the key to transcending reality, manifesting miracles and breaking free from the Matrix. The brain cannot achieve this alone, no matter what it imagines. It must be fired and energized by the power of the heart.

> Rudolf Steiner predicted that the greatest discovery of late-twentieth century science would be that the heart is not merely a pump but also a major source

[31]Jeremiah: 9:23,24.

of intelligence and that our greatest challenge would
be to allow the heart to teach us a new way to think,
which it seems, would open us to higher worlds.
Steiner pointed out that the heart picks up and re-
sponds to both the inner senses of our body and the
outer senses of the world. In order to view the world
anew, the task from the heart is to approach everything in the world with a sense of the knowing, as if
discovering it for the first time" – that is becoming as
a little child. Dropping our ideation and assumptions
that can reconnect us with the heart, a first step to
ever deeper consciousness connections with our life.[32]

Here are a few Scriptures among many regarding the heart. "Then
hear thou in heaven, thy dwelling place, and forgive, and do, and give
to every man according to his ways, whose heart thou knowest; (for
thou, even thou only, knowest the hearts of all the children of men;).
(I Kings 8:39) "And thou, Solomon my son, know thou the God of
thy father, and serve him with a perfect heart and a willing mind: for
the LORD [Yahuwah] searcheth all hearts, and understandeth all the
imaginations of the thoughts: if thou seek him, he will be found of
thee; but if thou forsake him, he will cast thee off for ever." (I Chronicles 28:9) "I will run the way of thy commandments, when thou shalt
enlarge my heart. The proud have forged a lie against me; but I will
keep thy precepts with my whole heart." (Psalm 119:32,69) "Search
me, O God, and know my heart; try me, and know my thoughts."
(Psalm 139:23) "Every way of a man is right in his own eyes; but the
LORD [Yahuwah] pondereth (weighs) the hearts." (Proverbs 21:2)
"The heart is deceitful above all things, and desperately wicked; who
can know it? I the LORD [Yahuwah] search the heart, I try the reins
[test the mind,], even to give every man according to his ways, and
according to the fruit of his doings." (Jeremiah 17: 9-10) And we all

---

[32] Joseph Chilton Pearce, *The Death of Religion and the Rebirth of Spirit.*

know this most important scripture ordained by the Holy One: "Thou shalt love the Lord thy God with all thy heart, and with all thy soul, and with all thy mind." (Matthew 22:37) Notice the first is heart. "Hearken unto me, ye that know righteousness, the people in whose heart is my law; fear ye not the reproach of men, neither be ye afraid of their revilings." (Isaiah 51:7)

The heart is mentioned from the beginning to the end of the Bible. In the first book of the Bible, Genesis, Yahuwah describes himself with a heart with enormous power and feelings. "And God saw that the wickedness of man was great in the earth, and that every imagination of the thoughts of his heart was only evil continually. And it repented the LORD [Yahuwah] that he had made man on the earth, and it grieved him at his heart." (Genesis 6:5-6) "And the LORD [Yahuwah] smelled a sweet savour; and the LORD [Yahuwah] said in his heart, I will not again curse the ground any more for man's sake; for the imagination of man's heart is evil from his youth; neither will I again smite any more every thing living, as I have done." (Genesis 8:21)

"Wherefore the Lord said, Forasmuch as this people draw near me with their mouth, and with their lips do honour me, but have removed their heart far from me, and their fear toward me is taught by the precept of men." (Isaiah 29:13)

"And I will kill her children with death; and all the churches shall know that I am he which searcheth the reins and hearts; and I will give unto every one of you according to your works." (Revelation 2:23)

> In our deepest moments of struggle, frustration, fear, and confusion, we are being called upon to reach in and touch our hearts. Then, we will know what to do, what to say, how to be. What is right is always in our deepest heart of hearts. It is from the deepest part of our hearts that we are capable of

reaching out and touching another human being. It
is, after all, one heart touching another hearts.[33]

Ah, the heart. The kingdom of God is within you. It is not somewhere
to go to. Where is the central you? Where is the electromagnetic energy force the strongest in our bodies? In the heart center.

> And when he demanded of the Pharisees, when the
> kingdom of God should come, he answered them
> and said. The kingdom of God cometh not with ob-
> servation: Neither shall they say, Lo here! Or, lo
> there! For, behold, the kingdom of God is within
> you. The kingdom of God is in your heart.[34]

"And thou shalt love the LORD (Yahuwah) thy God with all thine
heart, and with all thy soul, and with all thy might. And these words,
which I command thee this day, shall be in thine heart." (Deuteronomy 6:5-6) Again, in thine "heart."

Don Juan said, "For me there is only the travelling on paths that
have heart, on any path that may have heart. There I travel, and the
only worthwhile challenge is to traverse its full length. And there I
travel, looking, looking breathlessly." Don Juan Matus, a Yaqui Indian
shaman from Mexico, endeavored to make available to Carlos Castenada, who Don Juan called his apprentice, the teachings from ancient
times. Carlos Castenada wrote a series of books narrated in the first
person, relating his experiences with Don Juan Matus.

Below is a profound excerpt from one of his books in *The Teachings of Don Juan* series. Castenada uses the term "person of knowledge" to describe the individual who has successfully overcome the
obstacles to – in modern jargon – "living life to the fullest" or "realizing one's own potential". A "person of knowledge" is not necessarily

---

[33] Roberta Sage Hamilton.

[34] Luke 17:20-21.

one upon whom degrees have been conferred, or even one who has the ability to build on an education and venture forth into uncharted realms. We must open our minds and our hearts to All Possibility. Carlos describes below the four natural enemies one must defeat in order to become a person of knowledge:

He hesitated for a while, but then began to talk.

"When a man starts to learn, he is never clear about his objectives. His purpose is faulty; his intent is vague. He hopes for rewards that will never materialize, for he knows nothing of the hardships of learning.

"He slowly begins to learn - bit by bit at first, then in big chunks. And his thoughts soon clash. What he learns is never what he pictured, or imagined, and so he begins to be afraid. Learning is never what one expects. Every step of learning is a new task, and the fear the man is experiencing begins to mount mercilessly, unyieldingly. His purpose becomes a battlefield.

"And thus he has tumbled upon the first of his natural enemies: Fear! A terrible enemy - treacherous, and difficult to overcome. It remains concealed at every turn of the way, prowling, waiting. And if the man, terrified in its presence, runs away, his enemy will have put an end to his quest.

"What will happen to the man if he runs away in fear?"

"Nothing happens to him except that he will never learn. He will never become a man of knowledge. He will perhaps be a bully or a harmless, scared man; at any rate, he will be a defeated man. His first enemy will have put an end to his cravings."

"And what can he do to overcome fear?"

"The answer is very simple. He must not run away. He must defy his fear, and in spite of it he must take the next step in learning, and the next, and the next. He must be fully afraid, and yet he must not stop. That is the rule! And a mo-

ment will come when his first enemy retreats. The man begins to feel sure of himself. His intent becomes stronger.
Learning is no longer a terrifying task. When this joyful moment comes, the man can say without hesitation that he has
defeated his first natural enemy."

"Does it happen at once, don Juan, or little by little?"

"It happens little by little, and yet the fear is vanquished
suddenly and fast."

"But won't the man be afraid again if something new
happens to him?"

"No. Once a man has vanquished fear, he is free from it
for the rest of his life because, instead of fear, he has acquired
clarity - a clarity of mind which erases fear. By then a man
knows his desires; he knows how to satisfy those desires. He
can anticipate the new steps of learning, and a sharp clarity
surrounds everything. The man feels that nothing is concealed.
And thus he has encountered his second enemy: Clarity!

"That clarity of mind, which is so hard to obtain, dispels
fear, but also blinds. It forces the man never to doubt himself.
It gives him the assurance he can do anything he pleases, for
he sees clearly into everything. And he is courageous because
he is clear, and he stops at nothing because he is clear. But
all that is a mistake; it is like something incomplete. If the
man yields to this make-believe power, he has succumbed to
his second enemy and will fumble with learning. He will rush
when he should be patient, or he will be patient when he
should rush. And he will fumble with learning until he winds
up incapable of learning anything more."

"What becomes of a man who is defeated in that way,
don Juan? Does he die as a result?"

"No, he doesn't die. His second enemy has just stopped
him cold from trying to become a man of knowledge; instead,
the man may turn into a buoyant warrior, or a clown. Yet the

clarity for which he has paid so dearly will never change to darkness and fear again. He will be clear as long as he lives, but he will no longer learn, or yearn for anything."

"But what does he have to do to avoid being defeated?"

"He must do what he did with fear: he must defy his clarity and use it only to see, and wait patiently and measure carefully before taking new steps; he must think, above all, that his clarity is almost a mistake. And a moment will come when he will understand that his clarity was only a point before his eyes. And thus he will have to overcome his second enemy, and will arrive at a position where nothing can harm him any more. This will not be a mistake. It will not be only a point before his eyes. It will be true power. He will know at this point that the power he has been pursuing for so long is finally his. He can do with it whatever he pleases. His ally is at his command. His wish is the rule. He sees all that is around him. But he has also come across his third enemy: Power!

"Power is the strongest of all enemies. And naturally the easiest thing to do is to give in; after all, the man is truly invincible. He commands; he begins by taking calculated risks, and ends in making rules, because he is a master.

"A man at this stage hardly notices his third enemy closing in on him. And suddenly, without knowing, he will certainly have lost the battle. His enemy will have turned him into a cruel, capricious man."

"Will he lose his power?"

"No, he will never lose his clarity or his power."

"What then will distinguish him from a man of knowledge?"

"A man who is defeated by power dies without really knowing how to handle it. Power is only a burden upon his fate. Such a man has no command over himself, and cannot tell when or how to use his power."

"Is the defeat by any of these enemies a final defeat?"

"Of course it is final. Once one of these enemies over-powers a man there is nothing he can do."

"Is it possible, for instance, that the man who is defeated by power may see his error and mend his ways?"

"No. Once a man gives in he is through."

"But what if he is temporarily blinded by power, and then refuses it?"

"That means his battle is still on. That means he is still trying to become a man of knowledge. A man is defeated only when he no longer tries, and abandons himself."

"But then, don Juan, it is possible that a man may abandon himself to fear for years, but finally conquer it."

"No, that is not true. If he gives in to fear he will never conquer it, because he will shy away from learning and never try again. But if he tries to learn for years in the midst of his fear, he will eventually conquer it because he will never have really abandoned himself to it."

"How can he defeat his third enemy, don Juan?"

"He has to defy it, deliberately. He has to come to realize the power he has seemingly conquered is in reality never his. He must keep himself in line at all times, handling carefully and faithfully all that he has learned. If he can see that clarity and power, without his control over himself, are worse than mistakes, he will reach a point where everything is held in check. He will know then when and how to use his power. And thus he will have defeated his third enemy.

"The man will be, by then, at the end of his journey of learn-ing, and almost without warning he will come upon the last of his enemies: Old age! This enemy is the cruelest of all, the one he won't be able to defeat completely, but only fight away.

"This is the time when a man has no more fears, no more impatient clarity of mind - a time when all his power is in check, but also the time when he has an unyielding desire to rest. If he gives in totally to his desire to lie down and forget, if he soothes himself in tiredness, he will have lost his last round, and his enemy will cut him down into a feeble old creature. His desire to retreat will overrule all his clarity, his power, and his knowledge.

"But if the man sloughs off his tiredness, and lives his fate through, he can then be called a man of knowledge, if only for the brief moment when he succeeds in fighting off his last, invincible enemy. That moment of clarity, power and knowledge is enough.[35]

---

[35] Carlos Castaneda, *The Teachings of Don Juan: A Yogi Way Of Knowledge.*

Chapter 8

Three Commandments Blatantly Ignored

The Ten Commandments are so very important and three of them are being broken by people without them even realizing it. There were originally 613 commandments in the Old Testament, yet even Christians are not abiding by the Ten Commandments. Worshipping on Sunday, falsifying his name by replacing our Lord's name, Yahuwah, with LORD or GOD and the graven images that abound. The King James Version, translated in the 1500's, capitalizes LORD or GOD everywhere that once said YAHUWAH and this "version" is what most Christian churches base their gospel on.

1) Breaking the Sabbath - Fourth Commandment
   Keep the sabbath day to sanctify it, as the LORD (Yahuwah) thy God hath commanded thee. Six days thou shalt labour, and do all thy work: But the seventh day is the sabbath of the LORD (Yahuwah) thy God: in it thou shalt not do any work, thou, nor thy son, nor thy daughter, nor thy manservant, nor thy maidservant, nor thine ox, nor thine ass, nor any thy cattle, nor thy stranger that is within thy gates; that thy manservant and thy maidservant may rest as well as thou.[36]

---

[36] Deuteronomy 5:12-14

Notice in Yahuwah's world it is okay to have servants. That is where this whole Jewish supremacy comes in. If we are all born equal, why are there those delegated to be kings and queens and those delegated to be manservants and maidservants? That's why I want out of any kingdom and I want sovereignty and freedom from external control.

There is so much scripture regarding the Sabbath. "And madest known unto them thy holy sabbath, and commandest them precepts, statutes, and laws, by the hand of Moses thy servant." (Nehemiah 9:14)

I have shared this Sabbath breaking with so many Christians and they say, "Oh, the sabbath day is Sunday." I say, "No, the Sabbath is the seventh day, Saturday." One even had the audacity to say, "Oh, they didn't have calendars back then so the Sabbath has to be Sunday."

Sunday is the first day of the week, not the seventh. Calendars have been around for thousands of years. My sister JoAnn even said, "Oh, I don't think he cares what day we worship." The bible says, "Thou hast despised mine holy things and hast profaned my Sabbaths." (Ezekiel 22:8)

I looked in the New Testament to find out why the worship day was changed from the seventh day, Saturday, to the first day, Sunday. Why break the fourth commandment which is to honor the Sabbath when Jesus Christ and the apostles repeatedly said to honor the Father's commandments, not break them?

> Think not that I am come to destroy the law, or the prophets; I am not come to destroy, but to fulfill. Whosoever therefore shall break one of these least commandments, and shall teach men so, he shall be called the least in the kingdom of heaven; but whosoever shall do and teach *them*, the same shall be called great in the kingdom of heaven.[37]

---

[37] Matthew 17:19.

Paul (former name Saul) was not one of the twelve apostles of Jesus Christ (Yahushua). There were twelve apostles, not thirteen and Judas Iscariot was replaced by Matthias. Paul wrote in Colossians 2:16, "Let no man therefore judge you in meat, or in drink, or in respect of an holyday, or of the new moon, or of the Sabbath *days.*" What rubbish. The Sabbaths have been honored for thousands of years and now Paul says don't worry about the Sabbath. Paul starts most of the thirteen books he wrote in the New Testament with, "I, Paul, an apostle of Jesus Christ." The Merriam-Webster main definition of apostle is, "1: Anyone of the twelve men chosen by Jesus Christ to spread the Christian religion; 2: someone who believes in or supports a cause, mission etc." In Revelation 21:14, the new heaven and earth are described. "And the wall of the city had twelve foundations, and in them the names of the twelve apostles of the Lamb." Twelve not thirteen. These are the names of the twelve apostles: Simon/Peter, Andrew (brothers), James, John (brothers), Philip, Bartholomew, Thomas, Matthew, James, Lebbaeus, Simon, Judas Iscariot, replaced by Matthias.

> Now the names of the twelve apostles are these: The first, Simon, who is called Peter, and Andrew his brother; James, the son of Zebedee, and John his brother; Philip, and Bartholomew; Thomas, and Matthew the publican; James, the son of Alphaeus, and Lebbaeus, whose surname was Thaddeus; Simon the Canaanite, and Judas Iscariot, who also betrayed him.[38]

Paul is not one of the twelve apostles and is not even one of the seventy later named. His name is mentioned twice in the list of the seventy but he is not ordained an apostle. He is a self-proclaimed apostle. "And they gave forth their lots; and the lot fell upon Matthias; and he

---

[38] Matthew 10:2-4.

was numbered with the eleven apostles." (Acts 1:26) So tell me, does scripture lie? Matthias replaced Judas Iscariot. "It is the glory of God to conceal a thing: but the honour of kings is to search out a matter." (Proverbs 25:2)

Jesus Christ mentions the fake apostles in Revelation 2:2, "I know thy works, and thy labour, and thy patience, and how thou canst not bear them which are evil; and thou has tried them which say they are apostles, and are not, and hast found them liars." Yahushua (Jesus) did not need to teach to keep the Sabbath Day holy. It wasn't until about 300 years after his death that the worship day was officially changed in Christianity. He repeatedly said to keep the Father's commandments. There were originally over 613 commandments written. We are expected to at least obey the first Ten Commandments.

> And he came to Nazareth, where he had been brought up; and, as his custom was, he went into the synagogue on the Sabbath day, and stood up for to read. And there was delivered unto him the book of the prophet Isaiah. And when he had opened the book, he found the place where it was written, The Spirit of the Lord GOD [Yahuwah] *is* upon me, because he hath anointed me to preach the gospel to the poor; he hath sent me to heal the brokenhearted, to preach deliverance to the captives; and recovering of light to the blind, to set at liberty them that are bruised, To preach the acceptable year of the Lord. *(Isaiah 61:1,2)* And he closed the book, and he gave *it* again to the minister, and sat down. And the eyes of all them that were in the synagogue were fastened on him. And he began to say unto them, This day is this scripture fulfilled in your ears.[39]

---

[39] Luke 4:16-21.

When Jesus Christ/Yahushua walked this planet, his custom (or his habit, as some versions say) was to go to the synagogue on the Sabbath day.

> And he was teaching in one of the synagogues on the Sabbath. And, behold, there was a woman having a spirit of infirmity eighteen years, and was bound together and was not able to straighten herself at all. And seeing her, Yahushua called her near and said to her, Woman, you have been freed from your infirmity. And He laid hands on her. And instantly she straightened herself and glorified Elohim. But answering, being angry that Jesus (Yahushua) healed on the Sabbath, the synagogue ruler said to the crowd, There are six days in which it is right to work. Therefore, coming in these, be healed, and not on the Sabbath day. Then the Master answered him and said, Hypocrite! Each one of you on the Sabbath, does he not untie his ox or his donkey from the manger, and goes and waters it? And this one being a daughter of Abraham, whom Satan has bound, lo, eighteen years, ought she not to be freed from this bond on the Sabbath day?[40]

The Sabbath Day is so important it was even debated. There are more scriptures stating that Yahushua worshipped and taught on the Sabbath Day, the seventh day, not on Sunday, the first day.

The Sabbath is a covenant and a sign between Yah and his people. The Sabbath is particularly stressed under the everlasting covenant. The Sabbath is considered as being of the CHIEF evidences of "holding fast" God's Yah's covenant.

---

[40] Luke 13:10-16.

Speak thou also unto the children of Israel saying, Verily my sabbaths ye shall keep; for it is a sign between me and you throughout your generations; that ye may know that I am the LORD [Yahuwah] that doth sanctify you. Ye shall keep the sabbath therefore; for it is holy unto you; every one that defileth it shall surely be put to death; for whosoever doeth any work therein, that soul shall be cut off from among his people. Six days may work be done; but in the seventh is the sabbath of rest, holy to the LORD [Yahuwah]; whosoever doeth any work in the sabbath day, he shall surely be put to death. Wherefore the children of Israel shall keep the sabbath, to observe the sabbath throughout their generations, for a perpetual covenant. It is a sign between me and the children of Israel for ever; for in six days the LORD [Yahuwah] made heaven and earth, and on the seventh day he rested, and was refreshed.[41]

Isaiah mentions the COVENANT many times including 42:6, 49:8, 54:10, 55:3, and 56:4.

Blessed is the man that doeth this, and the son of man that layeth hold on it; that keepeth the sabbath from polluting it, and keepeth his hand from doing any evil. 6: Also the sons of the stranger, that join themselves to the LORD, [Yahuwah], to serve him, and to love the name of the LORD [Yahuwah], to be his servants, every one that keepeth the sabbath from polluting it, and taketh hold of my covenant.[42]

---

[41] Exodus 31:13-17.

[42] Isaiah 56:2,6.

"I am the LORD [Yahuwah] your God; walk in my statutes, and keep my judgments, and do them; And hallow my sabbaths; and they shall be a sign between me and you, that ye may know that I am the LORD [Yahuwah] your God." (Ezekiel 20:19,20)

In the wilderness, a man was gathering sticks on the Sabbath and the people brought him to Moses. Moses asked Yahuwah what he should do and Yahuwah said kill him.

> And while the children of Israel were in the wilderness, they found a man that gathered sticks upon the Sabbath Day. And they that found him gathering sticks brought him unto Moses and Aaron, and unto all the congregation. And they put him under guard, because it was not declared what should be done to him. And the LORD [Yahuwah] said unto Moses, The man shall be surely put to death: all the congregation shall stone him with stones outside the camp. And all the congregation brought him outside the camp, and stoned him with stones, and he died; as the LORD [Yahuwah] commanded Moses.[43]

Sure that is extreme, but Yahuwah is extreme. The worship day should not be Sunday but Saturday. It makes absolutely no sense to think that Yahuwah changes. "For I am the LORD [Yahuwah], I change not; therefore ye sons of Jacob are not consumed." (Malachi 3:6)

Many times there is scripture pertaining to the falsehoods being taught by priests and pastors and it is rampantly going on today. Yahuwah uses the word "conspiracy" in Ezekiel:

> There is a conspiracy of her prophets in the midst thereof, like a roaring lion ravening the prey; they have devoured souls; they have taken the treasure

---

[43] Numbers 15:32-36.

and precious things; they have made her many widows in the midst thereof. Her priests have violated my law, and have profaned mine holy things; they have put no difference between the holy and profane, neither have they shewed difference between the unclean and the clean, and have hid their eyes from my Sabbaths, and I am profaned among them. Her princes in the midst thereof are like wolves ravening the prey, to shed blood, and to destroy souls, to get dishonest gain. And her prophets have daubed them with untempered morter, seeing vanity, and divining lies unto them, saying, Thus saith the Lord GOD [Yahuwah], when the LORD [Yahuwah] hath not spoken.[44]

So many conspiracy theories in today's world and it has been going on with the churches, priests and pastors for thousands of years.

2) God's Name
"Thou shalt not take the name of the LORD [Yahuwah] thy God in vain; for the LORD (Yahuwah) will not hold him guiltless that taketh his name in vain." (Exodus 20:7)

The Third Commandment has also been broken unbeknownst to many believers. Yahuwah's name has been falsified. Thou shalt not use my name in vain. Vain translated in Strong's Hebrew concordance means having no effectiveness, falsify – change, empty, worthless. Many times Yahuwah mentions the importance of his name. "But I worked for my name's sake, that it should not be profaned in the eyes of the nations among whom they were, for I made myself known to them in their eyes, by bringing them out of the land of Egypt." (Ezekiel 20:9) The Creator's name is YAHUWAH and He states He

---

[44] Ezekiel 22:25-28.

will not give His glory to idols. I am the LORD [Yahuwah]: that is my name: and my glory will I not give to another, neither my praise to graven images." (Isaiah 42:8) When Judah went into captivity in Babylon from that time they stopped using the true name of the Creator YAHUWAH, and in doing so caused the nations and ultimately Christianity later to adopt the personal name of the Babylonian deity *god* or *gawd* instead of YAHUWAH. As I know I mentioned earlier, the King James Version, interpreted from the Greek in the 1500's, took his name out and replaced it with LORD and GOD in capital letters. "I will declare thy name unto my brethren: in the midst of the congregation will I praise thee." (Psalm 22:22)

The Father says many times, "Seek my name," and "Call on my name," "Know my name," "Praise thy name." Even Jesus Christ (Yahushua) mentions his name.

> I have manifested thy name unto the men which thou gavest me out of the world: thine they were, and thou gavest them me; and they have kept thy word. And I have declared unto them thy name, and will declare it: that the love wherewith thou hast loved me may be in them, and I in them.[45]

Well there are many gods and they have names…Moloch, Satan, Lucifer, Baal, Horus, Buddha, Allah, Baphomet. Why doesn't my God have a name? Also, many times Yahuwah has said, "and they will know my name," or, "because they know my name." "Because he hath set his love upon me, therefore will I deliver him: I will set him on high, because he hath known my name." (Psalms 91:14)

So many say that there is only one god, yet God, Yahuwah, says this profound scripture attesting that there are surely other gods: "For all the people will walk every one in the name of his god, and we will walk in the name of the LORD [Yahuwah] our God for ever and ever."

---

[45] John 17:6,26.

(Micah 4:5) Powerful scripture there. "Now therefore, what have I here, saith the LORD [Yahuwah], that my people is taken away for nought? They that rule over them make them to howl, saith the LORD [Yahuwah]; and my name continually every day is blasphemed." (Isaiah 52:5)

Here, Jesus (Yahushua) says he came in his Father's name. Hello? What's his name? I am come in my Father's name, and ye receive me not: if another shall come in his own name, him ye will receive." (John 5:43)

"Therefore my people shall know my name: therefore they shall know in that day that I am he that doth speak: behold, it is I." (Isaiah 52:6) How much clearer can that be? My people shall know my name and shall know that it his him. Can't you see the trick in taking his name out? "While I was with them in the world, I kept them in thy name: those that thou gavest me I have kept, and none of them is lost, but the son of perdition; that the scripture might be fulfilled." (John 17:12)

But on researching his name and re-reading the entire Bible, I found there have been changes to his name. Funny how none of this was ever taught in all the years of bible studies I attended. I mean years and never once was any of this discussed or ever read, especially the Old Testament. To Abraham he was *El Shaddai*. "And when Abram was ninety years old and nine, the LORD (Yahuwah??) appeared to Abram, and said unto him, I am the Almighty God [El Shaddai]; walk before me, and be thou perfect." (Genesis 17:1)

Now what average Christian is going to know that Almighty God was really a name like El Shaddai? Who would have known that God Almighty means El Shaddai and that the King James Version took El Shaddai out and replaced it with God Almighty? So in every instance in the King James Version is written God Almighty (at least forty times) rather than El Shaddai.

El is found 250 times in the Bible. The word *El* is the root of *Elohim* from which we get "mighty, power, omnipotence, the strong one." It certainly has a powerful meaning.

Upon further research of *El Shaddai* I found Wikipedia says the root word of *Shaddai* means "to overpower" or "to destroy". This would give *Shaddai* the meaning of "destroyer." A MIGHTY word!

When Moses asked the Lord what name he should be called, God said to Moses:

> I AM THAT I AM: and he said, Thus shalt thou say unto the children of Israel, I AM have sent me onto you. And God said moreover unto Moses, Thus shalt thou say unto the children of Israel, The LORD (Yahuwah) God of your fathers, the God of Abraham, the God of Isaac, and the God of Jacob, hath sent me unto you; this is my name for ever, and this is my memorial unto all generations.[46]

In Hebrew the name had four letters – YHWH – and may have been pronounced something like Yahweh. I say Yahuwah. We know his name is not "God". It may be Zeus for all we know. In Greek mythology, Zeus is the name of the God of thunder and lighting and Yah is described with a voice of thunder and full of lighting. It will be great when this great mystery is truly revealed for what it is.

Fear Of God

The Old Testament reveals much more truths about the nature of Yahuwah and what he is like and what his people are like. He is not all lovingkindness and demands fear, love and worship from his people. I kept reading sayings like "fear me," and, "those that fear the name of Yahuwah," and wondered how I was expected to both fear and love Yahuwah at the same time. Here are four scriptures that explain what the fear of Yahuwah is: "And unto man he said, Behold, the fear of the Lord, that is wisdom; and to depart from evil is understanding" (Job 28:28); "The fear of the LORD [Yahuwah] is the

---

[46] Exodus 3:14-15.

beginning of knowledge: *but fools* despise wisdom and instruction" (Proverbs 1:7); "The fear of the LORD [Yahuwah] is to hate evil: pride, and arrogancy, and the evil way, and the froward mouth, do I hate" (Proverbs 8:13); and "The fear of the LORD [Yahuwah] is the beginning of wisdom: and the knowledge of the holy is understanding." (Proverbs 9:10)

Isaiah wrote:

> Say ye not, A confederacy, to them to whom this people shall say, A confederacy; neither fear ye their fear, nor be afraid. Sanctify the LORD [Yahuwah] of hosts himself; and let him be your fear, and let him be your dread. And he shall be for a sanctuary; but for a stone of stumbling and for a rock of offence to both the houses of Israel, for a gin and for a snare to the inhabitants of Jerusalem. And many among them shall stumble, and fall, and be broken, and be snared, and be taken.[47]

Basically a confederacy is an alliance, group, or league. He says not to fear them, fear him. Fear Yahuwah with all your heart, soul and mind. Everyday pray for the truth in all things and for wisdom, knowledge, understanding, discernment and discrimination. Without Yahuwah holding me up with his right hand, I surely would have fainted and failed. This is after all, Yahuwah's game. Yet in Job 40:14, Yahuwah reveals this beautiful scripture: "Then will I also confess unto thee that thine own right hand can save thee." He told this to Job after he tells him:

> Cast abroad the rage of thy wrath: and behold every one that is proud, and abase him. Look on every one that is proud, and bring him low; and tread down

---

[47] Isaiah 8:12-15.

the wicked in their place. Hide them in the dust forever, and bind their faces in secret.[48]

I can't compel you enough, if your heart is being led to Yahuwah, read
the Bible yourself. Yahushua promised that after his ascent to be with
the Father, that he would send the Holy Ghost who would bring remembrance of all the things he said. Not everything written in the
Bible available to us today are things that Yahuwah and Yahushua said.
Not everything...but there are truths there and secrets written and
he has promised to open our eyes to things we never saw (not physical
eyes, spiritual eyes) and our ears to hear things we've never considered. "But the Comforter, which is the Holy Ghost, whom the Father
will send in my name, he shall teach you all things, and bring all things
to your remembrance, whatsoever I have said unto you." (John 14:26
) There are five more references to the Holy Ghost/helper/comforter
by Jesus (Yahushua) in the book of John alone.

There is much in the Bible, for astrotheology, alchemicals, stones
and gems are often mentioned and described by name and trees. A
good teacher on astrotheology is Santos Bonacci. He was a Jehovah
Witness for years, speaks many languages, and has YouTube videos
that show the astrotheology side of the Bible. It is so very interesting
to know that we are in the Age of Aquarius now. The Age of "I
Know". We were in the Age of Pisces, The Age of the Fisherman. A
long 26,000-year cycle and this transition is just now vamping up.

3) Thou shalt have no graven images.
   Thou shalt not make thee any graven image, or any likeness
   of any thing that is in heaven above, or that is in the earth
   beneath, or that is in the waters beneath the earth: Thou shalt
   not bow down thyself unto them, nor serve them: for I the
   LORD (Yahuwah) thy God am a jealous God, visiting the iniquity of the fathers upon the children unto the third and

---

[48] Job 40:14.

fourth generation of them that hate me. And shewing mercy unto thousands of them that love me and keep my commandments.[49]

The whole graven image boils down to what many Christians have on their walls, in their homes and churches - the picture of Jesus Christ. That picture was painted by many artists, most notably Leonardo da Vinci and Rembrandt. So all Christians have an image of what Jesus Christ looks like, and when and if this "anti-Christ" comes, all the Christians will recognize him as "Jesus Christ". There is a reason that Yahuwah said to have no graven images, as many believe an anti-Christ will come through the clouds as described in the New Testament.

"And then shall they see the Son of man coming in a cloud with power and great glory." (Luke 21:27) This all can be created and orchestrated through the secret Blue Beam Project and many will be fooled into believing this inter-dimensional being some call Sanada or St. Germaine is really Jesus Christ. Why? Because they all know what he looks like, right?

I personally have packed away the angels I used to collect and sold the gold cross I wore around my neck for years. I don't remember Jesus Christ (Yahushua) for dying on the cross, I remember him for showing us we don't die through his resurrection and love him for his wonderful teachings. He is truly a teacher of righteousness.

I'm not the only one who feels this way. I found this excerpt from a Sherry Shriner article after I typed the above months ago.

Is the Symbol of the Cross Good or Bad? The cross signifies death, a curse. Yahushua doesn't want us to remember his death but his LIFE, His Resurrection. Christians want to memorialize His death by wearing crosses, to many, it's simply remembering His redemption for us. However, HE doesn't want us to make graven images or "idolize" His death. I stopped wearing cross jewelry years ago once He

[49] Deuteronomy 5:8-10.

made me aware of how He feels about it. Satanists and Satanic groups have no problems wearing crosses, it reminds them of His death and they glory in it and that's what they celebrate. We worship a RISEN Savior, not one still in the grave.[50]

It was revealed to me a few years ago that wearing a cross is a graven image. Not surprisingly, the Catholic Church has changed the ten commandments. As shown below, the Catholic Church totally omitted the original second commandment. I guess that can justify all the idols and statues at the Catholic Churches.

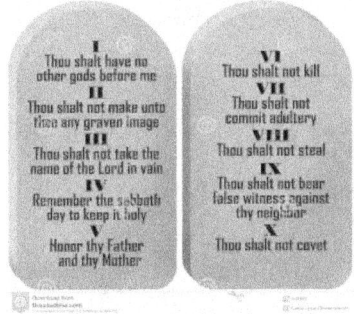

The traditional KJV Ten Commandments.

Catholic Commandments. Where did the graven images commandment go?

---

[50] Sherry Shriner. *Spiritual Warfare & Frequently Asked Questions,* www.sherryshriner.com.

Chapter 9

Through the Wilderness

God is said to have led the people for forty years through the wilderness by Moses with a cloud pillar by day and fire by night. "And the LORD (Yahuwah) went before them by day in a pillar of a cloud, to lead them the way; and by night in a pillar of fire, to give them light; to go by day and night; He took not away the pillar of the cloud by day, nor the pillar of fire by night, *from* the people." (Exodus 13:21) Seeing today what can be done in the skies with clouds, I am sure there was a cloud set out each day and to the uneducated slaves it was brought by God (a superior being). I see silent planes in the sky all the time creating clouds.

Moses, God's right-hand man, made the serpent, a symbol of the Reptilian. "He removed the high places, and brake the images, and cut down the groves, and brake in pieces the brasen serpent that Moses had made: for unto those days the children of Israel did burn incense to it: and he called it Nehushtan." (2 Kings 18:4) The New Testament even speaks of the serpent by Jesus Christ himself. "And Moses lifted up the serpent in the wilderness, even so must the Son of man be lifted up; That whosoever believeth in him should not perish, but have eternal life." (John 3:14)

Throughout those forty years in the wilderness, Yahuwah killed many of the Israelites and had the Israelites kill many people. At the time of death for man and animals the purest loosh is harvested.

And the LORD (Yahuwah) sent fiery serpents among the people, and they bit the people; and much people of Israel died. And the LORD (Yahuwah) said unto Moses, Make thee a fiery serpent, and set it upon a pole: and it shall come to pass, that every one that is bitten, when he looketh upon it, shall live. And Moses made a serpent of brass, and put it upon a pole, and it came to pass, that if a serpent had bitten any man, when he beheld the serpent of brass, he lived.[51]

Again, the serpent, sign of the Reptilian. Yahuwah killed some by fire during the forty years in the wilderness.

And *when* the people complained, it displeased the LORD (Yahuwah): and the LORD (Yahuwah) heard *it*; and his anger was kindled; and the fire of the LORD (Yahuwah) burnt among them, and consumed *them that were* in the uttermost parts of the camp.[52]

Yahuwah killed some by a plague during the forty years in the wilderness after they complained there was no flesh to eat.

Ye shall not eat one day, nor two days, nor five days, neither ten days, nor twenty days; *But* even a whole month, until it come out at your nostrils, and it be loathsome unto you: because that ye have despised the LORD (Yahuwah) which *is* among you, and have wept before him, saying, Why came we forth out of Egypt? And while the flesh *was* yet between their teeth, ere it was chewed, the wrath of the LORD

[51] Numbers 21:6,8,9.
[52] Numbers 11:1.

(Yahuwah) was kindled against the people, and the LORD (Yahuwah) smote the people with a very great plague.[53]

Then at the end of the forty years Yahuwah killed every man and woman over the age of twenty. "Your carcasses shall fall in this wilderness; and all that were numbered of you, according to your whole number, from twenty years old and upward, which have murmured against me." (Numbers14:29) Throughout many verses in the Bible, Yahuwah is constantly reminding his people that he brought them out of Egypt. "And remember that thou wast a servant in the land of Egypt, and *that* the LORD (Yahuwah) thy God brought thee out thence through a mighty hand and by a stretched out arm: therefore the LORD (Yahuwah) thy God commanded thee to keep the sabbath day." (Deuteronomy 6:15) Again we see the importance of the Sabbath day. By killing all adults, there could be a molding of the minds of the children, the same as today. Children are molded to become just the same as the society they are living in. The norm of life is what is taught to children from birth.

I've lived many lives being a child of God (Yahuwah), sinning nonetheless. The guilt from sinning is overwhelming. God, Yahuwah, is a superior being. The Bible is hypnotic and some very advanced entities wrote it to keep mankind in slavery. That is why it is so important to take inventory on all the deceitful, dishonest, low things you've ever done (otherwise known as repenting). Believe me, it isn't easy. I sat one night and counted how many men I had intercourse with throughout my life. I included all men that I was in love with, guys I dated for a few months, one-night stands, forced sex. The final count was about one hundred. I know it is give or take a few, but I will never go through that again. For the past twenty-five years I've read the Bible almost every day, at least a proverb per day which are mostly Solomon's words. The Freemasons base their secret knowledge on

---

[53] Numbers 12:19,20,33.

the keys of Solomon and of course Satan's seed Cain, yet Solomon toward the end of his lifetime set up altars to the gods of his favorite wives. Even a man who was given everything his heart desired still turned on Yahuwah. What does that tell you about being able to completely follow all the rules and regulations given by the Holy Father? No one can live up to it, especially with the manipulation of the aliens of society, just as it is designed to be so. Religions teach that man is nothing but a "worm" and born in sin and can never live up to God's standards. Humans are incarnated spiritual beings and are all that is, was and can be, eternal souls on a journey of discovery and freedom.

I found this scripture interesting since I live in the north country and am an offspring of Israel.

> Therefore, behold, the days come, saith the LORD (Yahuwah), that they shall no more say, The LORD (Yahuwah) liveth, which brought up the children of Israel out of the land of Egypt; But, The LORD (Yahuwah) liveth, which brought up and which led the seed of the house of Israel out of the north country, and from all countries wither I had driven them; and they shall dwell in their own land.[54]

The song of Moses and Miriam in Exodus reads, "The LORD (Yahuwah) is a man of war: the LORD (Yahuwah) is his name." (Exodus 15:3) Interesting how they put "man" of war. And yes, Yah is a warrior God. Doesn't that explain the endless wars, for thousands and thousands of years? We have to know whom we are worshipping.

The definition of worship from Merriam-Webster is "the act of showing respect and love for a god especially by praying with other people who believe in the same god : the act of worshipping God or a god : excessive admiration to someone."

---

[54] Jeremiah 23:7-8.

David Icke even named one of his many books *Human Race Get Off Your Knees: The Lion Sleeps No More*. I can hear him saying in one of his presentations with his British accent, "We're worshipping? We are all that is, was and can be and we're worshipping? Giving our power away? We're All POSSIBILITY." Something like that. Thank you to David Icke for all your dedication and work. David is a key player in helping me put the pieces of the puzzle together. I've read probably ten of his books.

Chapter 10

The Army of 144,000 Warriors (Elect) and the Watchman

Not much is written about this mysterious group of 144,000 prophesied in two chapters of the Book of Revelation. Even yet, some say there isn't really one group, but two separate groups of 144,000. Believe me, if there are 144,000 (the Elect), we will be counting heads and expecting the truth in all things. "Saying, Hurt not the earth, neither the sea, nor the trees, till we have sealed the servants of our God in their foreheads. And I heard the number of them which were sealed: *and there were* sealed an hundred *and* forty *and* four thousand of all the tribes of the children of Israel." (Revelation 7:3-4) It was done before as well. "And the LORD [Yahuwah] said unto him, Go through the midst of the city, through the midst of Jerusalem, and set a mark upon the foreheads of the men that sigh and that cry for all the abominations that be done in the midst thereof." (Ezekiel 9:4)

I had a friend with whom I discussed the 144,000. He went to church on the following Sunday and came back so proudly declaring, "My deacon told me the 144,000 are all virgin Jewish men who will be taken by Christ." I had to laugh.

> And I looked, and, lo, a Lamb stood on the mount
> Sion, and with him an hundred forty and four
> thousand, having his Father's name written in their

foreheads. These are they which were not defiled with women; for they are virgins. These are they which follow the Lamb whithersoever he goeth. These were redeemed from among men, being the firstfruits unto God and to the Lamb.[55]

The virgins of the nations. Those who know and love God Almighty and stay away from pagan holidays and idols, the gods of the nations, not literally 144,000 virgin men. Those who stepped out of the churches. The term women can symbolize a nation or even covenant as Paul uses a woman to symbolize the Old Covenant and the New Covenant. "Nevertheless what saith the scripture? Cast out the bondwoman and her son; for the son of the bondwoman shall not be heir with the son of the freewoman. 31: So then, brethren, we are not children of the bondwoman, but of the free." (Galatians 3:30,31) This army of 144,000 is a mixture of men and women. They are virgins in the fact that they are undefiled by the world's religious Jezebel system and spiritual adulteries. Feminine terms are often used in relation to spiritual terms. "They were not defiled with women" being religious whores and abominations. "And in their mouth was found no guile: for they are without fault before the throne of God." (Revelation 14:5) The Strong's Concordance lists #1388 as being "guile - craft or deceit." I'm sure the 'craft' being mentioned in Strong's is referring to witchcraft itself. How many ministries today are delving into witchcraft with their visions and angelic visitations? Many prophetic ministries, or those who claim to have prophetic gifts are being deceived by the angel of light himself. These will not make the group of 144,000 no matter how gifted yet confused they are. The craft will keep them out. Even those following after those leaders and adopting their practices and false teachings are guilty by association. A remnant will wake up to repent and realize they were deceived to qualify for and make the second group of 144,000 sealed here on earth.

---

[55] Revelation 14:1,4,5.

The 144,000 Elect and 144,000 of the Bride are coming from this 3D reality and souls that are in other dimensions (heavens). "And he shall send his angels with a great sound of a trumpet, and they shall gather together his elect from the four winds, from one end of heaven to the other." (Matthew 24:31)

"And then shall he send his angels, and shall gather together his elect from the four winds, from the uttermost part of the earth to the uttermost part of heaven." (Mark 13:27)

> And after these things I saw four angels standing on the four corners of the earth, holding the four winds of the earth, that the wind should not blow on the earth, nor on the sea, nor on any tree. And I heard the number of them which were sealed: and there were sealed an hundred and forty and four thousand of the tribes of Israel.[56]

The twelve sons of Jacob (renamed Israel) are Reuben, Simeon, Levi, Judah, Dan, Naphtali, Gad, Asher, Issachar, Zabulon, Joseph and Benjamin. The tribes of Israel named in Revelation 7:5-8 are Juda, Reuben, Gad, Asher, Nepthalim, Manasses, Simeon, Levi, Issachar, Zabulon, Joseph and Benjamin. Why Dan is omitted I don't know. Manasses is the son of Joseph. There are twelve land divisions from the sons of Jacob. Remember that Jacob was renamed Israel when God appeared to him when he was leaving Padan-Aram and blessed him.

> God said unto him, Thy name is Jacob: thy name shall not be called any more Jacob, but Israel shall be thy name: and he called his name Israel.[57]

---

[56] Revelation 7:1,4.

[57] Genesis 35:10.

During the periods of captivity, the sons of Jacob are divided into two kingdoms: the Northern Tribe and the Southern Tribe. Ephraim is the head of the Northern Kingdom (Tribes) and Judah is the head of the Southern Kingdom (Tribes).

"Moreover, thou son of man, take thee one stick, and write upon it. For Judah, and for the children of Israel his companions: then take another stick, and write upon it, For Joseph, the stick of Ephraim, and for all the house of Israel his companions." (Ezekiel 37:16) If you read on in Ezekiel, Yahuwah says that both sticks will be joined together as one and there will be no more divided kingdoms. The names of the twelve tribes of Israel will be written on the gates of the new city. "And had a wall great high, and had twelve gates, and at the gates twelve angels, and names written thereon, which are the names of the twelve tribes of the children of Israel." (Revelation 21:12)

Every person has to get in touch with their own God-consciousness and realize they are a part of God and God is a part of them. Get in touch with the spirituality of the universe. God is everywhere and in everything. I have learned much from the Holy Bible, but only after many years of reading and re-reading has interpretation become clear. It's clear that what many preachers, pastors and priests teach covers up the true spirituality of Yahuwah. "I have said, Ye are gods; and all of you are children of the most High." (Psalm 82:6) "Is it not written in your law, I said, Ye are gods?" (John 10:34) If we are all gods, then GOD Yahuwah is in us. We are eternal beings, all that is, has been, and can be. Yah wants us to know this. We are his children and his spirit is soaring through the universe at such a rapid pace. This universe is our university and Earth is one of its schools. That is the positive way to word it, but in this "school", I have learned that this is a virtual reality game and it is rigged and this plane[t] is actually a prison planet, loosh farm, slaughterhouse. We are here to grow, learn, and evolve which is almost impossible the way the world has accepted for thousands, probably hundreds of thousands, of years this slavery monetary system.

The words of the blessing of Enoch, wherewith he blessed the elect and righteous, who will be living in the day of tribulation, when all the wicked and godless are to be removed. And he took up his parable and said –Enoch a righteous man, whose eyes were opened by God, saw the vision of the Holy One in the heavens, which the angels showed me, and from them I heard everything, and from them I understood as I saw, but not for this generation, but for a remote one which is for to come. Concerning the elect I said, and took up my parable concerning them:

The Holy Great One will come forth from his dwelling.
And the eternal God will tread upon the earth, (even) on Mount Sinai,
[And appear from His camp]
And appear in the strength of his might from the heaven of heavens.

And all shall be smitten with fear
And the watchers shall quake,
And great fear and trembling shall seize them unto the ends of the earth.

And the high mountains shall be shaken,
And the high hills shall be made low,
And shall melt like wax before the flame

And the earth shall be wholly rent in sunder,
And all that is upon the earth shall perish,
And there shall be a judgement upon all (men).

But with the righteous He will make peace.
And will protect the elect,

And mercy shall be upon them.

And they shall all belong to God,
And they shall be prospered,
And they shall be blessed,

And He will help them all,
And light shall appear unto them,
And He will make peace with them.

And behold! He cometh with ten thousands of His holy ones
To execute judgement upon all,
And to destroy all ungodly;
And to convict all flesh
Of all the works of their ungodliness which they have ungodly committed,
And of all the hard things which ungodly sinners have spoken against Him.[58]

Jude, brother of Jesus/Yahushua quotes Enoch in the New Testament! How did Jude come to know the words of Enoch? They are not in the "modern" Bible.

And Enoch also, the seventh generation of Adam, prophesied of these, saying, Behold, the Lord cometh with ten thousands of his saints. To execute judgment upon all, and convince all that are ungodly among them of all their ungodly deeds which they have ungodly committed, and of all their hard speeches which ungodly sinners have spoken against him.[59]

---

[58] Enoch Chapter 1.
[59] Jude 1:14-15.

How blessed are we to have our eyes opened to things we could not see and our ears consider things we could not hear. The Book of Enoch was deliberately taken out when Constantine and the Roman Catholics took over Christianity. The true Christians had to go underground and the Christian/Gnostics were killed. All killed in the name of what? Technically, "freedom." We now are free to realize that a hard belief in any one correct "culture" or "mind control society," simply creates "divide and rule." We are all infinite beings deserving equal rights and choices. Human beings deserve some truth to this existence. If it is all for nought, why would I still be here, or for that matter why would I have taken the challenge and incarnated here into this diabolical matrix? It is indeed a challenge to want to stay here, typing this today when I have no contact with my own grandbabies and my own daughters hate me, but I must get this finished and hope to plant good seeds for myself and for whoever reads this. I don't want to harm anyone, steal, lie, have sexual impurity, or possessive wrath or anger. I am grateful right now, today, to be typing this and sharing whatever I am led to include in this book.

Call for the Watchman

"Awake, awake, put on thy strength, O arm of the LORD [Yahuwah]; awake, as in the ancient days, in the generations of old. Art thou not it that hath cut Rahab, and wounded the dragon?" (Isaiah 51:9) "Awake, awake; put on thy strength, O Zion; put on thy beautiful garments, O Jerusalem, the holy city: for henceforth there shall no more come into the uncircumcised and the unclean." (Isaiah 52:1) The watchman must be certain to warn as many souls as possible because if he doesn't the blood of the souls he didn't warn is on him. This is what he told Ezekiel:

> Son of man, I have made thee a watchman unto the house of Israel: therefore hear the word at my mouth, and give them warning from me. When I say

unto the wicked, Thou shalt surely die; and thou givest him not warning, nor speakest to warn the wicked from his wicked way, to save his life, the same wicked man shall die in his iniquity; but his blood will I require at thine hand.[60]

The entire chapter 33 of Ezekiel is devoted to the responsibility of the watchman.

Son of man, speak to the children of thy people, and say unto them, When I bring the sword upon a land, if the people of the land take a man of their coasts, and set him for their watchman: If when he seeth the sword come upon the land, he blow the trumpet, and warn the people; Then whosoever heareth the sound of the trumpet, and taketh not warning; if the sword come, and take him away, his blood shall be upon his own head. He heard the sound of the trumpet, and took not warning; his blood shall be upon him. But he that taketh warning shall deliver his soul. But if the watchman see the sword come, and blow not the trumpet, and the people be not warned; if the sword come, and take any person from among them, he is taken away in his iniquity; but his blood will I require at the watchman's hand.[61]

To anyone that is "watchman," this is profound scripture pertaining to waking up. It is quite a responsibility to be a "watchman."

How many thousands of years have there been "watchmen"? Revelation writes that the antichrist will rule earth for three and a half years. That means three thousand and a half years if what Peter said

---

[60] Ezekiel 3:17-18.

[61] Ezekiel 33:2-6.

is true about a thousand years to mankind is but a day to God. "But, beloved, be not ignorant of this one thing, that one day *is* with the Lord as a thousand years, and thousand years as one day." (2 Peter 3:8) "For a thousand years in thy sight are but as yesterday when it is past, and as a watch in the night." (Psalm 90:4)

My warning is to get out of the churches and rigid belief systems. How about Hebrews? It is most likely written by Paul and probably others since this book lacks his usual salutation such as "I, Paul, called to be an apostle…" There is much written in the New Testament about obeying government. "Obey your leaders and submit to them, for they are keeping watch over your souls, as those who will have to give an account. Let them do this with joy and not with groaning, for that would be of no advantage to you." (Hebrews 13:17) That is from English Standard Version of KJV. All the scripture I have written is from my Bible copyrighted in 1956, KJV Golden Glory. I've only added his name wherever it was omitted and replaced with LORD and GOD in caps. My version says this: "Obey them that have the rule over you, and submit yourselves; for they watch for your souls, as they that must give account, that they may do it with joy, and not with grief; for that is unprofitable for you." Our leaders care nothing about fairness or equality. Do not believe in the government that is in power today. Some believe the United States of America was founded on moral values and that may have been the true intent, but what is here and now in our faces, we cannot submit to. Plus, many founding fathers were Freemasons - George Washington, Benjamin Franklin, Thomas Jefferson and many others. Abraham Lincoln's best friend was a master mason. My gut tells me the United States was founded to become just like it is today. People are owned by the government. We have a birth certificate with our name in all caps. A name in all caps signifies ownership. We are each an owned corporation by the Republic of the United States of America. Hence, that is why when we die (depart these meat suits) we are called "corpses." Jordan Maxwell taught me a lot about etymology. Etymology is a chronological account of the birth and development of a particular word or element of a word, often delineating its spread from one language to another and its evolving changes in form and meaning. Also, our birth certificates are stamped with our sole. Interesting the chosen words for the soul (spiritual essence) and sole (bottom of the foot). Stamping the sole of the foot is binding the soul. The Asian, Japan or China (or maybe all of them) had the practice of binding females' feet. We're they binding the soul as well as the sole? There are chakras in our feet. Is the sole of our feet actually an entrance and exit way for energy in this experience? Words are spells. Growing up in elementary school we were taught spelling. It is no coincidence that learning to read and write words would be called spelling. All etymology of language.

We are just a commodity. Americans agreed to the social security system in 1935, just two years after the all-seeing pyramid on American currency was added with the New World Order inscription under it (in Latin of course). Because of the social security number, from birth, your parents, siblings, every residence you live at, every school attended, every job you have are all reported to the social security administration. A convenient tracking tool.

We must be truth seekers and courageous and strong. Remember that government is mind. Religion is mind. This is New International Reader's version which I am sure many churches use today:

> All of you must obey those who rule over you. There are no authorities except the ones God has chosen, Those who now rule have been chosen-by God. So whoever opposes the authorities opposes leaders whom God has appointed. Those who do that will be judged. If you do what is right, you won't need to be afraid of your rulers. But watch out if you do what is wrong! You don't want to be afraid of those in authority, do you? Then do what is right, and you will be praised. The one in authority serves God for

your good. But if you do wrong, watch out! Rulers don't carry a sword for no reason at all. They serve God. And God is carrying out his anger through them. The ruler punishes anyone who does wrong. You must obey the authorities. Then you will not be punished. You must also obey them because you know it is right. That's also why you pay taxes. The authorities serve God. Ruling takes up all their time. Give to everyone what you owe them. Do you owe taxes? Then pay them. Do you owe anything else to the government? Then pay it. Do you owe respect? Then give it. Do you owe honor? Then show it.[62]

Would you say our government of today, thieves, murderers, liars that they are proven to be, deserve such respect? Christians need to wake up just like everyone else and realize that we do have salvation; we are saved. Yahuwah wishes for none of the wicked to perish but for all to repent. This is the time - NOW - to take the blinders off and open our eyes to things we never saw before and make a difference. This is the separation of the wheat from the tares. The cowards from the braves. Question everything, prepare spiritually, and do what is right for not just yourself, but for others. There are millions suffering every day on this planet and our authorities, leaders, whatever you want to call the wolves in sheep clothing, know it and profit from it.

There is the issue of an anti-Christ coming in and pretending that he is Jesus Christ incarnated. "For false Christs and false prophets shall rise, and shall shew signs and wonders, to seduce, if it were possible, even the elect." (Mark 13:22) "For there shall arise false Christs, and false prophets, and shall shew great signs and wonders; insomuch that, if it were possible, they shall deceive the very elect." (Matthew 24:24) Why would this fake Christ be able to even fool the elect if it wasn't so well rehearsed? Such an outline. Now they have a name for

---

[62] Romans 13:1-7.

this fake Jesus – Sanada, a tall grey. A classic setup. It is impossible to believe anything today. The tactics for mind control have been around a very, very long time. Oh, of course, everybody knows what Jesus Christ looks like right…

This watchman wants to make a clear warning regarding taking the mark of the beast. Some think we already have the mark…the social security number. If so, that number wasn't by choice, it was by law, but when there is a chip offered to be implanted in the forehead or right hand in the future, don't take it.

> And he causeth all, both small and great, rich and poor, free and bond, to receive a mark in their right hand, or in their foreheads; And that no man might buy or sell, save he that had the mark, or the name of the beast, or the number of his name. Here is wisdom. Let him that hath understanding count the number of the beast: for it is the number of a man, and his number is Six hundred threescore and six.[63]

Much can be said about the "mark of the beast", the 666. Many will think that getting an all-knowing chip that carries all your identity, cash etc. would be so convenient. This chip hooks your body directly into the master computer. I have read there are actually two master computers created to track every move a person makes and can even control the mind through the computer. Stay prudent and watchful. It is not all conspiracy theory about the New World Order and the power of the beast that will take control.

Remember, Lucifer rules by deceit. If the job you work at installs a new system for entering the building or cashing your check via a chip implant, DO NOT TAKE IT. Also, if people are herded into FEMA (Federal Emergency Management Agency) Camps and then are demanded to take the chip/mark in your right hand or forehead,

---

[63] Revelation 13:16-18.

or starve, STARVE! There is absolutely no redemption for taking the mark, whether an RFID chip or tattoo in the right hand or forehead.

"And the third angel followed them, saying with a load voice, If any man worship the beast and his image, and receive his mark in his forehead, or in his hand, The same shall drink of the wine of the wrath of God, which is poured out without mixture into the cup of his indignation; and he shall be tormented with fire and brimstone in the presence of the holy angels, and in the presence of the Lamb." (Revelation 14:9-10)

"Behold, I come as a thief, Blessed is he that watcheth, and keepeth his garments, lest he walk naked, and they see his shame." (Revelation 16:15) To me keeping his garments is maintaining the full armor of God, as he is our shield and our buckler. Behold the bridgegroom comes at his own hour so always be ready with your pots full of oil (knowledge and love) and an extra bucket to last through the battle. This comes from the parable of the ten virgins waiting for the bridgegroom in Matthew chapter twenty-five.

We are in a spiritual battle. A battle for our souls. "And in that day shall the deaf hear the words of the book, and the eyes of the blind shall see out of obscurity, and out of darkness." (Isaiah 29:18) He has opened my eyes to things I never saw (spiritually) and my ears have considered things I never heard.

Getting the gospel spread to all nations first was the key to my realizing the mass mind control they were able to achieve. I guess people who suffered these last 2,000 years and figured it out and were killed or maybe escaped. I looked up the word *lawyer* in the Bible, as I could remember reading the word in the Bible.

> Then one of them, *which was* a lawyer, asked *him a question*, tempting him, and saying, Master, which is the greatest commandment in the law? Jesus said unto him, Thou shalt love the Lord thy God with all they heart, and with all thy soul, and with all they

mind. This is the first and great commandment. And the second is like unto it, Thou shalt love thy neighbor as thyself. On these two commandments hang all the law and the prophets. While the Pharisees were fathered together, Jesus asked them, Saying, What think ye of Christ? Whose son is he? They say unto him, The son of David. He saith unto them, How then doth David in spirit call him Lord, saying, The Lord said unto my Lord, Sit thou on my right hand, till I make thine enemies thy footstool? If David then call him Lord, how is he his son? And no man was able to answer him a word, neither durst any *man* from that day forth ask him any more *questions.*[64]

The above verses immediately reflected to me what the New Testament was made to do. What happened to the TEN COMMAND-MENTS? There's way more to it than just two commandments to get it right in this world. And the second commandment, how many people look at someone else and love them as they love themselves. To fully understand the needed protection and prayer for wisdom it is necessary to get through all the secret webs set up to snare the innocent. By first checking out scripture and saying, "Hey wait a minute, that doesn't sound right." After checking who wrote the books in New Testament, I found Paul to be a self-appointed apostle. He's not one of the first twelve, and mentioned only in the other seventy (which who appointed them) as being baptized and converted by two different named apostles. Now I have found some insight as to these fallen angels that were never discussed in church where I went. I never learned a thing about the Word when I went to church. Even hard to believe Paul wrote about celestial beings and terrestrial beings. Jude mentions the fallen sons of god. They definitely were still falling

[64] Matthew 22:35-46

after the flood. My gut tells me that God's first words were even written in a way to keep man under control.

I do have a Lord and I call him Yahuwah. I am faithful to him and to him alone. I will have no gods before me, especially those of the people which is his First Commandment in the Ten Commandments. Do you think Yahuwah went through all that trouble to write the Commandments just to have them overthrown by someone else? He is a jealous God. He is one God, our savior. No, I do not have the savior complex. I was born with my salvation. There has to be a ringleader to this circus, and I don't think I've come this far by myself. I know now about infinite consciousness and think I have some loving, watchful counterparts helping me.

The structure of society is broken and there is corruption everywhere. If, as the Scripture below states, people would eat their own children, how much more if a person is threatened with their life or offered money would a parent betray their child? Especially if they are promised, "Don't worry, we won't kill her/him"? People will do anything for money. Parents and children will turn on each other in a heartbeat. During a famine thousands of years ago, the following scripture describes the desperateness of human nature.

> And there was a great famine in Samaria: and, behold, they besieged it, until an ass's head was sold for fourscore pieces of silver and the fourth part of a cab of dove's dung for five pieces of silver. And the king said unto her, What aileth thee? And she answered, This woman said unto me, Give thy son, that we may eat him to day, and we will eat my son tomorrow. So we boiled my son, and did eat him: and I said unto her on the next day, Give thy son, that we may eat him: and she hath hid her son. [65]

---

[65] 2 Kings 6:25,28-29.

If Yah's own people can eat their own children, don't you think humans are mighty tasty to aliens?

Get out of the churches and let your heart lead you. Do your own work. All we take with us is our wisdom, understanding and knowledge. Your soul is too important to not open your mind to other possibilities and get out of a be[lie]f system. Notice the word lie is right in the middle of believe. They don't care what you believe as long as you believe in something bigger than yourself. We are not worms, born in sin. We are infinite beings born into an evil mind control trap. Religion is mind control. Why do you think a Christian religion net was put right into my programming at three years old through the compartmentalization of my brain? Christian churches don't teach the truth. Pastors and priests preach what they are told to preach and are told the interpretation of the Bible by the church, not by divine inspiration. "Woe unto you, scribes and Pharisees, hypocrites! for ye compass sea and land to make one proselyte, and when he is made, ye make him two-fold more the child of hell than yourselves." (Matthew 23:15:) The churches convert people into their doctrine and teach them incorrect interpretation and turn the people into ungodly persons. Christmas and Easter, for instance, are manmade Christian holidays. Nobody knows what month Jesus Christ [Yahushua] was born. Many believe it was in the month of September. The Christians just adopted December twenty-fifth to be his birth date and are actually following ancient religions that celebrated the winter solstice. Christmas was only declared a federal holiday in the United States on June 26, 1870. As for Easter, it is really a cover for worship to the fertility goddess Ishtar. The Easter bunny is nowhere in the Bible, but we all have heard the term "fucking like bunnies." The egg is also a sign of fertility.

Also never spoken about in the church is watching what you swear to Yahuwah. So many make promises to Yahushua and Yahuwah and never keep them or have any guilt for not keeping them. "When thou vowest a vow unto God, defer not to pay it; for he hath no pleasure in fools: pay that which thou hast vowed. 5: Better is it that thou shouldest not vow, than that shouldest vow and not pay." (Ecclesiastes 5:4-5)

> When thou shalt vow a vow unto the LORD thy God, thou shalt not slack to pay it: for the LORD thy God will surely require it of thee; and it would be sin in thee. But if thou shalt forbear to vow, it shall be no sin in thee. That which is gone out of thy lips thou shalt keep and perform; *even* a freewill offering, according as thou hast vowed unto the LORD thy God, which thou hast promised with thy mouth.[66]

Unfortunately, the evil ones/spirits watch us just as much as the righteous ones/spirits and the bad ones, including Lucifer (Lucifairy or Lucifaggot the mind maggot). I know Lucifer is the son of Yahuwah, just like Yahushua is. I don't want to give him a drop of glory as he is the master of deceit, the great masquerade party, and he can shapeshift into whomever he wants to.

Finally, I want to implore upon you the importance of the next years to come. The times are trying and there will be no warning. There have been many earthquakes since beginning of 2016 and a big one will be coming in the United States soon. "And great earthquakes shall be in divers places, and famines, and pestilences; and fearful sights and great signs shall there be from heaven." (Luke 21:11)

> And he spake to them a parable; Behold the fig tree, and all the trees; When they now shoot forth, ye see and know of your own selves that summer is now night at hand. So likewise ye, when ye see these things come to pass, know ye that the kingdom of God is nigh at hand. Verily I say unto you, This generation

---

[66] Deuteronomy 23:21-23.

shall not pass away, till all be fulfilled. Heaven and earth shall pass away; but my works shall not pass away. And take heed to yourselves, lest at any time your hearts be overcharged with surfeiting, and drunkenness, and cares of this life, and so that day come upon you unawares. For as a snare shall it come on all them that dwell on the face of the whole earth. Watch ye therefore, and pray always, that ye may be accounted worthy to escape all these things that shall come to pass, and to stand before the Son of man. And in the day time he was teaching in the temple; and at night he went out, and abode in the mount that is called the mount of Olives. and all the people came early in the morning to him in the temple, for to hear him.[67]

I bet that mount of Olives was a super-spiritually energetic place on earth.

---

[67] Luke 21:29-38.

Chapter 11

Aliens Have Been Around Forever

In the first book of the Bible, reference is made to giants (a/k/a hybrids). "There were giants in the earth in those days; and also after that, when the sons of God came in unto the daughters of men, and they bare children to them, the same became mighty men which were of old, men of renown." (Genesis 6:4) And also after that....after the flood. The giants were created by the fallen angels who left their heavenly estate to mate with women. "And the angels which kept not their first estate, but left their own habitation, he hath reserved in everlasting chains under darkness unto the judgement of the great day." (Jude 1:6) There have been thousands of huge skulls and some entire skeletal bones of giants excavated that are proven to be thousands of years old. Some call the giants the Nephilim.

After reading the Book of Enoch and the Gnostics texts, I realize that there are many multidimensionals in Yahuwah's family The Gnostics texts were found in clay jars in a cave in Nag Hammandi Egypt in 1945. The Book of Enoch was also found in a cave in the 1940's, although it had been found a couple hundred years before but kept hidden from the public. There are also the Dead Sea Scrolls. Enoch is the seventh of Adam and great grandfather of Noah. "By faith Enoch was translated that he should not see death; and was not found, because God had translated him; for before his translation he had this testimony, that he pleased God." (Hebrews 11:5) Such a great book deliberately removed from the Bible. Enoch wrote extensively about the 200 fallen watchers that came down and mated with human women. He wrote about being taken up to the luminaries and the chambers of the luminaries. He was taken up and down more than once. He never died. He was beamed up. He wrote about the cherubim and archangels who are around Yahuwah's throne day and night.

> Have courage, Enoch, do not fear; the eternal God sent us to you, and lo! You shalt today ascend with us into heaven, and you shall tell your sons and all your household all that they shall do without you on earth in your house, and let no on seek you till the Lord return you to them.[68]

The angels, cherubim, archangels and angels are all explained and revealed as spiritual beings, described in detail *i.e. wings, light, singing*. He describes the different heavens, what some call the dimensions of Earth:

> And the Lord summoned one of his archangels by name Pravuil, whose knowledge was quicker in wisdom than the other archangels, who wrote all the deeds of the Lord; and the Lord said to Pravuil: Bring out the books from my store-houses, and a reed of quick-writing, and give (it) to Enoch, and deliver to him the choice and comforting books out of your hand.[69]

> And Pravuil told me: All the things that I have told you, we have written. Sit and write all the souls of

---

[68] Chapter 1:10.

[69] Chapter 22:10.

mankind, however many of them are born, and the places prepared for them to eternity; for all souls are prepared to eternity, before the formation of the world. And all double thirty days and thirty nights, and I wrote out all things exactly, and wrote three hundred and sixty-six books.[70]

Isaiah describes the Seraphim:

Above it stood the seraphims; each one had six wings; with twain he covered his face, and with twain he covered his feet, and with twain he did fly. Then flew one of the seraphims unto me, having a live coal in his hand, which he had taken with the tongs from off the altar.[71]

Four beasts are described in Revelation Chapter 4, each having six wings. "And the four beasts had each of them six wings about him; and they were full of eyes within; and they rest not day and night, saying, Holy, holy, holy, Lord God Almighty, which was, and is and is to come." (Revelation 4:8) In Revelation, the four beasts do not rest day or night. So they never sleep. Doesn't sound too human to me. The seraphim (beasts) say to Yahuwah that he is all that was, is and to be. Obviously, they can't say that since they seem to be some artificial intelligence created to protect Yahuwah, but we infinite beings can say that we are all that is, was and can be. We are IsBes - all that IS and can BE - "IsBes". So if there are other creatures/species with our God than who knows how many other species are out there besides mankind?

Some spiritual beings can suck off our energy. The lower fourth dimensional beings are especially addicted to human energy ("loosh"), the low vibrational kind, i.e. fear, anxiety, depression. Satan demands

---

[70] Chapter 23:2,3.

[71] Isaiah 6:2,6.

worship from his followers just as Yahuwah does. When I worship I feel the holy spirit of Yahuwah. Satan and his worshippers have the same effect. It is all a game and because we don't know about these archons and multidimensionals, they are free to continue controlling and manipulating mankind into emotional energies that they prey on. Certain people are manipulated into our lives and cause mayhem in their victims' lives. It is true. I know. I lived it and am living it today.

Ezekiel describes a spaceship in the first chapter of his book:

> The appearance of the wheels and their work was like unto the color of beryl; and they four had one likeness: and their appearance and their work was as it were a wheel in the middle of a wheel. When they went, they went upon their four sides; and they turned not when they went. As for their rings, they were so high that they were dreadful; and their rings were full of eyes round about them four.[72]

Beryl as defined by Merriam Webster is "a mineral consisting of a silicate of beryllium and aluminum of great hardness that occurs in colorless hexagonal prisms when pure and in various colors (green, blue, yellow, or pink) when not pure, that is valued as a source of gems, and that is the principal source of beryllium." Beryllium defined thefreedictionary.com is "a high-melting, lightweight, corrosion-resistant, rigid, steel-gray metallic element used as an aerospace structural material, as a moderator and reflector in nuclear reactors, and in a copper alloy used for springs, electrical contacts, and nonsparking tools." Atomic number is 4. A hard gray material is what Ezekiel describes. I would say the eyes were windows.

There are many species of aliens. The Bible has made reference to alien names and always the serpent. In Jeremiah, Yahuwah says he

---

[72] Ezekiel 1:16-18.

will send serpents and cockatrices which could only mean the reptilian species commonly known as aliens. "For, behold, I will send serpents, cockatrices, among you, which will not be charmed, and they shall bite you, saith the LORD [Yahuwah]." (Jeremiah 8:17) "Ye serpents, ye generation of vipers, how can ye escape the damnation of hell?" (Matthew 23:33) "Our inheritance is turned to strangers, our houses to aliens." (Lamentations 5:2)

Isaiah mentions the cockatrice three times. "And the sucking child shall play on the hole of the asp, and the weaned child shall put his hand on the cockatrice' den." (Isaiah 11:8) "Rejoice not thou, whole Palestina, because the rod of him that smote thee is broken: for out of the serpent's root shall come forth a cockatrice, and his fruit shall be a fiery flying serpent." (Isaiah 14:29) "They hatch cockatrice' eggs, and weave the spider's web: he that eateth of their eggs dieth, and that which is crushed breaketh out into a viper." (Isaiah 59:5) A cockatrice is a reptilian egg. Dictionary.com on the internet defines cockatrice as "1. a legendary monster with a deadly glance, supposedly hatched by a serpent from the egg of a cock, and commonly represented with the head, legs, and wings of a cock and the body and tail of a serpent; 2. A venomous serpent." Thefreedictionary.com on the internet defines cockatrice as "1. a legendary monster, part snake and part cock, that could kill with a glance. 2. Another name for basilisk." Basilisk is defined in Merriam-Webster as "1. a legendary reptile with fatal breath and glance. 2. Any of several crested tropical American lizards (genus Basiliscus of the family Iguanidae) related to the Iguanas and noted for their ability to run on their hind legs. The Reptilians are real and are shapeshifters.

The Bible uses the term serpent many times and it does not literally mean snakes. From research and testimony of persons attending satanic rituals, it is my understanding that the reptilians do eat human flesh and drink human blood, especially adrenalized blood that is caused from terror immediately prior to death.

Also dragons are referred to in the Bible. The dragon is another interdimensional type being that manifests in the dragon form. The Chinese worship the dragon.

> For the pastors are become brutish, and have not sought the LORD [Yahuwah; therefore they shall not prosper, and all their flocks shall be scattered. Behold, the noise of the bruit is come, and a great commotion out of the north country, to make the cities of Judah desolate, and a den of dragons.[73]

"I am a brother to dragons, and a companion to owls." (Job 10:29) "Though thou hast sore broken us in the place of dragons, and covered us with the shadow of death." (Psalm 44:19)

When Yahuwah speaks directly to Job in Chapter 38, he mentions Pleiades, Orion and Arcturus. These are also in our solar system, yet never mentioned. "Canst thou bind the sweet influences of Pleiades, or loose the bands of Orion? Canst thou bring forth Mazzaroth in his season? Or canst thou guide Arcturus with his sons?" (Job 38:31-32) The Pleiadians are known to be another species. Blonde or in some cases brunette 'Nordic' type humans, high cheekbones, blonde hair and blue eyes, based in the Pleiadian Taygeta and other systems. The Orions which come from the stars in the Orion constellation are a group claimed to be working with the government on Black Op Projects. They are very heavily involved in influencing the world population through the use of mind control. "Arcturus is one of the most advanced civilizations in our entire galaxy".[74] The Arcturians teach that the most fundamental ingredient for living in the fifth dimension is love. They teach that negativity, fear and guilt must be overcome and be exchanged for love and light.

There are nine known planets in our solar system plus the sun and moon and most do not even know their names. The universe is

---

[73] Jeremiah 10:21-22.

[74] Edward Cayce.

so vast and our little solar system, the Milky Way, is just one of many galaxies. The planets starting from the closest to the sun are: Mercury, Venus, Earth, Mars, Jupiter, Saturn, Uranus, Neptune and Pluto. We do not even know the names of the many star constellations and Yahuwah names just a few in the Book of Job. How can man still believe that we are the only species in the universe? Yah also talks about Rahab. In Isaiah Chapter 51 Yahuwah reminds us when we cut Rahab and wounded the dragon. Rahab was a planet in our solar system and it was completely blown out. The dragon (Satan) was only wounded in that battle. That was thousands and thousands of years before the Book of Genesis. "Awake, awake, put on thy strength, O arm of the LORD [Yahuwah]; awake, as in the ancient days, in the generations of old. Art thou not it that hath cut Rahab, and wounded the dragon?" (Isaiah 51:9) "Thou has broken Rahab in pieces, as one that is slain; thou hast scattered thine enemies with thy strong arm." (Psalm 89:10) Some say that this planet was located between Mars and Jupiter, was the home of Lucifer and other angels, and that it was blasted out of our solar system and left the asteroid belt behind. I've read numerous articles regarding this mysterious planet and only say if it appeals to your curiosity, definitely look deeper into Rahab. There's also a scripture in the KJV from Job that omits the word Rahab, but others have shown it with Rahab in it. "The pillars of heaven tremble and are astonished at his reproof. He divideth the sea with his power, and by his understanding [He shatters Rahab] he smiteth through the proud." (Job 26:11-12)

Many reptilians that intermingle with mankind will pretend to be worshiping Yahuwah through the Catholic church. They have all the paraphernalia, i.e. the statues of Mary, the cross, statues of saints, etc. to show that they believe in God, when actually the Vatican is ruled and run by Satan himself. It is so important to quit using the shut-off mechanism when it comes to aliens. They are here and have been for thousands of years. There are many, many reptilians and others living in the earth in deep underground bases.

A whole book could be written about the deep underground military bases (DUMBs) and the deep underground alien bases (DUABs). Phil Schneider, a huge whistleblower regarding the deep underground military bases and deep underground alien bases, was a self-taught geologist and explosives expert. Of the 129 deep underground facilities Schneider believed the U.S. government had constructed since World War II, he claimed to have worked on thirteen. Two of these bases were major, including the much rumored bioengineering facility of Dulce, New Mexico. At Dulce, Schneider maintained, "gray" humanoid extraterrestrials worked side by side with American technicians. During August of 1979, Phil was commissioned to take part in a deep drilling operation in Dulce, New Mexico. Phil's job was to get rock samples, then recommend the explosive to deal with a particular rock. Upon arriving at the bottom of the shaft, a "horrible" discovery was made. It became immediately apparent that they had broken through into a large cavern that was infested with aliens. The creatures were described as a type-1, seven-foot tall "gray". In the ensuing shootout, sixty-six Secret Service, FBI and Black Berets were killed along with an unspecified number of grays. It was here he received a beam-weapon blast to the chest which caused his later cancer; many have confirmed that a large scar indeed existed. According to Phil, sixty-two of these bases are used for housing short and tall "grays", along with extraterrestrial craft.

Some of Schneider's more major accusations are worthy of attention:

1) The American government concluded a treaty with gray aliens in 1954. This mutual cooperation pact is called the Grenada Treaty.

2) The space shuttle has been producing special alloys in orbit. A vacuum is needed for the creation of these special metals, thereby justifying the mandate for a large, permanently manned space station.

3) Much of our stealth aircraft technology was developed by back-engineering crashed alien craft.

4) AIDS was a population control virus invented by the National Ordinance Laboratory, Chicago, Illinois.

5) Unbeknownst to just about everyone, the U.S. government has an earthquake device. Neither the 1995 Kobe earthquake nor the 1989 San Francisco quake had a pulse wave.

6) The Oklahoma City blast as achieved using small nuclear devices. The melting and pitting of the concrete and the extrusion of metal supporting rods indicated this. (Schneider's forte, he claimed, was explosives.)

Phil died on January 17, 1996, reportedly strangled by a catheter found wrapped around his neck – the bizarre death being dismissed by the authorities as suicide. He stated publicly he was a marked man and did not expect to live long. "If I ever 'commit suicide', Schneider told a close friend, "I'll have been murdered." He has lots of videos on YouTube sharing his work before he was murdered.

They are not coming, they are here and running the show under deep disguise. They are good, actually brilliant, to have gotten away with it for so many thousands and thousands of years. Some of the names of the fallen angels include Aliens, Watchers, Jedi, Dracos, Draconians, Anuk, Anunnaki, Reptilians, Enki, Enlil, Nephilim, Gibborim, and Locust. Some people call them demons but they are not demons. According to the Book of Enoch, demons are the spirits of the dead hybrid children of the Nephilim allowed to roam on earth. Demons are spirits and operate in the spiritual realm. Aliens have bodies, albeit usually grotesque because they lost their angelic beauty as part of their judgment. They can shapeshift – morph – transform into human bodies and look human.

Gnostic is defined as relating to, or possessing intellectual or spiritual knowledge. Gnostic ideas influenced many ancient religions that teach that gnosis (variously interpreted as knowledge, enlightenment, salvation, emancipation or 'oneness with God') means knowledge. The Gnostics were a group of people that were basically killed for their beliefs. The Gnostics talk about a demiurge, the archons, who have taken over the minds of mankind.

> They sought to overpower humanity in its psychological and perceptual functions…although they saw that human thinking was superior to theirs… For indeed their delight is bitter and their beauty is depraved. And their triumph is in deception (apaton), leading astray, for their own structure is without divinity.[75]

The passage is tight with ideas:

- Some group attempted to overpower humanity
- The field of attack was psychological and perceptual [Merriam-Webster definition of perceptual: of, relating to, or involving perception especially in relation to immediate sensory experience]. Hence the perception deception.
- Human thinking was superior to theirs
- Something about their pleasure and beauty is off
- They succeed, but only through deception because…
- …There is such a thing as "divinity"
- …It is implied that we have it
- …They lack it

[75] The Apocryphon of John II, a Nag Hammadi text.

The archons are spoken about in much of the Gnostic texts and I highly recommend reading them for yourself. There are great researchers on the texts, i.e. John Lash and Jay Weidner. There also are many interviews and books to be found on the topic. John Lash "Not In His Image" is an awesome book.

Anarchy - from the Greek prefix an-: without; the absence of & the Greek noun archon: master; ruler. Anarchy does NOT mean "without rules." It literally means "without rulers."

Don Juan, the Mexican Yaqui Indian shaman, tells Carlos Castaneda the following about our predator from The Active Side of Infinity:

> "We have a predator that came from the depths of the cosmos and took over the rule of our lives. Human beings are its prisoners. The Predator is our lord and master. It has rendered us docile, helpless. If we want to protest, it suppresses our protest. If we want to act independently, it demands that we don't do so… I have been beating around the bush all this time, insinuating to you that something is holding us prisoner. Indeed we are held prisoner!
>
> "This was an energetic fact for the sorcerers of ancient Mexico … They took us over because we are food for them, and they squeeze us mercilessly because we are their sustenance. Just as we rear chickens in chicken coops, the predators rear us in human coops, humaneros. Therefore, their food is always available to them."
>
> "No, no, no, no," [Carlos replies] "This is absurd don Juan. What you're saying is something monstrous. It simply can't be true, for sorcerers or for average men, or for anyone."
>
> "Why not?" don Juan asked calmly. "Why not? Because it infuriates you? … You haven't heard all

the claims yet. I want to appeal to your analytical mind. Think for a moment, and tell me how you would explain the contradictions between the intelligence of man the engineer and the stupidity of his systems of beliefs, or the stupidity of his contradictory behaviour. Sorcerers believe that the predators have given us our systems of belief, our ideas of good and evil, our social mores. They are the ones who set up our hopes and expectations and dreams of success or failure. They have given us covetousness, greed, and cowardice. It is the predators who make us complacent, routinary, and egomaniacal."

"'But how can they do this, don Juan? [Carlos] asked, somehow angered further by what [don Juan] was saying. "'Do they whisper all that in our ears while we are asleep?"

"'No, they don't do it that way. That's idiotic!" don Juan said, smiling. "They are infinitely more efficient and organized than that. In order to keep us obedient and meek and weak, the predators engaged themselves in a stupendous manoeuvre stupendous, of course, from the point of view of a fighting strategist. A horrendous manoeuvre from the point of view of those who suffer it. They gave us their mind! Do you hear me? The predators give us their mind, which becomes our mind. The predators' mind is baroque, contradictory, morose, filled with the fear of being discovered any minute now."

"I know that even though you have never suffered hunger... you have food anxiety, which is none other than the anxiety of the predator who fears that any moment now its manoeuvre is going to be uncovered and food is going to be denied. Through the mind, which, after all, is their mind, the predators inject into the lives of human beings whatever is convenient for them. And they ensure, in this manner, a degree of security to act as a buffer against their fear."

"The sorcerers of ancient Mexico were quite ill at ease with the idea of when [the predator] made its appearance on Earth. They reasoned that man must have been a complete being at one point, with stupendous insights, feats of awareness that are mythological legends nowadays. And then, everything seems to disappear, and we have now a sedated man. What I'm saying is that what we have against us is not a simple predator. It is very smart, and organized. It follows a methodical system to render us useless. Man, the magical being that he is destined to be, is no longer magical. He's an average piece of meat."

"There are no more dreams for man but the dreams of an animal who is being raised to become a piece of meat: trite, conventional, imbecilic."[76]

Interestingly, the Gnostic texts also talk about the spirit of planet earth. They call that spirit Goddess Sophia. The human body's frequency is attuned to the frequency of planet earth. I call this earth spirit Mother Gaia. Many Christians would never acknowledge that our planet also has a spirit, just like humans and animals. I mentioned to a Catholic that I love the spirit of the planet, Gaia, and he immediately told me I was worshipping a pagan god. The Gnostics taught that we are divine in nature, and we are in a consciousness trap. I highly recommend reading the Gnostic texts and Book of Enoch yourself.

An interesting document I came across in researching the Roswell incident is ALIEN INTERVIEW, by Matlida O'Donnell MacElroy,

---

[76] Castaneda, 1998.

edited by Lawrence R. Spencer. Matlida O'Connell was a nurse involved in the 1947 Roswell alien crash incident and had telepathic communication with the surviving alien, Ariel. It is definitely food for thought. Just google the roswell.pdf and it will come up. Very cleverly written if it is fake.

I had Greys come into my home in December 2014 and zap me with some type of wand on the temple while I was in bed. I was lying in bed late one evening and I said to myself, *They're here*. At the same instance two Greys were on the top of my lower legs and a Grey was on my chest. The Grey that was on my chest had a wand in his hand and zapped me on my temple. I remember when the wand was put to my head an electrical volt went through my body and I started shaking and convulsing. Then just as suddenly as they arrived, they were gone. I have learned that when the Greys come into contact with mankind that they most always come in threes.

Chapter 12

Human Sacrifice

I wanted to include the story of Jephthah's daughter from Judges 19 and found the great article below from "The Unspoken Bible" on the internet. I found the interpretation so accurate that I am sharing it. Human sacrifice has not stopped; it has only gone underground. I went to St. Patrick's Cathedral in New York City three days a week for three years (there are those 3s again) for Bible study and prayer in the basement of that church on my lunch hour. Yes, there is a basement under the main floor. There was a full basement under it and our group had chairs and a piano in a room in the front half of the basement. There were double doors leading to another part of the basement that were only open a few times. I remember seeing church pews and another alter under there. It is a vague memory, almost like I'm not supposed to remember but the image is there. Now that I have learned about all the ritual sacrifices that are held globally year round in churches and remote estates, I am sure there is an even deeper basement under that church.

Below is the article from The Unspoken Bible, www.usbible.com:

> Unlike the popular Abraham and Isaac in which an angel of God released Abraham from sacrificing his son, the story of Jephthah's daughter is left to be forgotten. The events

surrounding Jephthah can be found in Judges 10:6-12:7. The story of his daughter's sacrifice is covered in Judges 11:29-40.

Jephthah was one of Israel's judges who made a vow to God in exchange for a victory against the Ammonites. He would sacrifice, as a burnt offering, the first person who came out his house to greet him on his return. As fate would have it, it turned out to be his only child, his virgin daughter. He kept his vow.

To deflect comparison against Abraham and Isaac, this story is usually dismissed as a folk tale or a case of bad judgment. To those who take the Bible seriously, it can be neither-this is God's book. Jephthah made a deal with God. God kept his part of the bargain and he didn't release Jephthah from keeping his part for reasons that will be explained in the commentary section.

Jephthah vowed to God that if he is given victory over the Ammonites, he will make a burnt offering with whoever comes out to greet him when he returns victorious.

²⁹Then the Spirit of the LORD came upon Jephthah, and he passed through Gilead and Manasseh, and passed on to Mizpah of Gilead, and from Mizpah of Gilead he passed on to the Ammonites.

³⁰And Jephthah made a vow to the LORD, and said, "If thou wilt give the Ammonites into my hand,

³¹then whoever comes forth from the doors of my house to meet me, when I return victorious from the Ammonites, shall be the LORD'S, and I will offer him up for a burnt offering." (Judges 11:29-31)

So God gave him the Ammonites and twenty more cities.

³²So Jephthah crossed over to the Ammonites to fight against them; and the LORD gave them into his hand.

³³And he smote them from Aroer to the neighborhood of Minnith, twenty cities, and as far as Abel-keramim, with a

very great slaughter. So the Ammonites were subdued before the people of Israel. (Judges 11:32-33)

When he came home, his daughter came out to meet him. She was his only child.

³⁴Then Jephthah came to his home at Mizpah; and behold, his daughter came out to meet him with timbrels and with dances; she was his only child; beside her he had neither son nor daughter. (Judges 11:34)

He was shocked because he could not take back his vow.

³⁵And when he saw her, he rent his clothes, and said, "Alas, my daughter! you have brought me very low, and you have become the cause of great trouble to me; for I have opened my mouth to the LORD, and I cannot take back my vow." (Judges 11:35)

Who did he expect? A stranger?

She understood his dilemma and promised to cooperate. Jephthah honored her one final request for two months leave so she may bewail her virginity.

³⁶And she said to him, "My father, if you have opened your mouth to the LORD, do to me according to what has gone forth from your mouth, now that the LORD has avenged you on your enemies, on the Ammonites."

³⁷And she said to her father, "Let this thing be done for me; let me alone two months, that I may go and wander on the mountains, and bewail my virginity, I and my companions."

³⁸And he said, "Go." And he sent her away for two months; and she departed, she and her companions, and bewailed her virginity upon the mountains. (Judges 11:36-38)

She returned after two months and Jephthah kept his vow.

³⁹And at the end of two months, she returned to her father, who did with her according to his vow which he had

made. She had never known a man. And it became a custom in Israel

⁴⁰that the daughters of Israel went year by year to lament the daughter of Jephthah the Gileadite four days in the year. (Judges 11:34-40)

COMMENTARY

1. This is no folk tale. The last verse, 11:40, calls it a yearly four-day holiday. Obviously, it was once taken seriously.

2. Since his daughter was his only child, Jephthah must have been hoping some other family member would come out to greet him. Who could it be? His wife? His mother-in-law? We don't know. But the bottom line is that Jephthah was willing to sacrifice a family member in exchange for victory.

3. And what of God? No angel came down to stop the burnt offering like in the story of Abraham and Isaac. God delivered and Jephthah had to keep his vow. Deuteronomy tells us that vows must be paid for.

²¹"When you make a vow to the LORD your God, you shall not be slack to pay it; for the LORD your God will surely require it of you, and it would be sin in you.

²²But if you refrain from vowing, it shall be no sin in you.

²³You shall be careful to perform what has passed your lips, for you have voluntarily vowed to the LORD your God what you have promised with your mouth. (Deut. 23:21-23)

4. Another difference between Abraham and Isaac: Abraham's son was a male virgin; Jephthah's daughter was a female virgin. God seems to prefer virgin girls.

5. The Ammonites were major adversaries. Before Jephthah's victory, God was punishing the Israelites for worshipping idols. The Ammonites were oppressing them for eighteen years until Jephthah defeated them. We can be fairly

certain that the price of redemption for lifting the curse had to be someone clean and pure-a virgin girl.

⁷And the anger of the LORD was kindled against Israel, and he sold them into the hand of the Philistines and into the hand of the Ammonites,

⁸and they crushed and oppressed the children of Israel that year. For eighteen years they oppressed all the people of Israel that were beyond the Jordan in the land of the Amor-ites, which is in Gilead. (Judges 10:7-8)

6. Jephthah was the son of a prostitute. His father's wife disinherited him from any family property. This does not seem to have any relevance to his career.

¹Now Jephthah the Gileadite was a mighty warrior, but he was the son of a harlot. Gilead was the father of Jephthah. ²And Gilead's wife also bore him sons; and when his wife's sons grew up, they thrust Jephthah out, and said to him, "You shall not inherit in our father's house; for you are the son of another woman." (Judges 11:1-2)

Except according to Mosaic Law, he should not have been a Judge because he was a bastard.

²"No bastard shall enter the assembly of the LORD; even to the tenth generation none of his descendants shall enter the assembly of the LORD. (Deut. 23:2)

7. According to Mosaic Law, a vow once made must be kept no matter what the consequences.

²¹When thou shalt vow a vow unto the LORD thy God, thou shalt not slack to pay it: for the LORD thy God will surely require it of thee; and it would be sin in thee.

²²But if thou shalt forbear to vow, it shall be no sin in thee.

²³That which is gone out of thy lips thou shalt keep and perform; *even* a freewill offering, according as thou hast vowed unto the LORD thy God, which thou hast promised with thy mouth. (Deut. 23:21-23)

8. In the final analyses, Jephthah was chosen by God to fight Israel's enemies. An impious man would not have taken such a vow. He had every reason to believe that God kept his part of the vow BECAUSE it was embedded in his culture. Whether or not he would have won anyway, or if he made a mistake would be second guessing. He had to keep his vow as a sign of faith. For all he knew, there would have been worse consequences if he reneged. Maybe God was testing him. Especially, this story tells us that child sacrifice in the name of Yahweh was once a part of Hebrew culture. Excuses that Jephthah was irresponsible don't hold up.

EXCUSES, EXCUSES

Let's examine some of the usual excuses given for why Jephthah did not sacrifice his daughter.

Excuse 1: The chapter doesn't explicitly say God influenced Jephthah in any way.

Retort: If the sacrifice was Jephthah's idea alone, leaving God two bad choices, God did not register an objection nor channel him into a different vow. More so, not only did God accommodate Jephthah's request for victory over the Ammonites, he gave him victory over twenty more cities! How could Jephthah NOT take that as an endorsement?

And finally, if God did not know Jephthah's daughter would be first to greet him, then God has no prescience. On grounds of prescience, we could reasonably argue that knowing it would be Jephthah's beloved daughter and only child, God gave him twenty more cities as compensation! The story ends here, so we do not know if Jephthah had more children later, perhaps even a son.

Excuse 2: According to Leviticus 22: 18-19, burnt offerings have to be male.

[17]And the LORD said to Moses,

¹⁸"Say to Aaron and his sons and all the people of Israel, When any one of the house of Israel or of the sojourners in Israel presents his offering, whether in payment of a vow or as a freewill offering which is offered to the LORD as a burnt offering,

¹⁹to be accepted you shall offer a male without blemish, of the bulls or the sheep or the goats. (Lev. 22: 17-19)

Retort: The Leviticus passage assumes a freewill offering of an animal. A freewill offering under Deuteronomy 23:21-23 makes no exceptions.

²¹When thou shalt vow a vow unto the LORD thy God, thou shalt not slack to pay it: for the LORD thy God will surely require it of thee; and it would be sin in thee.

²²But if thou shalt forbear to vow, it shall be no sin in thee.

²³That which is gone out of thy lips thou shalt keep and perform; *even* a freewill offering, according as thou hast vowed unto the LORD thy God, which thou hast promised with thy mouth. (Deut. 23:21-23)

Excuse 3: According to Deuteronomy 12:31, human sacrifice was strictly forbidden by law.

³¹You shall not do so to the LORD your God; for every abominable thing which the LORD hates they have done for their gods; for they even burn their sons and their daughters in the fire to their gods. (Deut. 12:31)

Retort: Despite protestations to the contrary, the leaders and people of ancient Israel practiced human sacrifice at various times. See Child Sacrifice in Ancient Israel.

The Book of Judges emphasized the problems that precipitated the need for prophets and kings. As we see in 1 Samuel, some Judges were corrupt as Samuel's sons were.

¹When Samuel became old, he made his sons judges over Israel.

²The name of his first-born son was Joel, and the name of his second, Abijah; they were judges in Beer-sheba. ³Yet his sons did not walk in his ways, but turned aside after gain; they took bribes and perverted justice.(1 Sam. 1:1-3)

This motivated the elders to plead with Samuel for a king. When Samuel prayed to God, God complained that they had forsaken him to serve other gods.

⁷And the LORD said to Samuel, "Hearken to the voice of the people in all that they say to you; for they have not rejected you, but they have rejected me from being king over them.

⁸According to all the deeds which they have done to me, from the day I brought them up out of Egypt even to this day, forsaking me and serving other gods, so they are also doing to you. (2 Sam. 1: 7-8)

We have it on the highest authority that Judges were far from perfect. To argue that Jephthah would not sacrifice his daughter misses that salient point.

Chapter 13

All Will Be Dissolved and Recreated???

Yahuwah says he will destroy man by heat. There is scripture from Ezekiel and II Peter, and Revelations regarding the subject.

> Son of man, the house of Israel is to me become dross; all they *are* brass, and tin, and iron, and lead, in the midst of the furnace; they are *even* the dross of silver. Therefore thus saith the Lord GOD [Yahuwah]; Because ye are all become dross, behold, therefore I will gather you into the midst of Jerusalem. As they gather silver, and brass, and iron, and lead, and tin, into the midst of the furnace, to blow the fire upon it, to melt it; so will I gather you in mine anger and in my fury and I will leave *you there*, and melt you. Yea, I will gather you and blow upon you in the fire of my wrath, and ye shall be melted in the midst thereof.[77]

Here one can see Yahuwah comparing man to elements. After reading this I came across the following scripture.

---

[77] Ezekiel 22:18-21.

The Lord is not slack concerning his promise, as some men count slackness; but is longsuffering to us-ward, not willing that any should perish, but that all should come to repentance. But the day of the Lord will come as a thief in the night; in the which the heavens shall pass away with a great noise, and the elements shall melt with fervent heat, the earth also and the works that are therein shall be burned up. *Seeing* then *that* all these things shall be dissolved, what manner *of persons* ought ye to be in *all* holy conversation and godliness. Looking for and hasting unto the coming of the day of God, wherein the heavens being on fire shall be dissolved, and the elements shall melt with fervent heat.[78]

After I read Peter's words I wondered about the elements and realized it is the same as in Ezekiel. What a way to destroy much of the earth than by fire, especially the sun, with all the sun worship. In Ezekiel chapter eight, Yahuwah shows Ezekiel what abominations were being done in his sanctuary. He showed Ezekiel the four corners of the sanctuary. The last and worst abomination to Yahuwah is as follows:

And he brought me into the inner court of the LORD's [Yahuwah's] house, and, behold, at the door of the temple of the LORD [Yahuwah], between the porch and the altar, *were* about five and twenty men, with their backs toward the temple of the LORD [Yahuwah], and their faces toward the east; and they worshipped the sun toward the east.[79]

---

[78] 2 Peter 3:9-12.

[79] Ezekiel 8:16.

The sun worship. All that the Catholics did was continue with pagan sun-day-worship and tricked Christians into believing that it is because Jesus Christ arose that day. Yahuwah would never change his worship day. The Seventh Day is UniVersal.

Jesus Christ (Yahushua) gave Apostle John the book of Revelation. "And the fourth angel poured out his vial upon the sun; and power was given unto him to scorch men with fire. And men were scorched with great heat, and blasphemed the name of God, which hath power over these plagues: and they repented not to give him glory." (Revelation 16:8-9)

There is a planet in our solar system that comes into our solar system about every 3,500-3,600 years. The speculation of a planet headed into our solar system was first acknowledged and then later rejected by NASA. But further research reveals that NASA has known for the past 20 years that this planet was coming our way. The Vatican had even built a reservatory in Arizona in the 1980s just to watch its progress toward Earth. The planet is called Nibiru in the Sumerian Tablets and has been written about in several books. Nibiru has a long, slow orbit completely different from the other 9 planets in our solar system. The Hopi talk about the planet and call it the Blue Kachina. Some call it planet X and it is the planet wormwood in the book of Revelation. It has been pointed out that Nibiru will be exactly in the constellation of Virgo in September 2017 as described in Revelation: "And there appeared a great wonder in heaven; a woman clothed with the sun, and the moon under her feet, and upon her head a crown of twelve stars." (Revelation 12:1) The woman, virgin Virgo will have the moon at her feet, sun in her body and the twelve stars at her head in the constellation of Virgo in September 2017.

The arrival of Nibiru correlates with the seven trumpet judgments described in Revelation. Nibiru is five times larger than Jupiter and has its own 7 planet solar system called Nemesis. Nibiru has a huge red dust tail behind it. Why do you think there are so many deep underground military bases and deep underground cities with luxury accommodations. These people actually think that they will survive the destruction caused by this planet by hiding underground. They will just become food for the aliens.

There is a really informative man, Dr. Joseph Chiappalone, who has written many books and I've watched his presentations and listened to an interview. He calls the second sun that came in Planet X. He said it came in and has left and will be back by summer of 2016. This re-entrance is supposed to cause havoc on planet Earth. It is written in Isaiah that the Earth will rock to and fro like drunkard. "The earth shall reel to and fro like a drunkard, and shall be removed like a cottage; and the transgression thereof shall be heavy upon it; and it shall fall and not rise again." (Isaiah 24:20) Has the Earth already shifted and that is why all these truth vibrations are coming in? Dr. Chiappalone claims to have had contact with higher dimensionals since a small child. He says the entire solar system will be dissolved no later than 2035. My intuition senses something like 2025. He also stresses that this is a positive thing since the world has become so inherently evil and that is the only way to correct it. He was raised Catholic but says he now knows all religions are evil. He mentions the viables... those souls that have incarnated here many times and carry God-consciousness in their souls and are considered viable. The percentage he predicts for viable souls is pretty low. Something like one in eleven. However, he also said this some 650,000 million viables will have no memory of this earth experience. I am totally not agreeing to that if I am one of these viables. I don't want to forget my children or grandchildren, the beauty of this planet or to be able to remember and thus recognize evil. I don't want to forget the souls suffering here, all the knowledge I've tried desperately to acquire in a world where ignorance is the norm. If I don't remember the evil how can I protect myself when I face it again? I'm a firm believer in "forgive but DON'T forget". I'm all for having no more tears of empathy and sympathy to shed but I'm not agreeing to having no remembrance of the evil. That is the trick of the aliens – to wipe out our memories.

There is a second sun (planet) that came in a few years ago. Many saw it across the world. Of course, it didn't make any media headlines but one can find YouTubes with recordings from persons who saw it come in. Some call it Planet X. Enoch - Book 2(Parables) Chapter 70:3-4 "And he set me between the two winds, between North and the West where the angels took to the cords to measure for me the place for the elect and righteous and there I saw the first fathers and the righteous who from the beginning dwell in that place".

This is the same planet/star we see today and refer to as the Second Sun, Twin Sun, in the morning it rises with the Sun in the east and during the day it travels across the sky and sets in the West/Southwest when the Sun sets.

Many will claim it's Venus but it isn't.

In the last chapter of the last book of the Old Testament, Malachi says this:

> For behold the day cometh, that shall burn as an oven; and all the proud, yea, and all that do wickedly, shall be stubble: and the day that cometh shall burn them up, saith the LORD [Yahuwah] of hosts, that it shall leave them neither root nor branch. But unto you that fear my name shall the Sun of righteousness arise with healing in his wings; and ye shall go forth, and grow up as calves of the stall. And ye shall tread down the wicked; for they shall be ashes under the soles of your feet in the day that I shall do this, saith the LORD [Yahuwah] of hosts. Remember ye the law of Moses my servant, which I commanded unto him in Horeb for all Israel, with the statutes and judgments. Behold, I will send Elijah the prophet before the coming of the great and dreadful day of the LORD [Yahuwah]; And he shall turn the heart of the fathers to the children, and the heart of the

children to their fathers, lest I come and smite the
earth with a curse.[80]

Notice it says Sun. S-u-n, not S-o-n. The Sun, the Source where we
get reunited with God's spirit and our own souls reunite with our
higher selves and our true soul family.

Yah will send Elijah. Elijah was a prophet from the Old Testament
who never died. He was beamed up. "And it came to pass, as they still
went on, and talked, that, behold, there appeared a chariot of fire, and
horses of fire, and parted them both asunder; and Elijah went up by
a whirlwind into heaven." (Kings 2:11)

Many times God is quoted in the Old Testament that he bought
us and sold us. We are just sophisticated and domesticated cattle and
have been kept in the dark on purpose as to our real purpose for our
existence. I'm not the only person who believes humans are property
to be used and manipulated. How terrible to take our memories away
in order to incarnate here. Infinite beings being human have been
abused and deliberately dumbed down to our being eternal beings,
having a human experience.

I have to talk about the "host" of heaven. The "LORD of hosts",
"hosts of heaven", is referred over 200 times in the Bible. "Thus the heavens and the earth were finished, and all the host of them." (Genesis 2:1)
The word host as used in Genesis 2:1 is defined in Strong's Concordance
(6635) as "a mass of persons or things especially organized for war, an
army." Often it refers to human armies. So, yes, there were armies of humans when the earth was recreated from the last total destruction. "And
the earth was without form, and void; and darkness was upon the face of
the deep. And the Spirit of God moved upon the face of the waters." (Genesis 1:2) This is not the first time for anything. My take on the hosts of
heaven are like the "heavenly" beings (parasites) are sucking off the hosts.

Yahuwah is the top demiurge, the top archon, the top Dog/God of
this Milky Way and goes by many names to many people. We must keep

---

[80] Malachi 4:1-6.

our love strong and pure and have faith and trust that there is Universal Law to this planet being used as a loosh farm/slaughter house for thousands and thousands of years. Humans are given the illusion that this is real and that we're playing our hands from a fair deck of cards, when actually the worn out cards are stacked against us from the entry/birth part of the program. Yahuwah even said this has been done before.

> Thus saith the LORD [Yahuwah], The heaven is my throne, and the earth is my footstool: where is the house that ye build unto me? And where is the place of my rest? For all those things hath mine hand made, and all those things have been, saith the LORD [Yahuwah]: but to this man will I look, even to him that is poor and of a contrite spirit, and trembleth at my word.[81]

And all those things have been. See, all those things have been. This is a copycat world. This has all been done many, many times. So this isn't the first time infinite spirits have incarnated here and had to endure all this hypocrisy, the lies, deceit, delusion. Personally, my spirit is contrite and my heart is broken but there is good news. We are now on a positive timeline.

I spent probably three years of my life going to catechism classes every Wednesday evening for two to three hours in the Lutheran Church. I confirmed my faith in God in my teens through a formal ceremony. But many of those teachings were false. Deliberately being led away from the truth about the evil that is in this world. Being a Christian can be a death sentence for the soul. When I first learned that Christianity teaches false doctrines and deliberately leads believers away from the truth, I wanted to sue the Lutheran Church. Christianity molds children's minds into worshipping on the wrong day and to not question anything that is taught in the church.

---

[81] Isaiah 66:1-2.

None of what the powers that be ("TPTB") have done to me can stop my love for Yahuwah and Yahushua. They are the reason I am still alive in this three-dimensional frequency and not dead like so many of the other victims. It is clear that the perfect host doesn't know it has a parasite. That is why humans' energy has been continuously sucked out of them by the many multi-dimensionals. People are not aware that it is happening, just like the perfect mind control victim is not aware of the mind control.

If you are reading this book, then you probably already know about the nefarious crimes the United States Government has done and is doing to their own people. The biggest atrocity is what is being done to human beings' souls after their infinite spirit departs this human experience. Also, the alien factions were directly involved in making me a breeder and my daughter Amy a breeder. Amy even has the butterfly tattoo on her shoulder. My daughters have been a part of keeping me in the dark about my ritual abuse and mind control. Having to stay focused and wanting to stay a participant in this frequency is oftentimes difficult without a family. My three daughters won't even answer a text and I've only been allowed to see my two granddaughters for a couple hours once in over two years. That one visit was only because I sabotaged my daughter and showed up at their house with balloons and presents since it was Heidi, my first granddaughter's sixth birthday. That was the last time I have seen my grandbabies.

Chapter 14

Scripture Not Talked About in Church

Throughout all my years attending Sunday church services at many churches in many denominations, there was never a pastor or priest that shared any of the scriptures that you will be reading below. Sure, I understand that there is no perfect person, but to learn the capabilities of God's own people to hurt one another is mind boggling. Christians hardly ever even read the Old Testament. All my Bible studies growing up and throughout my adult life with Christians were always in the New Testament.

I know Yahuwah loved David because David was after Yah's heart. There is no perfect person, but being ruled by power hungry leaders is no longer an option. I personally declare myself sovereign. I don't want to rule or be ruled. David killed many people, supposedly enemies of his God but what about his own people? Just as today, lives of mankind are worthless to those in authority. Like his lieutenant and subordinate in the New World Order, Barack Obama, Dr. Henry Kissinger won the Nobel Peace prize – clear indication of an Orwellian world controlled by oligarchy propaganda. Henry Kissinger was quoted:

> "In Haig's presence, Kissinger referred pointedly to
> military men as 'dumb, stupid animals to be used' as

pawns for foreign policy." "The elderly are useless eaters."[82]

"Depopulation should be the highest priority of foreign policy towards the third world, because the US economy will require large and increasing amounts of minerals from abroad especially from less developed countries."[83]

Here is Scripture attesting to servants fighting to their death for entertainment. Here's a barbaric scene. The servants of David and the servants of Saul are ordered to fight each other to the death for entertainment by a pool.

> And Abner the son of Ner, and the servants of Ish-bosheth the son of Saul, went out from Mahanaim to Gibeon: And Joab the son of Zeruiah, and the servants of David, went out, and met together by the pool of Gibeon: and they sat down, the one on the one side of the pool, and the other on the other side of the pool. And Abner said to Joab, Let the young men now arise, and play before us. And Joab said, Let them arise. Then there arose and went over by number twelve of Benjamin, which pertained to Ishbosheth the son of Saul, and twelve of the servants of David. And they caught every one his fellow by the head, and thrust his sword in his fellow's side; so they fell down together, wherefore that place was called Helkath-hazzurim, which is in Gibeon.[84]

---

[82] Bob Woodward, Carl Bernstein, The Final Days, p 208.

[83] Henry Kissinger, National Security Memo 200, April 24, 1974.

[84] 2 Samuel 2:12-16

David killed Uriah, the Hittite because David had knocked up his wife Bathsheba and tried to hide it. David tried to trick Uriah into going to Bathsheba and having sex with her and thus concealing his adultery. But when Uriah wouldn't go be with his wife, David ordered Uriah be sent to the front lines of battle to be killed.

> And the woman conceived, and sent and told David, and said, I am with child. And David sent to Joab, saying, Send me Uriah the Hittite. And Joab sent Uriah to David. And when Uriah was come unto him, David demanded of him how Joab did, and how the people did, and how the war prospered. And David said to Uriah, Go down to thy house, and wash thy feet. And Uriah departed out of the king's house, and there followed him a mess of meat from the king. But Uriah slept at the door of the king's house with all the servants of his lord, and went not down to his house. And when they had told David, saying, Uriah went not down unto his house, David said unto Uriah, Camest thou not from thy journey? Why then didst thou not go down unto thine house? And Uriah said unto David, The ark, and Israel, and Judah, abide in tents; and my lord Joab and the servants of my lord, are encamped in the open field; shall I then go into mine house, to eat and to drink, and to lie with my wife? As thou livest, and as thy soul liveth, I will not do this thing. And David said to Uriah, Tarry here to day also, and tomorrow I will let thee depart. So Uriah abode in Jerusalem that day, and the morrow. And when David had called him, he did eat and drink before him; and he made him drunk: and at even he went out to lie on his bed with the servants of his lord, but went not to his

house. And it came to pass in the morning, that
David wrote a letter to Joab, and sent it by the hand
of Uriah. And he wrote in the letter, saying. Set ye
Uriah in the forefront of the hottest battle, and re-
tire ye from him, that he may smitten, and die.[85]

Cold and calculated, using his powers to kill whomever he chose.
David had Uriah deliver his own death message.

The man who reported to David the death of Saul and Jonathan
was killed by David for helping Saul end his own life.

He said unto me again, Stand, I pray thee, upon me,
and slay me; for anguish is come upon me, because
my life is yet whole in me. So I stood upon him, and
slew him, because I was sure that he could not live
after that he was fallen; and I took the crown that
was upon his head, and the bracelet that was on his
arm, and have brought them hither unto my lord.[86]

David inquired further, "And David said unto him, How wast thou not
afraid to stretch forth thine hand to destroy the LORD's (Yahuwah's)
anointed? And David called one of the young men, and said, Go near,
and fall upon him. And he smote him that he died." (2 Samuel 1:14-
15) David killed the man because Saul was one of Yahuwah's.

The Bible describes an emotionally close relationship between
David and Jonathan. You may or may not agree with the interpretation of the following scripture. I'm just sharing what I have learned
from reading the Bible for many years, especially the "ah ha" enlight-
enments that have been revealed to me since December 2012.

"And it came to pass, when he had made an end to speaking unto
Saul, that the soul of Jonathan was knit with the soul of David, and

---

[85] 2 Samuel 11:5-15.

[86] 2 Samuel 1:9-10.

Jonathan loved him as his own soul." (I Samuel 18:1) Most translations use the term "soul" rather than "spirit" to describe the bond. They speak of an "immediate bond of love", their souls being "in unison," their souls being "knit" etc. Genesis 2:7 as written in the original Hebrew describes how God blew the spirit into the body of Adam that God had formed from earth, so that Adam became a living soul. This means that "soul" in the ancient Israelite times represents a combination of body and spirit. Thus, the two men appear to have loved each other both physically and emotionally.

"Then Jonathan and David made a covenant, because he loved him as his own soul. And Jonathan stripped himself of the robe that was upon him, and gave it to David, and his garments, even to his sword, and to his bow, and to his girdle." (I Samuel 18:3-4) Since people in those days did not wear underwear, Jonathan stripped himself naked in front of David. That would be considered extremely unusual behavior (then and now) unless their relationship was sexual in nature.

"And Jonathan gave his artillery unto his lad, and said unto him, Go, carry them to the city. And as soon as the lad was gone, David arose out of place toward the south, and fell on his face to the ground, and bowed himself three times: and they kissed one another, and wept one with another, until David exceeded." (I Samuel 20:40-41) Some Bibles say "and they sadly shook hands, tears running down their cheeks until David could weep no more." The translators of the Living Bible apparently could not handle the thought of two adult men kissing, so they mistranslated the passage by saying that the two men shook hands! The original Hebrew text says that they kissed each other and wept together until David became large. The word which means "became large" in the passage is "gadal" in the original Hebrew. The same words are used elsewhere in the Hebrew scriptures to refer to King Solomon being greater than all other kings. Some theologians interpret "gadal" in this verse as indicating that David had an erection. However, the thoughts of David becoming sexually aroused after kissing Jonathan may have been too threatening for

Bible translators. They either deleted the ending entirely or created one of their own.

"I am distressed for thee, my brother Jonathan; very pleasant has thou been unto me: thy love to me was wonderful, passing the love of women." (II Samuel 1:26) In the society of ancient Israel, it was not considered proper for a man and woman to have a platonic relationship. Men and women rarely spoke to each other in public. Since David's only relationships with women would have been sexual in nature, then he must be referring to sexual love here. It would not make sense in this verse to compare platonic love for a man with sexual love for a woman; they are two completely different phenomena. It would appear that David is referring to his sexual love for Jonathan.

Lot, nephew of Abraham offered his own daughters to an angry crowd of men who wanted to have sex with the angels that were in his house in Sodom.

> And they called unto Lot, and said unto him, Where are the men which came in to thee this night? Bring them out unto us, that we may know them. And Lot went out at the door unto them, and shut the door after him. And said, I pray you, brethren, do not so wickedly. Behold now, I have two daughters which have not known man; let me, I pray you, bring them out unto you, and do ye to them as is good in your eyes: only unto these men do nothing; for therefore came they under the shadow of my roof.[87]

A man of "God" offered his own daughters to be raped and probably killed. "That we may know them" means to have sex with them.

Here a woman, a concubine, was thrown out and raped to death to appease a crowd of angry men that wanted to have sex with a man abiding in her master's house.

[87] Genesis 19:5-8.

Now as they were making their hearts merry, behold, the men of the city, certain sons of Beliah, beset the house round about, and beat at the door, and spake to the master of the house, the old man, saying, Bring forth the man that came into thine house, that we may know him. And the man, the master of the house, went out unto them, and said unto them, Nay, my brethren, nay, I pray you, do not so wickedly; seeing that this man is come into mine house, do not this folly. Behold, here is my daughter a maiden, and his concubine; them I will bring out now, and humble ye them, and do with them what seemeth good unto you; but unto this man do not so vile a thing. But the men would not hearken to him: so the man took his concubine, and brought her forth unto them; and they knew her, and abused her all the night until the morning: and when the day began to spring, they let her go. Then came the woman in the dawning of the day, and fell down at the door of the man's house where her lord was, till it was light. And her lord rose up in the morning, and opened the doors of the house, and went out to go his way: and, behold, the woman his concubine was fallen down at the door of house, and her hands were upon the threshold. And he said unto her, Up and let us be going. But none answered. Then the man took her up upon an ass, and the man rose up, and gat him unto his place. And when he came into his house, he took a knife, and laid hold on his concubine, and divided her, together with her bones, into twelve pieces, and sent her into all the coasts of Israel.[88]

---

[88] Judges 19:22-29.

Wow, took her home and chopped up her body.

I know I already included this scripture but feel it appropriate to include it again in this chapter.

> And there was a great famine in Samaria: and, behold, they besieged it, until an ass's head was sold for fourscore pieces of silver and the fourth part of a cab of dove's dung for five pieces of silver. And as the king of Israel was passing by upon the wall, there cried a woman unto him saying, Help, my lord, O king. And he said, If the LORD (Yahuwah) do not help thee, whence shall I help thee? Out of the barn-floor, or out of the winepress? And the king said unto her, What aileth thee? And she answered, This woman said unto me, Give thy son, that we may eat him to day, and we will eat my son tomorrow. So we boiled my son, and did eat him: and I said unto her on the next day, Give thy son, that we may eat him: and she hath hid her son.[89]

"God's" own people can eat their own children.

In the book of Nehemiah this is written, "Also the firstborn of our sons, and of our cattle, as it is written in the law, and the firstlings of our herds and our flocks, to bring to the house of our God, unto the priests that minister in the house of our God." (Nehemiah 10:36) Who knows what the priests would do with these firstborn sons. The prophet Nehemiah has a questionable character. Describing his zeal for "God", he wrote, "And I contended with them, and cursed them, and smote certain of them, and plucked off their hair, and made them swear by God, saying, Ye shall not give your daughters unto their sons, or take their daughters unto your sons, or for yourselves." (Nehemiah 13:25) God's own prophet killing his own people.

---

[89] 2 Kings 6:25-29.

I want to share this interesting scripture regarding Elisha. Elisha was the right-hand of Elijah and after Elisha saw Elijah get beamed up, Elisha took Elijah's mantle and started walking.

> And he went up from thence unto Bethel: and as he was going up by the way, there came forth little children out of the city, and mocked him, and said unto him, Go up, thou bald head; go up, thou bald head. And he turned back, and looked on them, and cursed them in the name of the LORD (Yahuwah). And there came forth two she bears out of the wood, and tare forty and two children of them.[90]

That sounds awfully cruel for some children doing what children are known to do....teasing. But the "go up" is probably them wishing him to die since Elijah went up and was gone. But really, killing little children for teasing.

The Christians always say Jesus Christ is the only begotten son of God. Yet here is scripture attesting to "sons" of God. "Now there was a day when the sons of God came to present themselves before the LORD (Yahuwah), and Satan came also among them." (Job 1:6) Again there was a day when the sons of God came to present themselves before the LORD (Yahuwah), and Satan came also among them to present himself before the LORD (Yahuwah)." (Job 2:1) When the morning stars sang together, and all the sons of God shouted for joy?" (Job 38:7)

It is also interesting that Satan is allowed to go to God's throne and present himself since he was thrown out of heaven. Apparently, God and Satan still converse. God (Yahuwah) is one who challenges Satan as to Job's integrity and lets Satan do horrible things to Job.

In Job, when God asked Satan where he came from, Satan specifically said "in the Earth." "And the LORD (Yahuwah) said unto Satan,

---

[90] 2 Kings 2:23-24.

Whence comest thou? Then Satan answered the LORD (Yahuwah), and said, From going to and fro in the earth, and from walking up and down in it." (Job 1:7) "And the LORD (Yahuwah) said unto Satan, Whence comest thou? Then Satan answered the LORD (Yahuwah), and said, From going to and fro in the earth, and from walking up and down in it." (Job 2:2) We know there are deep underground alien bases and reptilians and other species that live in the Earth.

There are also references that God speaks in plural as to himself and others. God speaks to Job saying, "Canst thou send lightnings, that they may go, and say unto thee, Here we are?" (Job 2:2) Why would he say here "we" are, if he doesn't have help? I've found at least six references in the Old Testament where Yahuwah uses the words "we" and "us." "And the LORD [Yahuwah] God said, Behold, the man is become as one of us, to know good and evil: and now, lest he put forth his hand, and take also of the tree of life and eat, and live forever." (Genesis 3:22)

Chapter 15

Government Control

We are all energy makers and money makers. Some of us are seeking the question of why we are here. With all the secrets in this world a truly enlightened soul doesn't stand a chance. The Freemasons have been around for thousands of years. Many powerful leaders are/have been Freemasons. Between the government, Freemasons, military and greed of every man, any person can be manipulated and exploited. Mankind is in prison and doesn't even know it. Because all information is filtered and altered to fit the agenda, it is hard to believe that a person can ever find the truth.

Since the beginning of civilization, those in power have tried to control people. Today it is largely accomplished through subliminal messages. Subliminal messages were first developed in the United States during World War II (1939, US joined in 1941). It was used on our pilots. In 1957, it was first used in movie theaters and television. Television is the perfect medium to use subliminal messages to control a population.

The word subliminal means below the perception of the conscious mind. Subliminal messages can be presented as visual, audio, or in the form of electromagnetic waves. The ultimate goal of any subliminal message is to manipulate a person by altering their perceptions to produce a change in thinking patterns resulting in modified behavior.

There are numerous types of subliminal messages. One type of visual subliminal message contains stimuli repeatedly flashed across a screen at fractions of a second, which is too fast for the brain to consciously perceive. Audio subliminal messages, played in music for instance, contain audio stimuli played at below or above the normal hearing ranges while others are barely audible. Sometimes two messages are delivered simultaneously into both ears which are directed to affect a particular part of the brain. Another type of audio subliminal message is known as backmasking which occurs when phrases are recorded backwards and embedded within a song or other sound recording. The last type of subliminal message is much more subtle than either the visual or audio. Electromagnetic waves whether they are extremely low frequency (ELF) or just low frequency (LF) affect the human body in various ways. By blasting the human body with electromagnetic waves, the brain wave patterns are disrupted which can have profound effects on the nervous system. Technology is currently available to stimulate areas of the brain to produce psychological and physiological effects.

The United States government is currently using HAARP to interfere with the earth's magnetic fields and your brain waves. The wave patterns in the ionosphere are identical to human brain waves. Therefore, interference in the earth's magnetic fields can affect the human body's magnetic field as well. Many patents that specifically state the intention of mind control, use these invisible waves to influence subjects. HAARP is short for High-Frequency Active Auroral Research Program and consists of antennae that emit electromagnetic waves into the ionosphere. High concentrations of these waves have shown to cause mood disorders. Long-term exposure can cause people to hallucinate, hear voices in their heads, develop psychic abilities or even to physically rock back and forth. There was a twenty-three-year old woman murdered in northern Michigan in the past couple years by a man who said he was playing a video game and it influenced him to kill her.

I was a child of the 60s, when public schools were thought to be safe. I had numerous hearing tests done in school with headphones put on my head. Probably upgrades to the programming performed during that mysterious hospital stay. There have been subliminal messages sent to my brain throughout my childhood. The television was my generations' best friend, just as it is today. I grew up worrying about the wrong things instead of the right things, worrying about being attractive, making money, sexual appeal, possessions.

Students were allowed to buy fluoride treatments when I was in third grade (about 1970). My parents didn't pay for the treatment and I still have my teeth. Where was this fluoride treatment funded from? Is that why so many Americans I grew up with (plus across the country) lost their teeth? Now I've learned fluoride damages the body such as slowing brain function.

In today's American world we have Craigslist, Facebook, reality shows - all mind control. It is documented that the Internet was developed in 1970 and initially used by the military. I am sure it was created and used decades before that "official" year. Now it is used to manipulate and allows people to be scammed all the time. Decades later it was "sold" to the public. This massive mind control has been going on since the introduction of the television (tel-lie-vision). The television was first invented in 1932 by three scientists from three different countries, Russia and America being two of those countries. In my school days I was taught that the Russians are our enemy but hand-in-hand the Russians and Americans created the television. I was taught fear through media manipulation and propaganda. Bill Hicks said, "Watching television is like taking black spray paint to your third eye." I have not watched television in over two years, I don't even own a television anymore. Why do you think the guide for television is called a program? Television is a programming tool for mind control.

As David Icke in his book *Phantom Self* explains:

All smart technologies are designed to wirelessly communicate with each other to form the global Smart Grid that would not only keep surveillance on everyone in the multiple ways I will explain, but would also feed information, perceptions and instructions to the human mind. Smart television, for example, are the Totalitarian Tiptoe (almost complete) to the Telescreens described by Dr. Richard Day nearly 50 years ago and by George Orwell nearly 70 years ago in his book 1984:

The telescreen received and transmitted simultaneously. Any sound that Winston made, above the level of a very lower whisper would be picked up by it; moreover, so long as he remained within the field of vision which the metal plate commanded, he could

There was of course no way of knowing whether you were being watched at any given moment. How often, or on what system, the Thought Police plugged in on any individual wire was guesswork. It was even conceivable that they watched everybody all the time, but at any rate they could plug in your wire whenever they wanted to.

You have to live – did live, from habit that became instinct – in the assumption that every sound you made was overheard, and except in darkness, every movement scrutinized."

In January of 2013, America was bombarded with news stories about the government's fiscal cliff. Then in July 2013, Obama went on a hundred million dollar safari. Madness. I don't understand how Americans can justify their extravagant government. The list goes on and on regarding Obama's (and all our presidents') lies. An average dollar that is spent in America is taxed at least sixteen times by the government. About one-third of yearly income is paid in taxes. Personal property is taxed. The mind has to open to all the billions of dollars collected daily/weekly by the U.S. government.

The custom of childbirth in hospitals began in the early 1940s. I was, like generations before me were, brainwashed to believe that it was safer in a hospital. Our babies were born and then taken away by the medical authorities. Did this subliminal messaging start at birth? What is really in the vaccinations our children are given. These are something like . No thought of their spirituality. Why has the soul and spirituality been ignored? We are mind, body and soul yet none of today's generation seems to care about their soul.

> This know also that in the last days perilous times shall come. For men shall be lovers of their own selves, covetous, boasters, proud, blasphemers, disobedient to parents, unthankful, unholy, Without natural affection, trucebreakers, false accusers, incontinent, fierce, despisers of those that are good, Traitors, heady, high-minded, lovers of pleasure, more than lovers of God.[91]

Most Modern KJV remove the word incontinent. I googled the definition of incontinent and its definition is as follows:

1. Having no or insufficient voluntary control over urination or defecation.
2. Lacking self-restraint; uncontrolled

Just as predicted in the New Testament that society would be as described. It was also predicted to be like that before the fall of Babylon in the Old Testament. It is so obvious and so devious.

[91] Timothy 3:1-4.

People have been secretly tested and monitored for years. They have been experimented with and totally unaware of the manipulation being done to their minds. The experimentation has constantly produced more effective results. Over the last sixty years, our generations have succumbed to such a terrible state Based on the Centers for Disease Control and Prevention's (CDC, 2017) Recommended Childhood Vaccine Schedule, children are to be administered 50 doses of 14 vaccines before age 6 and 69 does of 16 vaccines by age 18. The autism in children has risen A sure byproduct of this toxic cocktails on our children is the alarming increases for autism in the United States. About 1 percent of the world population has autism spectrum disorder (CDC, 2014). Prevalence in the United States is estimated at 1 in 68 births. (CDC, 2014) Prevalence of autism in U.S. children increased by 119.4 percent from 2000 (1 in 150) to 2010 (1 in 68). (CDC, 2014) Autism services cost U.S. citizens $236-262 billion annually (Buescher et al. 2014)

Tobacco, alcohol, and drugs were introduced into our society to be the norm.

Tobacco was given for free to American soldiers during the first wars (1914 and 1940). The government's plan worked to get our parents' generation addicted and their children will follow. Our children have it in their blood. My parents smoked, I struggled to quit smoking. It is like an electric collar on our necks. Try to quit and you will have severe mental and physical symptoms. Tobacco generates billions of dollars to the government every year and there are no laws on what the tobacco companies can put into a cigarette. Tobacco companies largely support our government. In the 1800's, the average American smoked forty cigarettes a year. Now that many is commonly smoked per day. Tobacco takes well over ten years off of life expectancy, something like thirteen years. The government is even funding quittobacco.gov help sites and 800 numbers. It's a scary monopoly with lives being discarded.

Alcohol abuse is at an all-time abuse rate. Yes, alcohol has been consumed for thousands of years. It was only harvested with the peoples' own resources (i.e., grapes, potatoes) and respectfully ingested, not meant for the abuse that is partaken of today. Beer is especially a tool to keep people numb. Its primary ingredient is water and water is fluoridated. I personally have stopped drinking beer made in the United States. For most of my life I've drank beer, some years on a daily basis. This awakening has led me to the power of beer in society. If you are going to make your own beer, use fresh well or spring water. You know nothing has been added to it. Beer has been abused for many decades. There are no ingredients listed on beer so anything can be added. My father drank beer every day of his life, I'm sure to numb himself. Characteristics of chronic heavy beer drinkers are those of an "I don't care" attitude.

Cocaine was discovered in the 1800's to be highly addictive. Sure no one put a gun to my head and made me ingest it, but because of our government letting it be introduced to the middle and upper classes, there was major addiction from the 60's to today. Crack was introduced in 1980. People addicted to drugs don't pay attention to what is happening in their world. Controlling humans is just like predicting a deer's behavior. We're tagged and managed. I even got in trouble and paid court costs, probation, all predicted to happen from drug addiction. I was addicted and was programmed to work and never questioned the monies going to the government. Just do what we are told. They harvest the money by us getting a job and trying to make the most money a day. We pay mindlessly into the government with hundreds of thousands of dollars coming from someone like me alone. We are taxed and re-taxed on our own property. This is slavery. There is no freedom. We are being watched and controlled every day.

I personally have been addicted to drugs, alcohol and tobacco - a product of how freely my government has been allowed to direct thoughts. I was also a work alcoholic. One firm I worked for gave a separate check for overtime of thirty-five hours or more. I got a separate check for six months in a row. That was bi-weekly so I worked seventy hours a month OVERTIME beyond my usual thirty-seven to forty hours per week. And here I thought I was raising my girls. Everything I did was in excess. People today are addicted and depressed. Millions of people have gone to rehab clinics. This all generates dollars to the government. Millions of people have died due to overdose on drugs.

Then there is excessive eating. The obesity rate in the United States is at an all-time high, yet there are still people starving in our country and in other countries. Why are these Americans all overeating? Mind control? Man is meant to use food to live not live to eat. The foods we eat are mostly processed, are probably not even safe. Hunger has been grossly misused. Overfeeding one country and starving other countries. Also, I wish to point out that from many awakened warriors I have learned that eliminating meat from the diet helps keep the human vibration up. I don't like labels and thus do not call myself a vegetarian, but I have almost completely eliminated meat from my diet. The animals are held in atrocious conditions and terrorized before and while being slaughtered. That meat, adrenalized with terror, is what humans are consuming and can't be good. Chickens are hung upside down by their feet, attached to a conveyor belt that carries them along to a blade that cuts their throats. Baby male chicks are thrown into a shredder since there is little use for male chicks. The chickens' beaks are painfully clipped and pigs' ears and tails are cut off since pigs are held in such close quarters and will chew each other's ears and tails off, all with no anesthesia. Cows are hung upside down by their legs, their throats cut and limbs chopped off while they are still conscious, bleeding to death. Once conscious awareness kicks in, a new empathy kicks in for the lives of animals that are held in horrible conditions and brutally slaughtered. At least bless and thank the animal for its flesh that is being eaten. Animals are spiritual beings, just the same as humans. Spiritual beings incarnating on planet earth in animal form or human form. We are spiritual beings first and foremost, having an earthly experience.

The human body and mind are extremely complex and we are guinea pigs. New prescription drugs are readily available. Humans are constantly being tricked by the constant commercials advertising prescription drugs. A typical commercial will advertise a drug, for example, for toenails. Then at the end of the advertisement, a list of possible side effects is named, including liver damage, heart disease etc., but your toenails will look good. All human sicknesses generate money to the U.S. government. We need insurance. Insurance companies are taxed, the medical supplies are taxed, shipping is taxed. Medical workers contribute their payroll taxes. Where is all this money going? Why has nobody questioned this system in our society? There are something like 300 mental disorders listed by the medical industry and there is a drug to "treat" each of them. This body was not made to be chemically destroyed, but drugs are so abundant here.

Today Americans are encouraged to file for social security disability and all their personal information is freely turned over to the government. Everyday there are commercials advertising assistance to get social security benefits. The social security recipient is then totally monitored by the government. Most people since Social Security was implemented in 1935 have not been able to enjoy the money paid in their entire lives since they died before or shortly after retirement. The statistics are there. The government does not want us to live. Uncle Sam wants you dead.

The Federal Reserve is owned by international, private banks and was established in 1913 on an Island in Georgia called Jekyll Island. I was taught that the U.S. Government owns and controls the Federal Reserve. Now I find out that the U.S. Government borrows from the Federal Reserve and pays them back with taxpayers' dollars, with interest. That alone is a bombshell. I sat in Government class in 1976 and distinctly recall being told the government owns and operates the Federal Reserve.

The government is controlled and operated by a shadow government/black government.

The Secret Government went into place in 1947,"
Mark explained to a caller. "As did the National Security Act. The Constitution of the United States
was founded in truth and justice for all, not for a few
self-appointed secret leaders operating on the phi-
losophy that 'secret knowledge equals power.' Secrets have now compounded to the point where
people no longer think to ask the right questions.
Technological secrets emerge as technological control. Ask what HAARP is about. Ask about DARPA.
Ask now while you can still think to do so because
technology is breeding itself through computeriza-
tion and it's time we took it out of the hands of the
Secret Government.[92]

There are so many groups, agencies and committees that most Americans have never even heard of. The Bilderberg Group, the Trilateral
Commission, the Trans-Pacific Partnership, Counsel on Foreign Relations. These groups have been around for a long time. The Council
on Foreign Relations (CFR) was created in 1921 and the Trilateral
Commission in 1973, an offshoot of the CFR. So, so many of the government positions are held by members from the CFR. Therefore,
the United States government is ruled secretly by a group rich aca-
demics, bankers, pharmaceutical executives, brokers, judges, lawyers,
scientists, inventors, etc. (just open your mind), with a membership
of only a little over three thousand. The CFR even has a "clubhouse"
in New York City. Jim Marrs, author of *Rule By Secrecy*, the "underground best seller," details the entire history of these groups. Did I
learn anything about these groups in high school? Almost a century
of being ruled and controlled by a shadow government. No, because
the education system is an indoctrination system. Even if a teacher

---

[92] Cathy O'Brien, *ACCESS DENIED For Reasons Of National Security: Documented Journey From CIA Mind Control Slave To U.S. Government Whistleblower.*

knew about something like the CFR, which most don't because they got the same indoctrination as we did, for the all-mighty dollar, they keep their mouths shut. I know. I lived it and I "believed" I was getting the "best" education of the world!!! Now I know everything is backwards. The terrorist group called ISIS. Ken O'Keefe, a former U.S. Marine and current whistleblower, is the YouTube to look up to learn more about ISIS. He says ISIS stands for Israeli Secret Intelligence Service and that ISIS is created and funded by the United States and Israel. There is so much evidence that ISIS is funded and armed by the United States government and Israel, and that no "ignorance is bliss" stance can be taken. The United States has used its veto power more than forty times in the UN to defend Israeli violation of international law.

Congressmen make $174,000 a year, for life. All they have to do is serve one day and they get paid that amount for life. What a joke. Many politicians hold dual citizenship with Israeli. What a hypocrisy. These politicians support Israeli and its interests, not the people of the United States. The United States government provides Israel $10.2 million in military aid each day, while it gives the Palestinians $0 in military aid.

> Since the October War in 1973, Washington has provided Israel with a level of support dwarfing the amounts provided to any other state. It has been the largest annual recipient of direct U.S. economics and military assistance since 1976 and the largest total recipient since World War II. Total direct U.S. aid to Israel amounts to well over $140 billion in 2003 dollars. Israel receives about $3 billion in direct foreign assistance each year, which is roughly one-fifth of America's entire foreign aid budget. In per capita terms, the United States gives each Israeli a direct subsidy worth about $500 per year. This

largesse is especially striking when one realizes that
Israel is now a wealthy industrial state with a per
capita income roughly equal to South Korea or
Spain.[93]

According to the Congressional Research Service's report *"U.S. Foreign Aid to Israel"* dated June 10, 2015 and written by Jeremy M.
Sharp, specialist to Middle Eastern Affairs, the Obama administration
gave Israel $3.1 billion for the fiscal year 2015 in direct bilateral mil-
itary aid (also referred to as Foreign Military Financing or FMF). The
U.S. government also gave $619.8 million for "joint" U.S.-Israel mis-
sile defense programs (designed to protect Israeli territory from potential outside threats), bringing total military aid to Israel to $3.7
billion per year.

Put another way, American taxpayers give Israel $10.2 million per
day (in 2015). By all accounts, the United States has given more
money to Israel than to any other country. The Congressional Research Service's conservative estimate of total cumulative US aid to
Israel (not adjusted for inflation) from 1949 through 2015 is $124.3
billion. I found that information on www.ifamereicansknew.org.

In an article by Michael B. Kelley entitled "Here's How Much
America REALLY Spends on Israel's Defense" dated September 20,
2012, he stated:

> Last week the Jerusalem Post reported that former
> Israeli's Defense Force (IDF) Commander-in-Chief
> Gabi Ashkenazi told a conference that U.S. taxpay-
> ers have contributed more to the Israeli defense
> budget than Israeli taxpayers in the past three years.
> This comment has been passed around everywhere.
> Alison Weir of Veterans News Now pointed out it
> was the first instance of an Israeli leader saying that

[93] John J. Mearsheimer and Stephen M. Walt, *The Israel Lobby and U.S. Foreign Policy.*

> U.S. taxpayers contribute more money to Israel's de-
> fense budget than Israeli taxpayers.

His article confirms the $3.7 billion per year but he noted that Israel still pays more for the entire Israeli military budget. To even have an article written about how much the United States supports such a vile country as Israel. That is money that should be given back to the hard-working United States citizens who "earned" it with their own sweat and time.

I also recently read that Israel has requested Congress to increase the budget for 2016. This American lie has to be ended. The American government is not for the American people.

I read sometime in 2013 about executive orders that were signed in the 1990's which allows big companies, like JP Morgan and Citibank to keep life insurance policies on employees no longer employed by them. Apparently, these companies do a weekly scan and match the ex-employee's social security number and collect life insurance dividends even when the person is no longer employed by that company. People are worth more dead than alive.

According to CNN, Bill and Hillary Clinton have earned a total of $153 million in lecture fees from addresses to pro-Israel organizations, including the Jewish National Fund (JNF), which directly participates in the ethnic cleansing of Palestinians and Bedouin citizens of Israel. An evaluation of Hillary Clinton's public disclosures from 2001 to 2015 shows that she and Bill, and their daughter, Chelsea, have earned roughly $4 million in speaking fees from pro-Israel organizations.

The National Security Agency "NSA" has records on all US citizens. The NSA also gathers information on anyone who might be of interest to any of the over 50,000 NSA agents. These agents are authorized by executive order to spy on anyone they deem of interest. The NSA has a permanent national security anti-terrorist surveillance network in place. This surveillance network is completely disguised and hidden from the general public. Tracking individuals in the US is easily and cost effectively implemented with the NSA's electronic surveillance network. This network covers the entire US and other parts of the world, involves tens of thousands of NSA personal, and tracks millions of persons simultaneously. NSA personal have quasi-public positions in our communities, and run cover businesses that can inform the intelligence community of persons of interest. NSA personal in the community tend to use occupations of social workers, lawyers and business owners as cover identities. Just a note, if you're an Rh negative individual and have had strange experiences with public officials, you may very well have been dealing with an undercover intelligence agent.

Chapter 16

Diseases, False Flags, Etc.

There have been generations upon generations of diseases. Many diseases were secretly brought into our society for population control. Of course, this has been going on for thousands of years. "Surely he shall deliver thee from the snare of the fowler, and from the noisome pestilence." (Psalm 91:3) The meaning for the word "noisome": 1. Having an extremely offensive smell. 2. Disagreeable; unpleasant. Synonyms: harmful, nasty, injurious, noxious, deleterious (which means causing harm or damage). The meaning for the word "pestilence": 1. A fatal epidemic disease, esp. bubonic plague. 2. A pernicious, evil influence or agent. Pernicious means: having a harmful effect, esp. in a gradual or subtle way. In my pursuit for truth, I even bought a Jan/Feb 2013 issue of Science Illustrated because it had "Top 10 of The World's Most Deadly Epidemics" on pages 54 and 55. And it just so happens this pestilence has been going on for thousands of years.

Measles dates back many centuries. Look up the statistics of deaths caused for last hundreds of years. The polio virus was first found in 1909 after an epidemic in Sweden in 1905. I don't know how it started in Sweden but I know this killing of innocent lives has been going on for centuries. There has been death and disease for centuries. Hence, for centuries people have been held on some type of bondage and it makes sense that this is the end of it. We have just been living with disease after disease for centuries. It has been complained about for hundreds of years. Jesus healed the diseased when he walked the earth. We don't know what laboratories these super geniuses may have had for probably hundreds more years than dates documented for discovery. They are super smart and super powerful. They've had this going on for centuries.

AIDS was brought into our society in 1981. A few men in New York and a few men in California suddenly came down with a disease never before known to mankind. The government said it was from monkeys. Homosexuality has been around forever and there were no people coming down with AIDS. The possibility of our government creating the disease in their secret laboratories and introducing it to an "undesirable" group of people for population control and more money generated from the medical field is very probable. Not surprisingly, it has affected Africa's population as well. Remove the people from land needed for others. Already, more than 30 million people around the world have died of AIDS-related diseases. In 2003, AIDS was the fifth leading cause of death in the United States among people twenty-five to forty-four, behind unintentional injuries, cancer, heart disease and suicide. This AIDS epidemic has been felt worldwide.

My brother Bobby is crying out to me, "Avenge my death." My brother's life partner, Chris, died from AIDS and my brother died from kidney failure due to treatment side effects of HIV. Bobby died alone in his apartment. He was only fifty-six years old. Worked all his life as a school teacher, never collected a dime of the Social Security he paid into since high school. He had no spouse or children so all that money went right back into the government's pockets. Confirming my enlightenment given to me by my deceased brother regarding the AIDS virus, I just saw Governor Jessie Ventura on a Howard Stern episode, recorded I believe sometime in 2011, and he stated he knows that two diseases in particular were created in the U.S. laboratories and introduced in the world. He stated AIDS and Lyme Disease. I feel Hep C as well. Then, just this morning, as soon as I woke up,

Chris, my brother Bobby's life partner who died from AIDS before Bobby passed away, told me to make sure I put that in my book. I wake up and there's Chris, smiling and happy but wanting to be vindicated. He was with me for about twenty minutes throughout the morning. I don't know where this telepathy came from. I just know it is real and has been happening since December 2012.

Why has homosexuality become so rampant involving children born in the 50's? Excessively gross statistics of child molestation. The government only knows that answer. Their DNA was altered during childhood? This behavior was written in the Word to become rampant:

> For this cause God gave them up unto vile affections: for even their women did change the natural use into that which is against nature; 27: And likewise also the men, leaving the natural use of the woman, burned in their lust one toward another; men with men working that which is unseemly, and receiving in themselves that recompense of their error which was meet.[94]

Could the medical industry make sure this happens by poking people with vaccinations geared to alter sexuality?

This is too rehearsed. Now we have millions of homosexuals, getting married. Oh yes, it is a revelation. All made up to fit the times. All been done over 2,000 years. Wait and watch. Wait and watch. Same movie, different channel.

Hepatitis C wasn't discovered until 1970. Again, a disease that is commonly found in "undesirable" drug addicts. Illnesses control population and make more money for the government. I was diagnosed with Hep C in 2006. I stumbled upon finding out. I had served twenty-three days in jail for violating my probation on a drug charge. When I got out, I was put on zero tolerance for six months. While

---

[94] Romans 1:26-27.

taking the weekly urine tests, my creatinine was low and I was accused of trying to alter my tests. Creatinine is a compound that is produced by metabolism of creatine and excreted in the urine. My program officer threatened to put me back in jail for three days. I was not altering my tests. I was going to meetings, jogging, really trying to stay clean. My attorney friend, Jack, suggested I go see a doctor to find out why the creatine level was so low. Because I shared my history of drug use with the doctor, unbeknownst to me he ordered a hepatitis blood panel. To this day, I have absolutely no discomfort or physical ailments due to Hep C.

I went to a specialist who immediately wanted to put me on treatment to cure it. Reading the side effects, probably fifteen in all, it was going to be a year of pure hell. Every patient gets at least three of the side effects. I decided that since I'm not sick, why make myself sick? I am just living with it. I am not inflicting my body to all the drugs necessary to remove something that is not bothering me. I was getting my liver monitored and all levels were in the normal range. An ultrasound revealed nothing abnormal in size or color of my liver. So why mess with the rest of my body? Medicine is not health.

There are numerous new flus discovered in the last twenty to thirty years as well. Where did they come from? Why didn't mosquitoes carry the West Nile virus hundreds of years ago? What is the flu shot? All vaccines and shots should be avoided. The vaccinations are loaded with mercury and other dangerous chemicals.

Cancer is so big that we all know about that disease. Many things are known to increase the risk of cancer, including tobacco use, certain infections, radiation, lack of physical activity, obesity, and environmental pollutants. All of these factors have been put into our lives since the turn of the twentieth century, but one factor was left out. There is a cure for cancer. David Noakes, a researcher, has promoted GcMAF which has been proven to cure cancer, and Big Pharma has continuously targeted him. GcMAF is a human protein all healthy people make that has twenty-one brilliant effects in the body including the most powerful seven attacks on cancer known to man. GcMAF turns cancer cells back into healthy cells. With no macrophages present, the cells cannot be eaten and destroyed, but GcMAF on its own, without the rest of the immune system, turns the cancer cells back into healthy cells. GcMAF has no side effects. Numerous studies have shown cannabis to cure cancer. David Icke just talked on his videocast in February 2015 about the wood of a grapevine that can cure all sorts of diseases and people can live decades longer than the average life span of today and that Big Pharma is creating it synthetically to sell in pill/drug form. Ironically, the packaging for the natural grapevine that David takes and sells on his website cannot list the uses and therapies it is useful for. It is against the "law" since it is a natural, herbal medication and not "BIG PHARMA." Cannabis has also been proven to cure cancer. Cannabis oil actually cures skin cancer. No wonder is it illegal in most of the United States.

The West Nile virus was first detected in the United States in 1999. The disease spreads to humans and animals via infected mosquitoes Mosquitoes become infected when they feed on infected birds. I remember learning about it sometime in 2006. That's how much I wasn't paying attention to the world, and I met a lady in 2011 who was paralyzed in one leg from the virus.

The new mosquito-carrying virus is "Zika" outbreak in Brazil, but facts are being disputed on this one. Obama has now asked Congress for $1.8 billion for mosquito control and of course, to create a "vaccine." Don't take any vaccines. They put toxic drugs in them and can even inject a microchip. There was the 2014 Ebola outbreak and now 2015 Zika outbreak. Interestingly, there was only $12 million spent on the investigation of the 9/11 event and $1.8 billion on a manufactured virus.

There was a television commercial I saw in 2013 or 2014 that said a thousand college students commit suicide every year. When did this dilemma begin? Are they being eliminated because their minds weren't moldable or are they the super geniuses that are not really dead and being transported and used for the future mankind? Suicides, people dying alone, how do we know they are not eliminations? Something goes wrong in their brain and they're eliminated. Suicides and deaths could be staged and those people living somewhere else, on a space station (there are many space stations being built by billionaires as well as governments) or another country, waiting for the northern hemisphere to be destroyed. There is definitely a conspiracy.

There were over seven mass murders in the United States in 2012 alone and that number has constantly gotten higher since 1999. On December 14, 2012, there was a supposed mass shooting in Newton, Connecticut. Twenty small children (twenty-six total deaths) were reported to have been slaughtered at Sandy Hook Elementary School. The mass murdering has been occurring worldwide. That American grade school class generated loosh all over the world. The principal of the school asked the children across the world to just make snowflakes. The amount of snowflakes received made by sad, low vibrational energy children and adults around the world was a great energy "crop". The school was bombarded with truckloads of snowflakes delivered from all over the world. All those children pouring out sadness thoughts. Saying to themselves, "I'm sure glad it wasn't me." The more loosh, the better. From the specials I've watched and articles I've read regarding the Sandy Hook (Hoax) mass murder, there were likely not even any children killed. It was all "false flag" actors and actresses (crisis actors), bought and paid for by the great United States government. One "witness" had three different versions of his story video recorded. The coroner was reported saying, "We can make anything look real." These mass murders are not just in America.

We humans have such a naturally greedy, selfish, self-important attitude. That bad gene can take over the kind genes in us and we can destroy each other. Who are these super genius bloodlines? I know they have been a part of our world since mankind started. There has been kings and queens from thousands of years ago, ruling the earth, generation to generation. David Icke did his research on the bloodlines of these rulers and it goes back a long, long time. These bloodlines are the rulers of today. It is too bad they got out of control, created greed and hatred. These persons have programmed us to work and pay into their pockets. Man has always worked. "Man goeth forth unto his work and his labor until the evening." (Psalm 104:23) Man's natural nature to work has been manipulated to produce money for our leaders. Today's wonderful technology has been used against us and hidden from us.

Abortion is used by many Americans. I had abortions and today am so very sorry for them. I pray for forgiveness for doing this. I know now they are wrong. This practice was also written about in the Word thousands of years ago. "For, behold, the days are coming, in which they shall say, Blessed are the barren, and the wombs that never bare, and the paps which never gave suck." (Luke 23:29) "Samaria shall become desolate; for she hath rebelled against her God; they shall fall by the sword; their infants shall be dashed in pieces, and their women with child shall be ripped up." (Hosea 13:17) Margaret Sanger, founder of Planned Parenthood, said in her own words, "The most merciful thing that a large family does one of its infant members is to kill it."[95] In her 1922 book, *Pivot of Civilization*, she wrote, "…human weeds, 'reckless breeders,' spawning….human beings who never should have been born," referring to blacks, immigrants and indigents, and poor people. Sanger exposed the thinking of eugenicists – similar to Darwin's "survival of the fittest" – but related the concept to human society, saying the genetic makeup of the poor and minorities, for example, was inferior.[96].

In 2015, it was reported that Planned Parenthood has been selling fetus limbs and organs in a black market for years. Planned Parenthood CEO Cecile Richards made a lot of public appearances in 2015 after her abortion business was caught selling aborted babies' body parts. Head of the largest abortion business in the U.S., Richards was forced to go on the defense as Americans called for the abortion giant to be

---

[95] Margaret Sanger, "Women and the New Race" (Eugenics Publ. Co. 1920, 1923)
[96] "Pivot of Civilization," by Sanger, 1922, p. 80.

investigated and defunded of more than a half-a-billion in taxpayer dollars each year. She testified before a U.S. Congressional committee and made numerous media appearances in an attempt to paint the abortion giant in a positive light. The Center for Medical Progress released its first video showing top Planned Parenthood employee Deborah Nucatola discussing how they crush and sell aborted babies' body parts as she ate lunch. Richards defended her abortion business in an interview with ABC News after the Center for Medical Progress released its first two undercover videos. The videos showed several top Planned Parenthood officials discussing the sale of aborted babies' body parts. Cecil Richards quoted, "Planned Parenthood has broken no laws. The healthcare and safety of our patients is our most important policy."

Every day I pray for the persons starving to death, who are cold because they have no heat, the captives in the ongoing sex slave operations, and all the poor children being held until they are used as sacrifices in the many rituals being done throughout the world. This is a worldwide problem and daily I pour out my prayers and hope to be able to somehow make a difference. This is not about me.

It is about us, our children and grandchildren and the future of mankind. There are thousands of adults and children reported missing every day in the United States alone. Every missing person has a story, has people missing them, loving them. All this creates negative energy. Negative energy is the most valuable loosh that can be harvested for the dark entities. In the summer of 2015, I googled statistics for missing children reported in the United States, a child being eighteen years old and younger. The number was staggering. It said in the last year alone (2015) over 700,000 were reported missing and only a little over 200,000 involved known family abductions, i.e., a mother or father steals the child from the other parent. Where are these children going? The government is doing its best to keep all this hidden from the public's eyes. In 2016 it was over 800,000 children reported missing.

There are children being born in homes from women held in captivity just for breeding these children to be used for almost daily rituals around the world. The children are delivered by midwives and since they are never put on a public record, there is no record of a missing child much less of the child ever being born. I pray for all their souls and pray that enough people becoming aware of what is going on behind closed doors will make a difference. There is so much that is going on and we are told, "Don't mind the man behind the curtain." Just go to work, pay your bills, get entertained…as long as it doesn't affect me personally, it doesn't matter. But it does matter. Infinite beings are from the infinite consciousness and we all just need to wake up and realize that all souls matter. Even just saying a prayer for them will heighten the vibrational level of our planet and open up more consciousness for many people. Prayer and meditation will definitely heighten your personal awareness and compassion.

The pedophilia is rampant. The atrocities being perpetrated every day on millions across this planet need to be exposed and stopped. I read two articles in 2015 regarding over 200 NASA workers caught ordering child pornography from a website in Europe with sex with children as young as three years old. Of course, the second article said that NASA was withholding the names of those government employees. The government covers it up because the government supports it. The CIA have "finders" books with names and addresses of children with descriptions etc. to go and grab these particular "high-dollar" children and sell them at auctions and use them for global prostitution, child pornography and, of course, the lovely "snuff" films for their weekly subscribers. Thousands of Syrian children have gone missing. Many children are also stolen for their organs. Global sex slave trafficking is a HUGE business. The children are used for trauma based mind control, sex, pornography, their organs, their blood, their flesh.

Probably half or more of humans are mixed with other species' DNA, particularly Reptilian DNA. I believe I have some. I don't know how to find out, but it would be interesting to know how many people are hybrids. Mankind has to open their minds and remember who they are. We have all had past lives. This is not our first rodeo. This is not the first time that man has evolved into a society such as this. This has all been done before. It is hard to sit back and just enjoy the ride when so many souls are being deceived and used. Yahuwah is revealing to his children the truth….there are many species mixed in with us humans here on planet Earth. This is an inter-dimensional world. We need to face that we are energy vibrating to a certain frequency and there are souls on other frequencies tied to this beautiful planet spirit. This is a spiritual battle and we have to get a warrior mentality. Yahuwah's "servants" are the best of the best. I was called Yahuwah's minion by my granddaughters' father when I told him in a text that I am Yahuwah's. He texted back, "You are Yahuwah's minion." Some may call me that and sometimes I feel like that, but I have faith and trust that this world can and will change.

Anything that breathes has a soul and that soul is energy. The energy of the soul is dispersed into the atmosphere and collected. All life on planet earth was created for this energy.

I've cried many, many tears in these last years. Finding out that mankind has been deceived for so many thousands of years has been the ultimate betrayal. Nothing else matters now, knowing that God uses people and lets them become afflicted. I just know if all this truth intuition had come many years ago, I would have directed my life differently. I know that I would have loved myself enough not to do drugs and would have got out of the self-destructive behavior way sooner. I'm sure if the controlling powers had their way, they wouldn't have anyone awaken to the truth. The fraud has been especially perpetrated on the westerners' beliefs. Uncle Sam is a big American con-artist. Land of the free, home of the brave. It is the land of cowards and secrets. Lies and deceit. The entire world has been deceived. The sheeple allowed it all to happen. If man doesn't get off his knees and take control for themselves, this cycle will never end. I know I was a sheeple in other lives. A perfect sheep with a pink studded color. I have thrown my collar into the fire and embrace critical, analytical thinking.

It is vital for humans to remember to breathe deeply for themselves. Our bodies are controlled by our energy. The breath is the symphony of the body. Proper oxygenation is vital to proper functioning of the body. The soul is energy and flows vibrationally through our bodies. Take control of something as simple as breathing. Maybe even only five or ten breaths, inhaling deeply, exhaling, feeling the air flow through your body. Open up the spinal cord. Remember the chakras. Mentally stimulate the pineal gland. This all helps to keep the connection with the higher dimension. I don't know if it's really higher since they are capable to keep mankind in servitude for all these thousands and thousands of years. Maybe I should call it the spiritual realm. All I know is that being out of this body is nothing to fear and will be going to another great experience and that the power of love is all that matters.

I only recently learned that there were three distinct brains that emerged successively in the course of human evolution and now cohabit the human skull. The reptilian brain (R-complex), the oldest of the three, controls the body's vital functions such as heart rate, breathing, body temperature, and balance. Our reptilian brain includes the main structures found in a reptile's brain: the brainstem and the cerebellum. The reptilian brain is reliable but tends to be somewhat rigid and compulsive. The R-complex brain is responsible for species-typical instinctual behaviors involved in aggression, dominance, territoriality, and ritual displays. The limbic brain emerged in the first mammals. It can record memories of behaviors that produced agreeable and disagreeable experiences, so it is responsible for what are called emotions in human beings. The main structures of the limbic brain are the hippocampus, the amygdala, and the hypothalamus. The limbic brain is the seat of the value judgments that we make, often unconsciously, that exert such a strong influence on behavior. The neocortex first assumed importance in primates and culminated in the human brain with its two large cerebral hemispheres that each play such a dominant role. These hemispheres have been responsible for the development of human language, abstract thought, imagination, and consciousness. The neocortex is flexible and has almost infinite learning abilities. The right and left cerebral hemispheres are connected by the corpus callosum. The left side deals with logic, language and reason. The right side deals with intuition and creativity. Many readers probably already knew this, but I did not and I thought it useful to share for those who do not know this. The human being has been evolving for probably a million years.

I had a dream about using drugs in July 2013. I actually used in that state. LOL. What a lesson I learned. The dream state was real. I was with a high school mate, David Buchanan, and we were sitting around a table waiting for the delivery. David is a person I went to high school with and graduated with in 1977. The drug delivery man showed up and threw an extra-large plastic bag with meth rocks in it and a pipe in each bag. I remember saying, "It's free. What do I have to lose?" and hitting that pipe and watching David put some in his pockets the way drug users will steal from each other. They take a little meth or crack and drop the liquid on their clothes. Then when it dries later, it can be scraped off and smoked again. I learned a huge lesson in that dream. No matter what, I can never again do drugs to alter my mind. I have deep regret for the years I spent wasting my time doing drugs. It is so strange how doing drugs makes you very much alone and now I am alone all the time and don't feel guilty for hiding any secrets. I have no secrets. Everything I do and have done is monitored anyway. It is possible that people being held against their will are given drugs to keep them complacent and controllable.

We experience life through the five senses, "the windows of the soul," and we're taught what capacity those senses have. Yet, each of them has a dimension that is many times deeper than what is normally perceived. Those dimensions will open for you as you move toward them. Meditation and deep breathing help to stimulate the pineal gland (the third eye in the middle forehead).

Technology is much more sophisticated than the common public is aware. I had birds flying into my window all the time back in 2013.

A bird landed on my screen in the kitchen window, stared at me for a minute, then flew away. At least two birds have crashed into my picture window in the living room. How can a bird tell a matter? A drone bird can. Yahuwah states which birds to eat and which birds to leave alone. There must be a reason why certain birds are to be left unharmed. "Curse not the king, no not in thy thought; and curse not the rich in thy bedchamber; for a bird of the air shall carry the voice, and that which hath wings shall tell the matter." (Ecclesiastes 10:20) Solomon has many verses of wisdom and I've read them all carefully and know that none of them were written without truths. Notice how he directs that a bird telling directly to matters of the kings (government) and rich people, all people in the world with money to expend on spy technology. After all, technology such as what is available today was created many times throughout the ancient years. The many satellites that have been around a long time can see a dime on your living room floor. A bird in the air can be metaphor for sound travel or an actual robotic bird. There's a billboard that shows a bumblebee with a camera on it with the slogan "Nature and technology coming together." It has been here just unbeknownst to the public, just like the mighty men of renown who have snuck in unawares and have taken control over every aspect of a person's life from cradle to grave. "For there are certain men crept in unawares, who were before of old ordained to this condemnation, ungodly men, turning the grace of our God into lasciviousness, and denying the only Lord God, and our Lord Jesus Christ." (Jude 4) This ungodly control has been going on for centuries:

> He sitteth in the lurking places of the villages: in the secret places doth he murder the innocent: his eyes are privily set against the poor. He lieth in wait secretly as a lion in his den: he lieth in wait to catch the poor: he doth catch the poor, when he draweth him into his net.[97]

---

[97] Psalm 10:8, 9.

Chapter 17

Food For Thought

When you depart this biological computer body, you are intercepted by the controllers in the fourth dimension and basically persuaded that you have to come back for another life. Realizing that you have a choice and being reunited with oneness is what they don't want you to know or do. There are other dimensions where they hold you until you come back to earth for another incarnation. Of course, if you choose to agree to come back without trickery, then that is your choice. The world is not a wonderful, happy place for many billions of people. Just because your life is comfortable does not mean there are not others without shelter and food. With all the wealth of the world, there should not even be poverty anymore.

The past, present and future are all one in the same. There is no time or space in the other dimensions. Many people believe dreams have no relevance. However, what most people do not know is that dreams are not just dreams but while sleeping the higher entities share information with you. Also, dreams can be planted in your head to deceive you. I have had very many dreams in the sleep state and images while meditating in the last few years. There are two very prophetic dreams in particular that I have to share. The first was a scene of a bunch of very happy people gathered together in what reminded me of people gathered together before they enter an event at an amusement park. As the place moved forward toward the sun or a very bright planet, a very loving being akin to Jesus Christ in front of all us asked, "So, are you ready?" All the people yelled and screamed, "Yessss!" There was no hatred, greed, guile or envy. We all knew what we were there for and were so happy to be leaving planet earth. Then we flew directly into the light and exploded into bliss.

In another dream, I was going through buildings akin to a street in New York City. I reached a particular building and went to the eighth floor. I walked in and the receptionist telepathically acknowledged me, turned to the office behind her, and said telepathically to the man in the room behind the desk, "She is here." I walked around the desk and into the office and telepathically the man with gray hair and beard said, "So you figured us out." In the dream, I perceived that the eight floors of the building were akin to eight lives I had lived or perhaps eight compartments my mind was put into during electroshock treatment as a child. I'm sure that telepathic communication is not far away. The Bible refers to dreams in many instances. One in particular that I think confirms that dreams are implanted is from the book of Job. Although the words were not from God nor Job but a friend of Job's, I believe there is relevance to higher powers being able to manipulate man through dreams. "In a dream, in a vision of the night, when deep sleep falleth upon men, in slumberings upon the bed; Then he openeth the ears of men, and sealeth their instruction." (Job 33:15-16) The Book of Enoch also has Enoch's dreams and visions. Scripture says Yahuwah spoke to Solomon in a dream and asked Solomon his heart's desire.

The plain truth is this is a prison planet, leaving all important spirituality from our earliest development, giving us the impression that this life is all there is or was or can be. This life and every lifetime is so important. Recognizing we are all spiritual beings on a human journey, and that we do not die, changes the perspective of most human beings. Nothing is taught about the soul and its power. The minds of mankind are trapped in anxiety, fear and oh, of course, vanity. Vanity is one of the top ten worst issues on this planet. The Bible refers to vanity many times, but when taught since early childhood how important the looks of the body are, how can one not become vain?

Also, I discovered all the television shows depicting people who are clinically dead and their stories of the experience. I did a book report in high school on people who were clinically dead and what they experienced. The books I read said they all went through a tunnel toward a light. The light was all loving kindness. Some say they saw deceased relatives. My mother had an emergency gall bladder operation. While on the operating table she almost died. She woke up with gray hair and attributed it to what happened to her while she was being operated on. She said Jesus came over a beautiful ocean and said, "Come on, Virginia. It's time to go." She said, "Oh no, I can't. I have a husband and five children to raise." He said, "OK, then I'll wait," and floated back up over the ocean. That was a hologram. Jesus never said he was going to float over an ocean to greet you when you go to the other side. At first I thought, *Well that confirms it. Jesus Christ does exist.* But now that I'm enlightened, it only confirms the use of holograms in man's minds throughout life and after this human experience as well. Nowhere in the Bible does it say that Jesus Christ will appear and take you personally to heaven upon departing this 3D reality.

A nun, Elizabeth Kuebler-Ross, wrote a book on experiences patients had at a hospital she worked at while they were clinically dead. All described pure bliss and a tunnel or tube. One story in particular about a very young boy who had a near death experience makes me sure that a lot is controlled after our deaths for people who don't know what to expect. He said that Jesus was with him. When the nun asked the parents if he had any religious upbringing, they replied, "No." How then would he know Jesus?

There are so many contradictions in the Bible, especially the New Testament. I certainly love Yahuwah more than anyone or anything on this planet, but we are taught to love thy neighbor as thyself. How much more a child loves their parents and parents love their children.

It is uncontrollable to love them so much, but according to Jesus Christ you can't love them more than him. Not many can live up to that. "He that loveth father or mother more than me is not worthy of me: and he that loveth son or daughter more than me is not worthy of me." (Matthew 10:37) Hence, after death they are shown their life and shown how they prayed to live with their family more than die and be with the Holy Father and are told they have to come back. It's all a headgame.

It also says in the same book of St. Matthew how easy it is to follow God's commandments, which is a straight out lie. Jesus says:

> Come unto me, all *ye* that labour and are heavy laden, and I will give you rest. Take my yoke upon you, and learn of me; for I am meek and lowly in heart; and ye shall find rest unto your souls. For my yoke is easy, and my burden is light.[98]

A bit hypnotic. The commandments of Yahuwah are so watered down in the New Testament. I read that there are three hundred errors in the Old Testament and three thousand errors in the New Testament of the King James "Version" (translation). Whoever believes that the Bible was not altered by man is a fool. Just because the Book of Revelation says a curse will be on anyone who subtracts or adds from the Book does not mean the entire Bible. The Book of Revelation wasn't in existence until a couple thousand years ago. That sentence pertains to the Book of Revelation only, not the entire Bible. There are so many translations of the Holy Bible, one would have to learn Hebrew and that might not even help.

The chemtrail program is an issue that needs to be addressed - all the chemtrails, every day, since I first observed them in 2012. I was walking the property and noticed the first chemtrails back in October and November of 2012. I started researching cloud seeding and chem-

---

[98] Matthew 11:28-30.

trails. The government and military have been controlling weather around the world for much longer than common people are aware. I am told the earth orbits the sun and that the earth is closest to the sun in the northern hemisphere's winter time. The earth orbits around the sun and due to the earth's axis, when earth circles nearest the sun, the northern hemisphere is closest to the sun. Hence, the need for man-made winters. Our planet is getting so hot; there were country-wide record-breaking statistics in 2012. The chemtrail planes have been quietly polluting our air with heavy metals for at least a couple decades. Global warming has been discussed without much media attention since the 1990s. The geo-engineering is a part of the secret government/military operations. Dane Wigington, a weather geo-engineering expert, has many YouTubes and a website (geoengineering-watch.org) exposing the massive geo-engineering, especially the chemtrails and the harm it is producing on the planet. He can give an in-depth presentation on the climate engineering issues and how critically this nefarious agenda is effecting life on earth.

A world of scientific discovery had already been being used before my birth - inventions and technologies that to this day I am unaware. "I wisdom dwell with prudence, and find out knowledge of witty inventions." (Proverbs 8:12) I was never taught that our weather can be controlled by man. I was taught that Mother Nature controlled it. The first cloud seeding was successful in 1946. Snow was made from the clouds. November of 2012 was the first I ever had even heard of cloud seeding, a form of weather modification. Operation Popeye was a program used in the Vietnam War during 1967 – 1972 and it extended the monsoon period by an average of thirty to forty-five days. China used weather modification for the 2008 Olympics to clear pollution. The United States and China have the most carbon emission, 40 percent polluting our planet. This important scientific discovery was not included in public school curriculum since its discovery and if it was, it very well could have been forgotten due to subliminal messages. I (born in 1959), my daughter (born in 1979), nor my daughters (born in 1989 and 1991) were ever taught about weather modification, i.e. cloud seeding, in school. Most of the American population is unaware of this cloud seeding today. Most people, if not every person I've asked about cloud seeding, have never heard of it. Why the big secret? Was it because of global warming and the power to manipulate weather to produce horrible disasters. I have to wonder if any of my weather growing up was truly from nature.

In 1952, London was almost destroyed from weather modifying experiments. Why is London always foggy? I believed it was a natural happening, but with all this extensive weather being modified today, secretly, how can a person know? There are generators changing the weather from the ground, planes flying overhead altering the clouds. This can't be good for Earth. This practice has been kept so secret from the public and has been going on for a very long time.

HAARP (High-frequency Active Auroral Research Program) is a program worth checking out. It is a weapon which is closely connected with Nikola Tesla's discoveries. HAARP is not just a one experimental station in Alaska. This program is also conducted by many laboratories, universities and other military facilities across the United States and other countries. It is widely known and stated in many publications that this weapon has an influence on the weather, earthquakes, and human brain. There are many YouTubes and books to be read regarding HAARP and its capabilities.

One Saturday in February 2013, the sky was a clear blue backdrop. There was not a cloud in the sky, only at least six planes flying in various directions overhead, leaving their chemtrails across the sky. Then two hours later in the sky, there were many clouds shaped into arch angels and locusts and whatever else they would want the mind to believe at the time of attack.

There has been thunder and lightning in the winter months the last few years. In 2014 it was so bad that I thought my home was getting bombed. Thunder and lightning in the winter! I remember a friend living in Kentucky told me about the fearsome storm there in

December 2013. CBS News had a story about the winter thunder and lightning. Not a usual phenomenon at all. The ability to control the weather is a little-believed reality.

Growing up I remember Malaysia as being a country with disease and death, not really giving much thought to why these people were left to die. Why did my government, with its massive quantity of American dollars, do nothing? Lower Africa's mortality death rate is forty to every thousand. In 2010 alone, 950,000 - almost 1 million women - died in childbirth in Africa. What happened to those babies? Millions have died in Africa since the AIDS epidemic was introduced into society in 1981. Indonesia lost almost 300,000 people from the Tsunami storm in 2004 and their death rate is still high. South America's death rate is nine in every thousand. All these countries are in the southern hemisphere. Are these people being wasted to make room for the chosen humans who can live there if the Northern Hemisphere is destroyed? "Their line is gone out through all the earth, and their words to the end of the world, in them hath he set a tabernacle for the sun." (Psalm 19:4) I've read articles about billionaires across the world investing in spaceships. Escape the catastrophe via flight off the planet. Live in space for a while.

Is the entire planet going to be destroyed for a time and people are going to live on space stations until it is habitual again? Is that why the world treasuries have been based on gold? Gold is more valuable to the higher powers than people and often spoken about in scripture. "More to be desired are they than gold, l yea, than much fine gold: sweeter also than honey and the honeycomb." (Psalm 19:10) Gold has been valued since the beginning of man. Our great King Solomon had much gold:

> Now the weight of gold that came to Solomon in one year was six hundred and threescore and six talents of gold. And King Solomon made two hundred targets of beaten gold: six hundred shekels of beaten

gold went to one target. And three hundred shields made he of beaten gold: three hundred shekels of gold went to one shield. And the king put them in the house of the forest of Lebanon.[99]

The Word has many references to gold. Gold is the most valuable resource for space exploration. Russia and Mexico alone bought $1 billion worth of gold in March 2012. Gold, in December 2012, was at an all-time high per gram in the United States. Gold rush is and has been on since the beginning of mankind on earth. There is also information regarding white powder gold, some kind of mono-atomic drink that some are drinking. This drinkable gold product is said to enhance longevity, health and vibrancy.

Death rates are huge in countries in the southern hemisphere. Life appears to be meaningless there. Perhaps it is because the land will be needed. Africa lost almost one million mothers in childbirth in 2010. Nobody cares. It is all planned. All the gold is being bought and used for spacecraft. There is also powdered gold. A guest on my show I broadcasted through Conscious Consumer Network, Winston Shrout answered a question a asked him. I told him back when I was watching television there was all these gold rush shows about digging for gold in the earth and in the oceans. I said isn't it amazing that gold has been harvested for thousands of years on mother Gaia and she never seems to run out. Winston shared that gold is actually biologically, naturally grown or regenerates on this planet.

So all the distraction with threats of world war III. When our planet collides into the sun and destroys much of the life on this planet, people will think it was a nuclear bomb and that the other countries did it. Southern hemisphere death rates are much higher than northern hemisphere death rates. Is this to make room for the people who will be needing land when they come out of their bunkers? Deep Underground Military Bases (DUMBs); Deep Un-

---

[99] 2 Chronicles 9:13,15,16.

derground Alien Bases (DUABs). They are real. This is not a joke. FEMA camps have been built. Just because the Nazis built the concentration camps, backed by bankers in other countries before they herded up the Jews does not mean they are meant to be used for the same purpose. These FEMA camps may be used for multiple purposes. The underground bases and secret underground cities built under many buildings are going to be used. Under the Denver Airport there is a deep underground base.

During a full moon in November 2012. I clearly saw two ships on either side of the moon. I remember saying, "If that is the international space station, it is huge." I took pictures and sent the picture to a few people. They saw exactly what I was talking about. In January or February 2013, I looked out at the full moon and could clearly see the same size formations on either side of the moon but then they were covered with a cloud. One was cigar- or submarine-shaped and the other oval. It was so obviously covered that I showed Brian, my boyfriend living with me at the time. He agreed that they were indeed suspicious looking clouds. There have been stars that I looked at with the binoculars and could clearly see them zig zagging back and forth. What I would see with the binoculars looked nothing like a star. Then one evening in June 2013, I was outside at dusk and a few "stars" appeared. When I looked at them with the binoculars they looked the same as the stars zig-zagging, but this time they clearly moved across the sky. They definitely were not stars but spaceships. There is always overhead activity all day and night long. Many times the aircraft can be heard and not seen or seen and not heard.

In July 2013, when Brian's grandsons came to stay at my house and property, one evening we had a fire and we ALL saw several "stars" moving in zig zag directions. Even Brian, who has such negativity about the possibility of UFOs couldn't deny what he saw. It is important not to associate fear with the extra-terrestrials. They are definitely smarter than most humans, but because we really do not die spiritually, there is nothing to fear. They may be able to kill our bodies but our souls live on. It is up to the individual where they go after this life. There are many dimensions beyond earth and the person who is aware of them while living can be prepared and aware that many of the other dimensions are traps for the soul to stay in enslavement.

There is a lot of different information written in this book. My main objective of this writing is to help people become aware, especially those who are waking up, that it has all been planned. They know who we are. We need to remember who we are. This is now become a learning game for me. Gathering as much knowledge about this world as a person can, but unfortunately not through the education system, through following higher consciousness and seeking alternative information. I believe the main objective of the mind control programs and the persons targeted for them are the persons who they knew were going to wake up. They are watching the process of our evolution and documenting everything. I feel the energies all around me. I see auras of people and energy vibrating through and around trees, flowers, etc. If we are all that has been, is and will be, then the future is already predicted. If we choose our own destiny, I refuse to consider myself a victim. I did dreadful and stupid things but I have been lucky enough to live long enough to understand the process and the agenda.

I realize that this is a war for the soul. We all have an infinite consciousness and only a handful of people are aware of it. I was studying this stuff during my teens and remember reading Shirley MacLaine books and watching her movie where she left her body and was held by a cord. There are even incidents in the Bible that refer to the cord, a silver cord. "Because he hath loosed my cord, and afflicted me, they have also let loose the bridle before me." (Job 30:10) This is the same cord that people exploring the meaning of our existence have described during their outer body experiences – experiences of being attached to a silver cord. "Or ever the silver cord be loosed, or the golden bowl be broken, or the pitcher be broken at the fountain, or the wheel broken at the cistern. Then shall the dust return to the earth as it was: and the spirit shall return unto God who gave it." (Ecclesiastes 12:6-7)

Edgar Cayce had an encounter with the Angel of Death while preparing to undergo one of his otherworldly journeys. Edgar Cayce had lost consciousness and had a dream. Usually, he would travel through a tunnel toward the light, but in this instance, he met the Angel of Death and learned about the silver cord. The following is his experience described in his own words:

> "As I went out, I realized that I had contacted Death, as a personality, as an individual or as a being. Realizing this, I remarked to Death: 'You are not as ordinarily pictured – with a black mask or hood, or as a skeleton, or like Father Time with the sickle, instead, you are fair, rose-cheeked, robust – and you have a pair of shears or scissors.'
>
> In fact, I had to look twice at the feet or limbs, or even at the body to see it take shape.
>
> The Angel of Death replied:
>
> "Yes, Death is not what many seem to think. It's not the horrible thing which is often pictured. Just a change – just a visit. The shears or scissors are indeed the implements most representative of life and death to man. These indeed unite by dividing – and divide by uniting. The cord does not, as usually thought, extend from the center – but is broken from the head, the forehead – that soft portion we see pulsate in the infant.
>
> Hence we see old people, unbeknown to themselves, gain strength from youth by kissing there; and youth gains wisdom by such kisses.
>
> Indeed the vibrations may be raised to such extent as to rekindle or reconnect the cord, even as the

Master did with the son of the widow of Nain. For
he did not take him by the hand (which was bound
to the body as was the custom of the day), but rather
stroked him on the head – and the body took life of
life itself! So, you see, the silver cord may be broken
– but the vibration…"[100]

I personally have had numerous out-of-body experiences without even
concentrating on having the experience. The first time I was frightened because I was not prepared for it. I remember it like yesterday. It
was an evening after dinner. I was out at my mom's, having moved back
in with her when I left my husband after he molested my niece. My
mom was out back working in her yard and I had laid down after clean-
ing up dinner dishes. I was just relaxing and then suddenly I heard lots
of electrical type wind. I floated out of my body to the Harrington
Hotel where I had a job in the bar, The Red Fox Tavern. I went
through the hotel lobby, up the stairs and down the hallway. I saw the
mirror at the end of the hall and was at Bobby's door (the guy I had already started dating right after leaving my husband). Then, just as suddenly, I was back in the bedroom. I could see the wallpaper and my
body lying on the bed. I remember saying to myself, *Sandy, you're going
to have a heart attack.* Then, as I was slipping back into my body, I heard
a female voice say three times, "You'll be back, you'll be back, you'll
be back." I jumped up off the bed and ran through the house.

My mother was just coming in the back door. She said, "Sandy,
what's the matter? You are as a white as a ghost."

I told her I thought I was going to have a heart attack I was so
frightened and proceeded to tell her what happened. I never will forget that incident.

I have also discovered that sleeping with the head facing north really
helps to expand astral dreaming (learning) and memory of the experiences become more consistent as a person concentrates immediately

---

[100] Edgar Cayce's Near Death Experiences 5. Cayce meets the angel of death

upon awakening what the dream experience was. There are lessons to be learned in our astral dreams, out of body experiences. Although some researchers proclaim that sleeping with the head to the north is dangerous, I personally found after making sure my head was directed to the north, that I had way more vivid and memorable astral dreams.

I don't bother trying to relax enough to have it happen again. My total focus is on gathering as much knowledge of this world and its lies and deceit, so I can do something about it in the afterlife. These multidimensionals are everywhere. Whether its entrapment by gods or aliens, it does not matter.

It is definitely going on today. Having out-of- body experiences and heightened telepathy are known byproducts of the mind control program.

There are dates and months that people are born that coincide with their behaviors. I noticed a pattern that most of the men I speak about that were key players in my mind control were born in May, Taurus. Tommy Byrnes, the biggest player in my mind control manipulation, was born September 9, 1966 (09091966). The religions teach that horoscopes go against God and leading their flocks from believing in energy alignments at birth. If we all have energy to be harvested during our lives and at the time the spirit leaves the body, why can't the energy field of the planet affect our personality characteristics? Dates are very important to the controlling aliens and the importance of the date of our birth is something that needs to be acknowledged globally.

Chapter 18

We Don't Die

Every day I meditate and more understanding comes to me. Meditation is never taught in church, yet scripture indicates the need to meditate and tap into our consciousness which takes us closer to God-consciousness and the infinite truth. "And Isaac went out to meditate in the field at the eventide: and he lifted up his eyes, and saw, and behold, the camels were coming." (Genesis 24:63)

In the third book of Moses, Leviticus, scripture describes booths that were built in which Yahuwah's people would go and meditate during the feast in July. I would imagine that these were solitary places for people to go and meditate and spiritually bond with Yahuwah.

> And ye shall take you on the first day the boughs of goodly trees, branches of palm trees, and the boughs of thick tress, and willows of the brook; and ye shall rejoice before the LORD [Yahuwah] your God seven days. Ye shall dwell in booths seven days; all that are Israelites born shall dwell in booths. That your generations may know that I made the children of Israel to dwell in booths, when I brought them out of the land of Egypt: I am the LORD [Yahuwah] your God.[101]

---

[101] Leviticus 23:40,42-43.

> And they found written in the law which the
> LORD [Yahuwah] had commanded by Moses, that
> the children of Israel should dwell in booths in the
> feast of the seventh month; And all the congregation
> of them that were come again out of the captivity
> made booths, and sat under the booths: for since the
> days of Jeshua the son of Nun unto that day had not
> the children of Israel done so. And there was very
> great gladness.[102]

Yahuwah is in space and is a spiritual being. "GOD [Yahuwah] *is* a Spirit: and they that worship him must worship *him* in spirit and in truth." (John 4:24) Without relaxing and breathing and meditating, it is almost impossible to hear his voice. "When I remember thee upon my bed, and meditate on thee in the night watches." (Psalm 63:6)

My biggest relief is knowing that I will never die. That I and all spiritual beings are immortal souls. We are souls being tried and tested in a prison-like planet. What a revelation to find out I've been in prison since birth. Imprisoned with lies and deceit. People say the luckiest people on earth live in the United States. The United States is one of the biggest culprits of manipulating man's thoughts and beliefs from birth. I am not proud to be an American. At fifty-three years old, I find out that most of my education was a lie. I worked so hard for that diploma, just to find out that what was taught in my history and government classes was manufactured. The United States is not the land of the free and the brave. In my opinion, it is the land of lies and cowards.

Throughout my entire life I have read the Bible. I now know that religions are there to keep people away from spirituality and under bondage of guilt. Although I don't label myself a Christian anymore, I have found truths in the Bible that have brought me closer to the God consciousness. The early holy ones were known as Elohim in

---

[102] Nehemiah 8:14,17.

Hebrew. These were the gods. Man has been manipulated to believe that this physical body and this incarnation is all there is or was or will be. Souls have been in existence for probably close to a million years and all that is happening today has been done before. Atlantis existed and was destroyed. Babylon existed and was destroyed. Many souls in this earth world today lived in bodies during those times. "That which hath been is now; and that which is to be hath already been; and God requireth that which is past." (Ecclesiastes 9:15) The controllers of the world know what souls are coming through and whose lives they can manipulate or destroy. I've also found evidence in the Bible dismissing the belief that man returns to dust. Yes, the body breaks down and returns to the dust but the soul lives on. Even the highly questionable New Testament has a verse stating that God is not the God of the dead but of the living. The soul lives on after death. It is undeniable. The Sadducees, asking about resurrection and whose wife a woman would be in heaven if she were married seven times in her lifetime:

> And Jesus answering said unto them, Do ye not therefore err, because ye know not the scriptures, neither the power of God? For when they shall rise from the dead, they neither marry, nor are given to marriage; but are as the angels which are in heaven. And as touching the dead, that they rise: have ye not read in the book of Moses, how in the bush God spake unto him, saying, I *am* the God of Abraham, and the God of Isaac, and the God of Jacob? He is not the God of the dead, but the God of the living; ye therefore do greatly err. (underline added)[103]

The body dies but the soul is resurrected into the higher dimensions. "Your father Abraham rejoiced to see my day: and he saw it, and was

---

[103] Mark 12:24-26.

glad." (John 8:56) So Abraham rejoiced at the birth of our Savior, Jesus Christ, Yahushua. If he rejoiced, he is not dead but alive in the heavens.

There are multiple heavens (dimensions) as Yahuwah is in the heaven above the heavens. "In my Father's house are many mansions; if it were not so, I would have told you. I go to prepare a place for you." (John 14:2) It is so important at this time in the world to wake up and truly repent of wrongdoings. I've read the Bible and there are revelations that are happening today. The Bible has an agenda and it must come true. There is going to be a drastic climate change. It is going to happen to depopulate the planet. What an appropriate way to destroy many peoples than by the sun. With all the Sunday worship, it makes total sense that Yahuwah would use the sun.

I know that sounds farfetched, but look at the world today and look how individual spiritualism is suppressed. How can I explain all the out-of-body experiences (dreams) that I know actually happened? Our memories are constantly being altered and erased. It's virtual torture. Realizing all the sheeple follow one another blindly. This has all been done before. Many have already been implanted in one way or another. There is no privacy for anyone. Many persons are being watched by the fourth dimension as well as by government surveillance. Every website we go to is monitored. Anybody who is awakened and realizes what is really going on is being watched. All the blinking towers (they are everywhere) emit many frequencies to disrupt our thoughts and emotions. The intelligence of the prison wardens is incredible.

Every time I pray and mediate and come in contact with the other dimensions, my nasal passages will twitch and click. I often feel my hair move and something near my back or wispy webs along my arms. My heart will start to beat rapidly and I feel chilly air around me. The five senses cannot perceive the spiritual beings all around, but the sixth sense can. Mankind's perception is very limited in this human existence. Only a quarter of the energy that surrounds us is perceived by the five senses. Our DNA is made that way, and then our bodies are bombarded with electromagnetic waves and poisonous foods to hinder any infinite awareness or desire for infinite awareness. I am saying that infinite awareness does not lie, but time, prayer, and meditation are the avenues to tap into all the beautiful truth vibrations.

A beautiful book I read by Brian L. Weiss called *Many Masters, Many Lives* reveals the truth to our everlasting existence. Brian is a psychiatrist who felt compelled to write his book after his experience with a client. After he hypnotized her, he found that she was able to recall other lives and experiences between lives. She tells about the "masters" who would greet her between lives. There is so much evidence to the fact that we don't die. There are many testimonies from near death experiences and out of body experiences.

If we don't die, then all is accounted for. Everything we do or don't do in this lifetime is written in the universe. Since people do not know this, and it all comes back to them at the time of leaving the biological body, the feeling of guilt overwhelms them and they stay on a lower plateau and agree to come back for another incarnation. "But I say unto you, That every idle word that men shall speak, they shall give account thereof in the day of judgment. 37: For by thy words thou shalt be justified, and by thy words thou shalt be condemned." (Matthew 12:36-37) Are we going to wake up and stand up and not be afraid to open our minds to other avenues, even if it challenges our "belief" systems? To realize that this is one of the most exciting privileges to be alive and awake, functioning in the matrix, indestructible, because we don't die, thus, all that we learn and share with Source is valuable to the creative energy of the universe. It does not mean we have to love our God Source any less. We love him more because he has chosen us. He let us wake up. I am so eternally grateful to know my redemption is here. The following paragraphs ending this chapter are a little article I wrote and shared on my website in early 2017.

It was a summer day in 2013 that I sat on the hill overlooking a beautiful pond surrounded by birch and oak trees on the back of the 20 acres property I had owned when I heard a voice. The sun was setting through beautiful clouds and the sky was almost apricot in color. The voice was clear and full of authority, call it my higher spirit, God, Yahuwah, Yahushua, Gaia, it doesn't matter. I had been sitting on the hill sobbing, tears running down my face, a small droplet of snot began running down from my nose. My stomach was heaving up and down with pains of sorrow and empathy for the all the evil in the world (especially the children being held against their wills in global sex slave rings). I had just put my head down between my legs and wiped my face on my jeans. Then, clear as a bell ringing, I heard, the voice "Sandy, Look Up, look up, your *Redemption* is here." I said WOW! This is big. I've gotten clear messages before but this one was different.

I kept hearing those words over and over in my head. Sandy, your redemption is here. Sandy, your redemption is here. Inner voices were telling me "Open your eyes Sandy, redemption's not far. Remember who you are." I contemplated redemption and its meaning, its origins, so I googled the definition of redemption. This is what was received:

Google definition:
re-demp-tion
/R dem(p)SH( )n/
Noun

1. the action of saving or being saved from sin, error or evil; "God's plans for the redemption of this world" *synonyms*: saving, freeing from sin, absolution
    "God's redemption of his people"
    -   A thing that saves someone from error or evil
2. the action of regaining or gaining possession of something in exchange for payment, or clearing a debt
    synonyms: retrieval, recovery, reclamation, repression, return archaic
    the action of buying one's freedom

Origin:
LATIN – buy back

ENGLISH – redeem
LATE MIDDLE ENGLISH – redemption

Redemption / Definition of Redemption by Merriam-Webster
www.merriam-webster.com/dictionary/redemption

Simple Definition of redemption: the act of making something better or more acceptable : the act of exchanging something for money, an award, etc. Christianity : the act of saving people from sin and evil " the fact of being saved from sin or evil.

Redemption / Define Redemption at Dictionary.com
www.dictionary.com/browse/redemption
1. an act of redeeming or atoning for a fault or mistake, or the state of being released.
2. deliverance, rescue...atonement for guilt

So immediately after I read the definition for redemption, it was clear to me that there are two beautiful experiences that the word redemption represents. Some people relate redemption only to the religious concept but have no clue of the connotation that redemption also means taking control of something...reclaiming, fulfilling a contract. My awareness quickened as memories flooded in and spiritual contact became an everyday occurrence.

The words redemption, redeem, redeemable, redeemer, redeeming appear 139 times in the KJV Bible per Christian Apologetics & Research Ministry (CARM) www.carm.org.

Luke 21:25-28: 25: And there will be signs in the sun and in the moon and in the stars; and upon the earth distress of nations, with perplexity because of the roaring of the sea and the waves, 26: Men's hearts failing them for fear, and for looking after those things which are coming on the earth; for the powers of the heavens shall be shaken. 27: And then shall they see the Son of Man coming in a cloud with power and great glory. 28: **And when these things begin to come to pass, then look up, and lift up your heads; for your redemption is drawing near.** (bold emphasis added)

Redemption means to free someone from bondage. It often involves the paying of a ransom, a price that makes redemption possible. Christians beLIEve that redemption is only achieved through the blood shed by Jesus Christ/Yahushua. Yes, he did die for the forgiveness of our sins and redemption of our souls. We are redeemed. Accept redemption. We are all that was, is, and can be. We are all possibility. A destiny of redemption isn't just for me. It is for ALL who want to be free. UNIVERSE is just waiting for us to open our eyes to all there is to see.

So, if my redemption is here, why can't your redemption be here as well? The following is a little affirmation that I say:

I am redeemed under the authority of Yahuwah's and Yahushua's names and acknowledge that Yahushua is my salvation and that I am and have always been saved. I am not waiting on a savior to take me to heaven. I am claiming my redemption and reclaiming ownership of my soul. I am sovereign. I don't want to rule, and I don't want to be ruled. I want friends. Infinite BROTHERS/SISTERS in divine bliss; with truth, love, liberty, knowledge, learning, safety, creativity, imagination and PEACE. I will not accept the things I cannot change; I WILL CHANGE the things I CANNOT ACCEPT. I will serve in an army of righteousness, yes I will be a servant to truth, liberty and justice for ALL.

All contracts are now fulfilled and if they are not fulfilled the contracts are null and void and no longer hold any authority over my soul. My soul is free from any bonds or contracts previously agreed upon. I ask the spirit guides, archangels or higher selves to now cut the cords to all souls tied to me who choose to serve the darkness rather than the light and choose to continue in their malevolent ways. Please cut the ethereal and energy cords and throw them into the abyss. So it is DONE. Thank you UNIverse. Gratitude and love for the ALL the lessons I learned in your school called Earth, but now it is time for the CHANGE.

It's time to LOOK UP, LOOK UP, YOUR REDEMPTION IS HERE!!!!

Our contracts are fulfilled. The 26,000 tour of service ends in this incarnation. My goodness, there are 4,200 known religions per Google. All you do is ask how many religions there are in the world and 4,200 is what "she" says. Technology is a tool for both good and evil. Those that have been held in the vice of the perpetual hamster wheel of life and death....in the illusion of death...in the illusion of birth...claim your REDEMPTION. Be joyful and happy as there is no death, only getting over the finish line and completing the game. I will reiterate this forever "The best part of my awakening is the KNOWING that there is no such thing as death." We take with us all our wisdom, knowledge, understanding and information. Consciousness/subconsciousness is energy and energy cannot be destroyed only transferred or contained. Get out of the Earth school Matrix. We come in to play, but "they" have a cheat sheet. Remember, there is nothing new under the sun. We have all been through this before. It's time for a [r]Evolution of the soul and mind. Open our minds, awake our awareness. Reclaim our souls I don't know who taught me this prayer, but I prayed it as young as two-years old. "Now I lay me down to sleep. I pray the Lord my soul to KEEP. If I should die before I wake. I pray the Lord my soul to TAKE." What? Brainwashed to give my soul to a LORD I know nothing about except through religion brainwashing. I would pray that and then turn and have sex with my cousin and brother and other older boys. Everything being filmed. It was sickening how much and how often and the things I did at such a young age. Night after night, year after year. It's all I knew. Anyway, bits and pieces of my trauma will come out in my articles but I have an entire book that shares in the best chronological order some of things I went through.

Many are afraid to proclaim their redemption. There are those who hold on so tightly to their servitude and slavery to the corrupt system that they demand to be governed and ruled. Those are the ones who choose to put their head in the sand and never look up. To them ignor[ance] is indeed bliss. But to the many that are awakening and realizing that we have been exploited for our energy and money, I say proclaim your redemption. Know that you can reclaim your soul/spirit and return to Source and get reunited with your higher selves.

Here's to meeting at the cast party. Glad you are on my Ride!

Chapter 19

The Illusion Factor

I keep repeating Albert Einstein's words, "Reality is merely an illusion, albeit a very persistent one," or David Icke's words, "Infinite love is the only truth. Everything else is illusion."

I, as many others, know that ultimately, infinite love is the only truth. Everything else is an illusion. I looked up the word *illusion* at dictionary.search.yahoo.com and found the following definition: "1. An erroneous perception of reality. 2. An erroneous concept or belief. 3. The condition of being deceived by a false perception or belief." My first interpretation of the word *illusion* was that the world itself is being generated as a false perception, but looking at the definition it clearly is the perception of our reality that is false. Our perception is that this life is all there is. All Christian religions teach us that reincarnation is against believing in Yahuwah. This is another hypocrisy to keep the sheeple under control. A mind control victim is under the illusion that they are making their own decisions. Now that my programming has broken down, I am positive that I have been controlled by governmental aliens and the freemasons. I hope to be able to outline this in such a way that makes it clear so that I can somehow help others who have been manipulated and used their entire lives.

I love this quote from Bill Hicks:

This is where we are at right now, as a whole. No one is left out of the loop. We are experiencing a reality based on a thin veneer of lies and illusions. A world where greed is our God and wisdom is sin, where division is key and unity is fantasy, where the ego-driven cleverness of the mind is praised, rather than the intelligence of the heart.[104]

Every American I meet knows the famous saying, "All you have to do is die and pay taxes." No, you do not die. My seeking wisdom and truth has only just begun in this human experience. My quest for truth and freedom will go on into the other dimensions and that is why I find this so important. This is for all the starving people around the world. Twenty thousand people a day worldwide die from starvation. This pathetic world still has people starving to death. There are people waiting at the dumpster for their next meal. There are people that are homeless, cold and frightened.

There are sex slave victims and sacrifice victims. To the thousands of persons reported missing every day across the world, this is for all the victims of 9/11. Anyone with half a brain can tell by the evidence that that was an inside job. Yet, I've been practically thrown out of bars for saying that. Do your homework. There were explosives heard and military explosive powders in the debris. Why did the third tower fall? Follow the money trail by owner Silverstein and his insurance scam. The perfect problem-reaction-solution. There are whole books written on that scam and many videos, and I've read a few and watched many videos. Those persons killed that morning were just collateral damage. Millions have been killed since in countries that the hijackers were not even from. The supposed hijackers were from Saudi Arabia. There possibly weren't even any planes since drones were already being used by the military way before 2001. The Pentagon's hole was not even wide enough to have a plane with wings. It

104

had to have been a missile. Interestingly, the Pentagon had been reported just the day before 9/11/2001 to be missing over 6 trillion dollars and were going to be audited for the missing money. No more paperwork, no audit for the bombing of the Pentagon. Not much is said about the missing money or the endless wars causing so much death, fear and sadness. This is a prison planet, and mankind must wake up to this fact in order to make a change.

We need to open our eyes, our inner eyes. There are those with perfectly good eyesight yet are blind inside. To restore sight to the blind is not to the literal blind but to those blinded by hypocrisy and lies.

> To open the blind eyes, to bring out the prisoners
> from the prison, and them that sit in darkness out of
> the prison house. 8: I am the LORD [Yahuwah]; that
> is my name: and my glory will I not give to another,
> neither my praise to graven images. 16: And I will
> bring the blind by a way that they knew not; I will
> lead them in paths that they have not known: I will
> make darkness light before them, and crooked
> things straight. These things will I do unto them,
> and not forsake them.[105]

The illusion is that we people are weak and powerless. Every soul on this planet is all possibility. The illusion is the deception programmed into each individual from birth. Children are taught that parents can lie. Santa Claus, the Easter Bunny, all being fed to our children from their parents and society. This conditions the child to just take lies with a grain of salt. American children, as I am sure in other countries are programmed to believe the government is necessary for existence. Once one is awakened to this massive lie, the illusion begins to dissolve.

I am writing this to make a difference with the true incidents of my childhood and throughout my life. I am nothing like the person I

---

[105] Isaiah 42:7-8,16.

was. During a David Icke video, he says, "What are you going to say to your children and grandchildren when they ask, 'Mommy, Daddy, what were you doing while all this truth awakening happened?'" During my daily meditations, I keep getting led to write it all down. It does make a difference. Why didn't this awakening happen when I lived in New York City? I lived there for sixteen years. I have lived in California, Alabama, and South Carolina as well. I have traveled over forty states of America and have been to Mexico, Jamaica, Canada and England.

A message from David Icke in his last book The Phantom Self goes something like this. We are wavelength, electro-magnetic, digital, mathematical, holographic, infinite awareness having a human experience. I don't have the book anymore, as I borrowed it, but I always have remembered reading that and it really makes sense to me and I wanted to share that. We are spiritual beings having a human experience, ah experiment, no its supposed to be experience.

An incident happened in Clare County, Lake, Michigan in February 2015. I watched a cloud grow up from the ground over the trees as I was doing dishes that morning, looking out the window to the west of my property. I thought there was a fire as the cloud looked like it could be a smoke cloud. I listened for sirens. Then I dried my hands, grabbed my phone, and took a picture. Later that day, when I sat down and zoomed in on the picture, it became apparent it was some type of ship. The picture showed above this cloud plume eight lights and the shape of an oval type ship with a hatch on the top. It is true that holograms are released to disguise a ship in the sky. Many UFOers say that Michigan is known for its many alien stations especially in the Great Lakes. Others have seen ships up there and that wasn't the only ship I saw in my three years at that property. Does this belong in the illusion chapter? I don't know but I wanted to share it. The picture was taken through the window so no possibility of sunlight glare. I have the picture below, but I have shown others and they could clearly see what I saw.

The cloud mushroom grew from below to rise above the trees. There are eight lights above and the shape of the ship.

Chapter 20

My Spiritual Contacts (Several of at Least Thirty)

This is an amazing story that I have to share. I met Elliott Haines III at Serpent Mound Spring Seed and Water Peace Summit weekend of March 17-20, 2017. Elliott and I talked and shared some time together. During a conversation I told him I thought he has a spirit by him. He said maybe it is Patrick. Elliott explained that he knew someone who was killed on the USS Cole. Elliott explained that Patrick was like the step-son of his heart. I said it is definitely a male. Before the event ended Elliott and I exchanged telephone numbers.

A few days after the event I called Elliott and we were talking on the telephone. He brought up Patrick Howard Roy and my throat tightened and hair stood up on my arms and the air changed. I said to Elliott, Patrick is here. Through that communication Patrick indicated to me he was very young when he was murdered. I said to Elliott, he wasn't 20 years old yet. Elliott confirmed that Patrick died at 19 years old, 7 months and 6 days. Patrick also showed me 36 and I perceived that to be his age today and Elliott confirmed that he turned 36 this March. Then I said the 3 and 6 is also his birth month and day and Elliott confirmed that that he was born 03/06/1981. It was shown the date of the attack, 10-12-2000 on the USS Cole and the supposed terrorist attack on the Twin Towers in New York City on 9-11-2001, are one digit difference for the month, day and year of the attacks.

A couple weeks later I went to Elliott's home in West Virginia. On April 8, 2017, I was in Elliott's living room when an orb came flying across the room and stood in the foyer and I could see the shape of a man manifest in front of my eyes. One of the first times I actually saw the outline of the spirit that was communicating with me. I called Elliott from his room and told him Patrick was here. Well what Patrick shared with me was amazing. All he shared with me proved true when I watched the docudrama that is available on YouTube. Patrick said that the USS Cole was never blown up by terrorists in a boat. He showed me a panel on the inside of the boat where the explosives were placed. He showed the hole in the middle side of the ship, which was very small. When I asked Elliott about that he said the ship had a huge amount of damage and almost sank. Elliott said that the news showed a huge amount of damage when he watched the media coverage back in 2000. But when I watched the docudrama, "Untold Story of the USS Cole (Docudrama), the picture of the hole was exactly what Patrick showed. I mean Patrick showed me that same image of the picture shared on the docudrama of the damage on the ship. Then Patrick showed me his coffin, closed with a flag over it. I said to Elliott "You never viewed Patrick's body?" Elliott said no, the family NEVER saw Patrick's body. Elliott said that the Navy told Patrick's family that Patrick's body was one of the last that was recovered. That blew my mind since Patrick was indicating to me that there was malicious activity. Patrick was telling me that he never died on that ship. Now this is going to sound far-fetched but he showed me Mars. Not sure yet exactly what Patrick was trying to tell me. It feels to me that Patrick and some others were taken to Mars. While watching the docudrama, it was revealed that the USS Cole went missing for 55 days after leaving Norfolk, Virginia in August 2000 until it showed up in Yemen on 10-12-2000. The route to Yemen was less than 7,000 miles.

It is apparent that the USS Cole was another false flag attack orchestrated by the Elite to prepare the public for the 9-11-2001 "terrorist" attack. It is a forgotten tragedy. Patrick indicated to me that he wants his family and countrymen to know the truth about the USS Cole. If you think the idea of forcing men and women to go to Mars is not possible, Laura Magdalene Eisenhower was invited to go to Mars in 2006. The USS Cole tragedy was only 6 years previous to Laura's invitation. Let's not forget about the Philadelphia Experiment and all the other ships involved in false flag operations to instigate war.

The most recent profound spiritual contact I have had was with Sonny Bono. He came clear as day in February 2016. He knew my skepticism so he said, "Sandy, I was born in the age of Aquarius." He said, "They said I died in 1998 (January 5, 1998) but I really died in 2001." He indicated he was murdered. I looked up his info and he was born February 16, 1935...Aquarius in Detroit, Michigan. The same city, and state as my mother was born. She was born October 14, 1932. He showed me the mind control was going on back then with children, himself, and my mother. He showed me the peace sign. Sonny and Cher were pushing the peace sign in the 1960's. He said that the symbol inside the sign should be facing upwards rather than downwards. That by placing it upside down it is a sign for death, hatred, power, greed and death. He simply confirmed that everything is backwards and the importance of symbology to confuse the masses. After this encounter with Sonny, I looked up and found a lot of information about the peace symbol. It is an ancient symbol and the inside is a cross with broken arms. Apparently, the cross with broken arms inside should be facing upward to signify love, harmony, etc. The supposed reason for putting the peace symbol into our minds in 1958 was for nuclear disarmament but the symbol used against Christians goes back thousands of years.

Whitney Houston has come through two times. The higher powers planned and set her up with drug addiction, killed her before she woke up. She said, "Tell MiMi I'm sorry." After she was there, then gone, I thought she meant MiMi was her mother. I wondered to myself if I had ever heard Whitney's mother's name. Then a few days later, while meditating about and pondering my drug abuse, Whitney came through again. She said to include this in my book. She knew that I was doubting her presence and said, "Ask MiMi about the yellow dress." She indicated to me that MiMi would know from the yellow dress incident it was indeed Whitney. Whitney wanted me to tell MiMi that she is alive and well. Trapped, but alive and well. I can only relay what was said to me. If there is any way to get a message to MiMi and ask her if a yellow dress would mean anything between herself and Whitney, I'd love to know. Of course, because of all this mind control all my life, I'm still questioning whether people are really coming through or just my imagination. I was always amazed through my life how someone as famous and wealthy as Whitney Houston couldn't get off drugs. She said to me, all telepathically of course, that they know who is coming through and they set people up for failure with weaknesses known about that person from other lives.

Having been a drug addict myself, when the energy flows through my body and I feel the higher dimension, it is very similar to taking a hit from drugs. That is why people like Whitney and myself were so addicted to drugs. It is so amazing when the energy force comes through. The heart starts racing, you can feel the energy around like cobwebs touching the arms and head. Taking a hit of crack cocaine can give very similar experiences. A good way to keep enlightened souls suppressed is to have them become drug addicts. The words sung by the late and wonderful Whitney Houston's song "The Greatest Love Of All" was written by composers Michael Masser (music) and Linda Creed (lyrics). It was originally recorded in 1977 by George Benson:

I believe the children are our future
Teach them well and let them lead the way
Show them all the beauty they possess inside
Give them a sense of pride to make it easier
Let the children's laughter remind us how we used to be

Everybody searching for a hero
People need someone to look up to
I never found anyone who fulfill my needs
A lonely place to be
So I learned to depend on me
I decided long ago, never to walk in anyone's shadows
If I fail, if I succeed
At least I'll live as I believe
No matter what they take from me
They can't take away my dignity
Because the greatest love of all
Is happening to me
I found the greatest love of all
Inside of me
The greatest love of all
Is easy to achieve
Learning to love yourself
It is the greatest love of all

Sometime in May 2014 a friend of my ex-husband Tommy, Michael DePrineo, came to me. He appeared in my mind smiling with the same type of T-shirt type clothing and curly hair I remember him having. His nickname was Boo. The communication was clear and strong. I was a passenger on a beautiful Saturday morning drive. It was so clear and so real. I was like, "Hey, Boo, wow! Didn't expect you." (All telepathically, of course.) He asked me to tell Debbie (who I acknowledged as his wife), Michael Jr. (his son), and his daughter that he was alive and watching them. I said (telepathically), "Oh, Boo, I don't remember your daughter's name." He showed me Nikki on the left of my mind and Mia on the right. I said (all telepathically), "I really can't remember, Boo. How will I be able to relate your visit if I don't have your daughter's name?" Then the next day around the same time, he appeared again and said, "No, no, her name is Nina." Part of the name

Nikki and part of the name Mia spells Nina. I nervously texted my ex-husband and asked him if Boo Boo's daughter was named Nina. He said yes. I didn't want to ask Tommy what her name was. I wanted to confirm the name given to me. It was Nina. I have absolutely nothing to gain by making this up. He said that there are many in the other dimensions watching us. and they are being taught from what people on earth are learning about the falsehoods of this world and the world governments. He didn't know that the world was such a lie when he departed this existence but has since been watching and learning. He indicated he was killed by an induced heart attack by the TPTB. He was only in his forties. He is very interested in this world still since his children are here. He said to tell Tommy hello, and he acknowledged Tommy's young son Thomas, Jr. He told me to tell Tommy this world is not what it appears to be. I told Tommy that Boo Boo had a message.

Tommy said, "What, that he's out of rolling paper?" I laughed and said Boo would love that response and to give me a call if he wanted to know. I didn't hear from him again until a few months before Thanksgiving weekend of that same year. Many people don't want to believe that the soul never ever dies even though the body does.

I have had contact with Michael many times since that first incident. It was through Michael that I met Tommy. Michael was dealing coke and Tommy was one of his runners. I got Michael's number and ordered a gram and Tommy delivered it. I was immediately attracted to Tommy. I had no idea all these years that Tommy was brought into my life deliberately to distort my life. Now I know why Tommy didn't want to hear what Michael had to say, because Tommy works for the government.

When I met Tommy, he was an apprentice for the elevators. After we got together, he was laid off and went to other jobs. One year he had at least five jobs. All the time with Tommy, I was the main breadwinner. After we got divorced, he got back into the elevator union. Then he got a job working for the city of New York as an elevator repair inspector. Now he has a job with Con Edison and says there are sixty elevators that he is working on maintaining. He drives a fancy car and has loads of money. He says he is very good at what he does. He has manipulated me since the day I met him.

While visiting in New York over Thanksgiving weekend, I asked him what his new baby was going to be. He pointed at our daughter Michelle and said, "One of those". The feminine spirits are especially hated by the aliens and the Freemasons. Women are just sex toys to aliens and most men. The Catholic Church only in the 1500s acknowledged that women have souls. Now I have three daughters and two grandchildren in this world. I can only pray for their souls. They are so deeply imbedded in this manipulation and they have no clue. Sorry, I got off the spiritual contact. Below are a few more I'd like to share.

I had a communication with John Lennon. He came through and, of course, this is all telepathically, so it comes through in thoughts to my energy. The spirits lower their vibrations and I raise mine and we get a connection. Please keep in mind I was never a big Beatles or John Lennon fan in the past. I knew very little about John Lennon before this communication. Prior to this remarkable communication I had been noticing a spirit around and felt like it was the presence of John Lennon. Every store I would go into or whenever I turned the radio on, the song "Imagine" by John Lennon would play. That was for about two weeks before this happened out of the blue in my living room around 11:30 at night.

This is the first time we communicated. I have had numerous communications with others, and before John came through my brother-in-law, Jessie Parker came, which is not uncommon to me. Jessie is a Vietnam vet and he asked me to please forward a message to his children, my nephews, and nieces. He wanted me to tell his son Thomas that Grandpa is with his daughter. I couldn't remember his granddaughter's name as she had passed over about eight years ago. He told me her name was Maddy. By relaying the message, I was told her name is Madison. That is least ten communications that included names I had never known or couldn't remember. They each turned out to be the names of the persons I was acknowledging from the spirit or the names of the spirits themselves.

Then all around Jessie, I felt spirits of Vietnam soldiers and then John Lennon's spirit was there. They all were cheering for John and saying, "John is leading us. He's our hero."

I could feel the spirits' energies saying, "We were drafted, forced to go to war and be slaughtered." Project Popeye, Agent Orange, some false flag event (I now know as Gulf of Tonkin) all flowing from them.

So during John's communication, he showed me a man, John Lennon. I was like, "Okay, that's your son." He was right. I thought at that time he was showing me Julian and that I had the name wrong, as I had heard he had two sons.

Then I saw a picture of him playing in water with a boy and he said, "Sean." I was like, "That's right, I recognize him." It was a dark-haired boy that I recognized from pictures of Sean in magazines. He was adamant on showing all the water fun and swimming.

Then an image of a third person. He said, "My son Julian," and they were in a music studio with him playing the guitar.

I was like, "John, you're showing me three sons."

He said, "Yes, yes, that's right. I was only forty when they killed me. You're still in the material world and can communicate to my children, to all the children how important it is to wake up." He was so excited to be able to communicate so clearly with someone still in this dimension.

I said, "Why me?"

He said, "Because I have been watching you and see how you have no fear of death or ridicule." He even knew a few months earlier I had gone online and looked up his quotes. Never had I read his biography and I didn't put together the importance of the Vietnam soldiers until I read it.

I pondered all this for a while, thinking I may be hallucinating or wishing it to be true, and I decided to see what the internet had to say about John Lennon. Wow. Reading about his anti-Vietnam stance made me understand all the soldiers spirits I felt. Reagan didn't even want to let John back into the United States after holding a bed and breakfast event protesting the Vietnam War in Europe. Then I read about his children and he and Yoko had a baby that died...John Ono Lennon. Oh. so that's why he said, "Yes, three sons." Reading about his relationship with Sean, at the end of a quote, he said, "and I taught him how to swim like a fish." Goosebumps went up on my arms. He was so enjoying the water. Reading about his relationship with Julian, Julian said the best times he had with his father was playing music with him. And sure enough, he was indeed forty years old when he was killed, just as he told me. He was born October 9, 1940, and he died December 8, 1980. John Lennon is quoted as saying, "You're all geniuses, and you're all beautiful. You don't need anyone to tell you who you are. You are what you are. Get out there and get peace, think peace, and live peace and breathe peace, and you'll get it as soon as you like."

I have had many people come through who knew I could get messages to their loved ones so they came through when I was in their loved one's presence or was going to be seeing them. I'm not making any of this up. Most spirits that have come through are spirits that personally have known me or spirits associated with an individual I am with. Most things end up being correct, i.e., a friend's mother, who I never knew or whose name I never knew, started coming around when I was with him. I knew it was his mother but waited for her to give me her name before I told him the message. Her name, Janie Mary, was indeed her name. There is a funny story how we communicated back and forth before I was sure what name she was saying because of course, I thought I could be imagining the entire experience.

I have absolutely nothing to gain by making this up. It is just that it happens so much, and I have so many astral dreams, I know there are other dimensions and our loved ones are only in a different frequency range of this, what I can only call "earth dimension."

I sent an outline of the experience to Yoko's website Imaginepeace.com but, of course, didn't hear anything back. I am sure I will hear from him again. Whitney just said, "Tell MiMi I'm sorry and she'll know it's me because of the yellow dress incident." I think she named an album "MiMi" and then I basically didn't go any further. I just figure no one would believe me anyways. He specifically asked me to somehow contact Yoko. This is so cool, knowing we don't die, but I am not the Long Island Medium and much of this so-called spiritual contact could by synthetic. At this point, remaining grateful, aware and alert are all I can hope for.

I could share the other stories of how people contacted me and we were able to get the information correct and prove it. My first husband, Cliff came with his father, who I had never known, never thought about. My goodness, Cliff was killed in 1980. His father died when Cliff was about twelve years old.

He was so excited when he appeared with his father. He said, "I found him! I found him! He can tell you more." Cliff's dad told me about the Masons and the involvement they have with the government, that he was a pedophile and got caught molesting a neighborhood girl. The authorities came and he sold his son, Cliff, my first husband, to the program rather than go to jail. Telepathically he said his name plain as day…Ernie. Well, the next day I asked my daughter to check her father's death certificate for his name and she said she couldn't find it but asked his half-sister Shirley what his name is. Sure enough, Shirley said his name is Ernael but they called him "Ernie." That's just one example. Any soul that has communicated with me and asked me to share their everlasting existence with another, I have done. Otherwise, none of it is worth it. They are feeding off my energy just as the energy vampires do, but what a good cause to let it happen.

I know there are many spirit warriors working in the other dimension and species from other galaxies, and we will get out of this prison planet.

Sometime in 2014, I was in a good standing yoga position with my palms up, chakras open, praying to Elohim, energy soaring through me, tears pouring down my cheeks - and something squeezed my shoulder. I mean, I felt my shoulder get squeezed hard, and I turned and gasped as I was the only one in the house. The interdimensionals are so much around me and watching me. I know they have satellites that can see a dime on the living room floor. I know they can come right into my house. There is a sulfur smell that comes into the room when spirits are around as well.

I feel so blessed to know all these spirits who still care about their offspring and want the world to change. Not all spirits are interested in breaking out just as in this earth dimension. I am not afraid of them killing me and I will not go down without waking up as many people as possible. Otherwise, none of this is worth it. I'm ready to depart now. It is so hard knowing I am under 24/7 watch. My telephone was tampered with again. My contacts have changed and an email I forwarded to Zen Gardner disappeared from my sent messages. So many of the awakened are targeted individuals. They knew who was going to wake up and when. My life has been under alien control since birth. This will go on from cradle to grave. Even though I know Yahuwah and Yahushua are another species, I still have confidence and love for them. This is probably one of the hardest lifetimes I've ever been through and I've been through many. Mind control is ancient knowledge. This is old school. Anything that hath been will be and anything that will be has already been. There is nothing new under the sun. Solomon's inspired words. The phrase under the sun occurs twenty-nine times in the book of Ecclesiastes. "The thing that hath been, it is that which shall be; and that which is done is that which shall be done: and *there is* no new *thing* under the sun." (Ecclesiastes 1:9)

So this has already been done before. "That which hath been is now; and that which is to be hath already been; and God requireth that which is past." (Ecclesiastes 3:25) "That which hath been is named already, and it is known that it is man: neither may he contend with him that is mightier than he." (Ecclesiastes 6:10)

Through meditation I've had glimpses of past lives. I know I lived in about the year 1000 in London and had an administrative position for the Parliament. I was killed when I was about forty years old. I was an actress in a past life. My mind was also fragmented in another life and I fell on the scripture and became a nun. I was violently raped and killed at a mission in Brazil. My best lives were that of European Native Indians and American Native Indians. In one life, I was called Little Flower. I've spoken with ancestors from that life and in those days we called the Great Spirit in the Sky "Grandfather." These glimpses did not just happen overnight. These five past lives have been revealed in bits and pieces in the last three years. It really does take more than a few minutes a day of meditation to get to the point of recollecting past lives. I've meditated some days up to three hours, but again, it takes time and dedication. Even fifteen minutes before you get out of bed in the morning or before you go to sleep at night is a great start. If you want, you can simply lay on your bed and close your eyes, envision the chakras opening and spinning, push the breath through the nose and down into the belly. Fill the lungs up. Exhales can be slow through the nostrils and cleansing through the mouth. Light some sage or sweet grass to enhance the meditation mood and light candles. Add some meditation chanting or frequency healing like the 528 healing frequency or Native American Indian or Eastern Indian meditation music. These all can be found on YouTube.

Chapter 21

Zen's Manifesto

I am going to close with this reminder. Technology is forty years more advanced than the public is aware. I know I was tracked, photographed, and filmed and even right now am being watched and filmed. On the property I had for three years, across to the east is a pole to a barn with four electronic devices on it. I was constantly zapped with extremely low frequency ("ELF") and electromagnetic frequency ("EMF") rays. I've had men ("handlers") in and out of my life. Probably at least sixteen, maybe eighteen. This is a frequency, mind control matrix and we just have to take the ride!

Zen Gardner is an activist that apparently pulled out from the public eye when he was called out for lying to his listeners and readers about his involvement with a Church of God cult for twenty odd years. I don't even know the exact name of the church he was involved with but it was known that the leaders agreed to sex with underage children. He claims innocence for the involvement and I understand. I was just disappointed that he painted a different picture of his life before becoming a website activist, author etc. I participated in churches as well which led the herd into false teachings. He wrote this and offered all who read it to share it with as many people as we want to. So I'm adding it here:

To the Few Whom This Concerns:

Re: The deliberate subjugation of our people and planet

While you continue to hypocritically blame humanity for the dire plight of our world, we hereby put you on notice that we are well aware that it is you, the financial, corporate, military, scientific and governmental agents and most of all the dark shadow forces behind you, that we know full well comprise and empower the destructive global power grid, that are responsible for our current engineered crises and overall social condition.

You've brought us and our planet to the precipice. If you do not cease and desist, what is soon to come will be blood on your hands, cause untold suffering, and all for naught as far as your designs are concerned. You too will shrivel up in the dustbin of history as just another invasive parasite that couldn't succeed in its self-serving designs for all its efforts.

Know that.

We hereby officially notify all those complicit in this massive control program that:

- We are aware of your efforts to dumb down, anesthetize and control the world's populations.

- We are aware of your destructive programs to sicken and alter humanity through the chemical, electromagnetic and genetic modification of our food, plants, animals and ourselves.

- We are aware of your wanton destruction of our earth, skies and oceans through resource exploitation, geo-engineering and weather modification.

- We are aware of your many false flag events and surreptitious "strategy of tension" schemes purposely designed to keep the world in perpetual fear and continual wars against fabricated outside enemies for control and profit.

- We are aware of your fascist medical designs to drain and destroy humanity via the decrepit allopathic medical system based on profit and ill health at every level, including the proliferation of pharmaceuticals, invasive and debilitating treatments and deliberately damaging vaccines.

- We are aware of your moves toward a worldwide police state based on hyperbolized fear and disinformation to manipulate humanity in order to get an unspoken imprimatur to execute your program of control and subjugation.

- We are aware that your political crony establishment is all staged and designed to distract from the real issues and keep the populace occupied and feeling like participants while you work your nefarious program.

- We are aware of your falsely imposed vampiristic taxation system to fund further bureaucratic bloat, controls and an overarching agenda of genocidal wars on innocent peoples, and that it is arbitrary and our sovereign choice to simply not participate in any longer.

- We are aware that a select few major corporations with vested interests in this global agenda now control almost all media and that mass media is nothing more than a mouthpiece of propaganda to these ends.

- We are aware that your "entertainment" industry is simply socially engineered entrainment towards personal and social distraction, chaos and degradation.

- We are aware of your AI, electromagnetic grid and mind manipulating designs and technologies that are being imposed to further expand your psychopathic control program.

- We are aware that you repress emerging technologies that threaten existing parasitic profitable ones, such as the hazardous petroleum and nuclear industries, when alternative energy sources and other such solutions have arisen for many decades which you have suppressed.

- We are aware that you sequester knowledge and information in a vast array of fields to keep the general populace in the dark and thereby disempowered as to our true historical context, while you are coveting secret information and carrying out advanced covert research for your own ends.

- We are aware that you have stigmatized, marginalized and seek to outlaw any form of criticism, questioning or dissent using whatever excuse you can manufacture.

- We are aware of your oppressive, enslaving monetary and legal control scams, private fractionalized banking pillaging, and twisted cravings for money and power in an imposed control system that never needed to exist in the first place.

- We are aware of your falsely postured institutions, foundations, institutes, charitable organizations and international bodies such as the so-called United Nations and its many agencies and agendas being used to further develop your global control plans and programs.

- We are aware of your secret societies, blood line allegiances and luciferian, freemasonic, Babylonian and otherworldly roots that propel the wickedness of your self-appointed leaders. We are aware of your ritual sacrifices, pedophilia and bestiality inclinations and other sordid practices, all of which are anathema to our conscious race.

- Ad nauseum…

This will be tolerated no longer.

Furthermore…

- We are aware that you know we are on to you. We stand fearless, fully committed to humanity's well being. You are shallow, self-serving and seriously misled guns for hire working for a control system being engineered by powers beyond your knowledge that will devour you, just as you seek to devour us.

- We are aware of who you are. Your days are numbered. Your designs will soon be visited upon your heads if you do not drastically change your ways. Universal law dictates it. You know it, and we know it. Hence your sloppy, miscreant behavior being so thoroughly exposed which you so furiously attempt to deny and suppress. This futile lashing out only works toward the exposure of open truth and the awakening's favor.

If there is an ounce of humanity left in any of you, defect and help us expose and bring down these life ending forces. You, your children, your grandchildren and anything you may still hold dear are already suffering and will also perish in the catastrophe we are soon destined for if you do not respond.

Now.

A last warning.

We are aware. We are awake and activated. We will do everything within and without our personal power to see our race and planet survive and shake this parasitic invasion. Our planet itself will not take this attempted overthrow. Know that, and expect repercussions from Her, as well as us, a gathering storm of sacred truth you cannot possibly fathom.

Your opposition, resistance and puny, short-sighted efforts are dwarfed by what awaits you.

Will you find your humanity in time? We think many of you could, and those of you who do will be welcomed amongst the awakened. However, we realize many are beyond redemption.

But don't try to fool us. We're more on to you than you could ever imagine.

Just watch and see. We will surprise you, just as you fear.

We're here. We live. We cannot be stopped nor thwarted by any means despite your flimsy efforts.

The truth and love we bear are coming for you. Truth and cosmic resonance cannot be denied and any aberration from it will be mitigated.

That's just the way it is.

Think about it. If you dare.

Signed,
The Eternally Awakened

My Lord's Prayer:

Heavenly Father, righteous Father, loving Father, who art in heaven and in space;
Holy, and hallowed and pure be thy name, Yahuwah
Thy Kingdom Come, in my Heart
Thy will be done, as above as below, in all dimensions
Give me this day my daily bread, my daily manna,

knowledge, love
And forgive me of my trespasses, as I forgive those
who trespass against me
And lead me not into temptation; but deliver me
from evil
For thine is the power, the glory and the dominion
forever and ever. Amen

Yahuwah's blessings to All!!!

I want to be called a friend of the Most High! And yes I will call myself a servant to righteousness, liberty and justice. To serve peace, love, and beings of light, yes I will be a servant.

"Ye are my friends, if you do whatsoever I command you. 15: Henceforth I call you not servants; for the servant knoweth not what his lord doeth: but I have called you friends; for all things that I have heard of my Father, I made known unto you." (John 15:14-15)

Thank you and I hope this helps all Mankind. Peace - no war. Harmony and love - infinite, unconditional pure, pure, real, true LOVE.

Bibliography

Bachman, Samantha, www.samanthabachman.com.

Bartley, James www.theuniversalseduction.com.

Bible, Holy, King James Version, *Guiding Light Edition*. Good Counsel Publishing Company, Chicago, Illinois 1956.

Bonacci, Santos, www.universaltruthschool.com

Brzezinski, Zbigniew, *The Grand Chessboard*, Basic Books, A Member of the Perseus Books, New York 1997.

Castaneda, Carlos, *The Teachings Of Don Juan: A Yaqui Way Of Knowledge*. Fourth printing, Pocket Books, New York 1975.

Castaneda, Carlos, *The Active Side Of Infinity*, Pocket Books, New York 1999.

Cayce, Edgar, *Reading 3744-5*, Phillips Hotel, Dayton, Ohio, February 14, 1924.

Cayce's, Edgar, *Near Death Experiences 5. Cayce meets the angel of death*

Cayce's, Edgar A.R.E., *Readings Advice On Personal Spirituality, Meditation, and Prayer.*

Chiappalone, Dr. Joseph, www.jchiappalone.com.

Dictionary.com

Einstein, Albert, Letter to Jost Winteler (1901) quoted in *The Private Lives of Albert Einstein* by Roger Highfield and Paul Carter, March 15, 1994.

Enoch, Book of, www.forbiddengate.com/BookOfEnoch.pdf.

Epstein, Orit Badouk, *Ritual Abuse and Mind Control: The Manipulation of Attachment Needs*.

Fly, Freeman, www.freemanflytv.com.

Gardner, Zen, www.zengardner.com.

Gnostics Texts, Ng Hammadi, Egypt.

Halgamuge , Malka N., *Oxford Journals*.

Hamilton, Roberta Sage, www.wisdomquotes.com.

Hersha, Cheryl, *Secret Weapons: How Two Sisters Were Brainwashed To Kill For Their Country*, New Horizon Press, Far Hills, New Jersey, p. 52.

Hicks, Bill, *Sane Man*, 1989.

Hicks, Bill, www.brainyquote.com.

Igan, Max, www.thecrowhouse.com.

Icke, David, *Infinite Love Is The Only Truth, Everything Else Is Illusion: Exposing the Dreamworld We Believe To Be Real*, England, David Icke Books, England, April 1, 2005.

Icke, David, *Phantom Self.*, David Icke Books, England, 2016.

Icke, David, www.davidicke.com.

Johnston, Miles, www.thebasesproject.org.

King, Jr., Martin Luther, *Letter from the Birmingham Jail*. April 16, 1963.

Kissinger, Henry, National Security Memo 200. April 24, 1974.

Lennon, John, *Beatles Interviews Database: John Lennon Interview: Release June 6,1968*.

Marrs, Jim, *Rule By Secrecy: The Hidden History That Connects the Trilateral Commission, the Freemasons, and the Great Pyramids*. Harper Collins, New York April 2001.

McCraty, Rollin, Raymond Travor Bradley, Dana Tomasino, *The Social Heart Energy Fields and Consciousness*. Boulder Creek, CA; HeartMath Research Center Bulletin, Institute of Heartmath, 2004.

Mearsheimer, John J. and Stephen M. Walt, *"The Israel Lobby and U.S. Foreign Policy"*.

Merriam-Webster, www.merriam-webster.com

Miller, Alison, *Healing the Unimaginable: Treating Ritual Abuse and Mind Control*, Computer Files, Kamac, 2012

Monroe, Robert, *Far Journeys*. Anchor Press, New York December 1, 1992.

O'Brien, Cathy, *ACCESS DENIED For Reasons Of National Security: Documented Journey From CIA Mind Control Slave To U.S. Government Whistleblower.*

O'Keefe, Ken, www.worldcitizen.solutions.com.

Orwell, George, *1984*. Penguin Classics: New Ed. Edition 2004, first published 1948.

Patton, Ron, *Project Monarch: Nazi Mind Control.*

Patton, Ron, *The Evolution of Project MKUltra Project Monarch, Nazi Mind Control.*

Pearce, Joseph Chilton, *The Death of RELIGION and the Rebirth of SPIRIT*, Rochester Vermont, 2007.

Phillips, Mark, *Operation Monarch.*

Sanger, Margaret, *Pivot of Civilization*. 1922.

Shriner, Sherry, www.sherryshriner.com.

Schneider, Philip, *The Underground: A Hidden Reality and the True Story of Phil Schneider.*

Springmeier, Fritz, *Project Monarch.*

Springmeier, Fritz & Wheeler, Cisco, *The Illuminate Formula Used To Create An Undetectable Mind Control Slave, Chapter 1: The Selection & Preparation Of The Victim.*

Springmeier, Fritz & Wheeler, Cisco, *The Illuminate Formula Used To Create An Undetectable Mind Control Slave, Science 5. The Skill of Lying, The Art of Deceit.*

Tesla, Nikolas, 1926 interview with Collier's magazine reproduced by Twenty-First Century Books, titled *When Woman Is Boss.*

Vonnegut, Kurt, *Palm Sunday: An Autobiolgraphical Collage.*

The Unspoken Bible, www.usbible.com.

Williamson, Marianne, *A Return To Love: Reflections on the Principles of a Course in Miracles.* pg. 190-191, Harper Collins, 199.

Wigington, Dane, www.geoengineering.org.

Woodward, Bob, Bernstein, Carl, *The Final Days*, quoting Henry Kissinger.

CPSIA information can be obtained
at www.ICGtesting.com
Printed in the USA
BVHW04s1941190618
519442BV00013B/89/P